Praise for

The Rifle

"Andrew Biggio stayed true to his warrior ethos by not forgetting those who fought before him. I am beyond impressed with his work interviewing some of America's last World War II veterans and am grateful for the service he has rendered a new generation of veterans."

—**ROBERT O'NEILL**, U.S. Navy SEAL and *New York Times* bestselling author of *The Operator: Firing the Shots that Killed Osama bin Laden and My Years as a SEAL Team Warrior*

"These are the stories that all Americans, especially veterans and the families of those who fought in World War II, have been waiting to hear. Biggio tells emotional and heartwarming stories punctuated with accounts of the terror of war and the thrill of combat. This book honors every Marine and soldier who never lived to share their stories."

—**MAJOR SCOTT HUESING, USMC (Ret.)**, bestselling author of *Echo in Ramadi: The Firsthand Story of US Marines in Iraq's Deadliest City*

"*The Rifle* is not just a story of the heroism and abiding patriotism of the Greatest Generation, it is a fine recounting of forgotten history. Andrew Biggio is a war historian on par with Seymour Hersh, able to bring the trials and tribulations of armed combat to life."

—**MICHELE McPHEE**, bestselling author of *Maximum Harm: The Tsarnaev Brothers, the FBI, and the Road to the Marathon Bombing*

"Andrew Biggio has a remarkable ability to form meaningful connections with veterans of wars that were fought decades before his birth. *The Rifle* is his way of thanking those men for their service, and we all owe him a debt of gratitude for dedicating his whole being to lifting up the veteran community."

—**JIM "DOC" McCLOUGHAN**, combat medic for the U.S. Army and Medal of Honor recipient

"*The Rifle* represents all our World War II veterans. The author, Andy Biggio, has travelled the world to find specific World War II veterans to honor them. Their signing the actual rifle helps solidify their tangible place in our history. This book belongs on everyone's coffee table as a tribute to our World War II veterans."

> **—CHARLEY VALERA**, National Indie Excellence Award–winning author of *My Father's War: Memories from Our Honored WWII Soldiers*

"Andrew Biggio is a loud and effective voice for veterans not only here in Massachusetts but now around the country. His experience as a combat veteran gives him credibility. I applaud him for relating the stories of veterans."

> **—TOM KELLEY**, co-author of *The Siren's Call and Second Chances* and Medal of Honor recipient, Vietnam War

The Rifle

The Rifle

Combat Stories from America's Last WWII Veterans, Told through an M1 Garand

ANDREW BIGGIO

**Foreword by Medal of Honor Recipient
Hershel "Woody" Williams**

REGNERY
HISTORY
Washington, D.C.

Regnery History™ is a trademark of Salem Communications Holding Corporation
Regnery® is a registered trademark and its colophon is a trademark of Salem Communications Holding Corporation

ISBN: 978-1-68451-305-5
LCCN: 2020953030

First trade paperback edition published 2022

Published in the United States by
Regnery History, an Imprint of
Regnery Publishing
A Division of Salem Media Group
Washington, D.C.
www.RegneryHistory.com

Manufactured in the United States of America

10 9 8 7 6 5 4 3 2

Books are available in quantity for promotional or premium use. For information on discounts and terms, please visit our website: www.RegneryHistory.com.

To the eighteen- and nineteen-year-old kids who gave their lives in the Second World War, whose names we may never know. Still buried in Europe and the Pacific Islands where they fell, they are seldom visited, as their counterparts who survived also faded through time. Even as their family members and friends disappear with the ages and the cemeteries seem empty, their legacy will last forever.

For Andy

July 16, 1925–September 17, 1944

"Some serve, others fight."

Andy Biggio. *Photo courtesy of the author*

CONTENTS

Author's Note

The stories in this book all come from the veterans' memories of personal experiences they had, recalled 75 years after the events occurred. While every effort has been made to verify the details of these stories, the veterans telling them were between 92 and 101 years old, so some details may have been lost to the passing of time. That is why it is so important to preserve these heroes' stories now, while we still can.

Foreword

Andrew Biggio has recorded the stories of a generation of men who made tremendous sacrifices to contribute to our shared American history. Through their eyes, *The Rifle* offers lessons of military and civilian life that will grip anyone who reads it. Biggio, a veteran himself, knows the importance of remembering the courage and sacrifices involved in preserving peace and our American way of life. His dedication to that task is a testimony to his character.

I am fortunate and honored to have played a small part in that history and to contribute to his efforts to record the experiences of America's greatest generation. Most of these individuals have never had the opportunity to share their personal conflicts and vivid combat experiences. They are a part of history that has made America the place we call home, but they often go unrecognized.

As important as our stories are, we veterans were among the lucky ones. We returned home to our loved ones, and our sacrifices don't stack up to the ones made by those who didn't. We as a people must never forget those who didn't get to come home or their loved ones who have a vacant chair at the table.

CWO2 Hershel "Woody" Williams
U.S. Marine Corps World War II Medal of Honor Recipient,
Iwo Jima

Prologue

When my fifth grade class took a field trip to the Chelsea Soldiers' Home—an assisted living facility for veterans—in 1998, my teachers introduced us to a man who was 106 years old. He was a World War I veteran. I had the chance to talk to him, but at age eleven I was more concerned with switching out the batteries to my Game Boy than learning the name or story of this prehistoric old man.

The importance of that visit wouldn't hit me until many years later, when I found myself thrown into American history as part of the newest generation of veterans. I came to regret that fifth grade field trip thirteen years later, when Frank Buckles, America's last World War I veteran, died in 2011 at the age of 110.

It was too late to get that World War I vet's story, but I set out on a mission. I wasn't going to let another generation of veterans disappear without telling their stories. I wanted to get any knowledge or advice from them that I could and memorialize their service.

The Rifle is the product of my commitment to that task. It's a chronicle of combat stories from America's World War II veterans, a compilation of their lessons from war and life afterwards. Their stories are a testament to the rich experience veterans have to offer us. Remembering and honoring them enriches us as much as it ennobles them.

What I discovered from the men and women I interviewed goes against what mainstream media and the movies show us. World War II is the most marketed, profitable, and popular war of all time. It's unbelievable to think that a war that killed an estimated 80 million people has made so many others rich.

But there was more to World War II than the famous scenes of D-Day in France and the flag-raising on Iwo Jima. The men in the 101st Airborne are not the only ones who fought in Normandy, and the Marines did not win the Pacific on their own. Not every soldier who fights earns a Medal of Honor. Not every wounded soldier gets a Purple Heart. The men who opened up to me in the last stages of their lives had fought in overlooked skirmishes in unsung divisions and units. They were heroes who often went unrecognized.

Today, the average World War II veteran is found in a nursing home. Very few are able to live on their own, and most have outlived their spouses. They are hardly able to walk, eat, answer the door, or take care of themselves. They are the old men in the neighborhood, the ones who do not come out much, the ones whom kids playing "ding-dong ditch" like to cause trouble for. In 2018, a thousand of these veterans died every day. They were not always this vulnerable. They were, at one time, the strongest warriors the world has ever encountered.

These writings aren't just meant to memorialize heroes from the past. They aim to show younger veterans—who are often labeled as "broken" or blanketed with the stigma of being mentally ill—that they can live long, successful lives after combat. A new generation of heroes needs the tutelage of the previous generation. And with time running out for America's greatest generation, the people who can offer our veterans guidance will only become harder to find.

Some of the men in this book have never told their stories until now. The oldest veteran interviewed was 101. The youngest was 92. Their lives in combat and after combat tested them beyond anything we can imagine. That they survived is sometimes miraculous, often inspiring.

Giving these World War II veterans this platform to share their stories changed the direction of my own life. Over the course of dozens of interviews, often travelling across the country to meet veterans, I learned a tremendous deal about my nation's history, my family, and my own service. My experience is living proof that paying respect to veterans can shape the way you view the world. And it all started because of a rifle...

The Mission

I enlisted in the Marine Corps in the spring of 2006. A year later, I received orders to deploy to Iraq. At that time, deploying into a combat zone was exactly what I wanted. It was what everyone wanted who enlisted during that time. We knew exactly what was going on in the world. We were not drafted; we volunteered.

I was able to return home before my deployment. As I drove around my childhood neighborhood, I started to notice things that I had long overlooked. At the stoplight down the street from my house, my dad's car idled as we waited for the light to turn green. To our immediate right was a sign that read "Andrew Biggio Square," a dedication to my grandfather's brother who was killed in World War II. Andrew Biggio was my namesake, and my father's as well. We were named after a man whom we had never met.

As I looked at the sign, thoughts of my own deployment raced through my head. The last Andrew Biggio who went off to war left from the same house, hugged his family on the very same porch, and did not return.

The thought came and went, and so did my tour in Iraq. Before long I was slated to deploy again. In the summer of 2011, I found myself in

Afghanistan. The improvised explosive devices (IEDs) were never-ending, far more dangerous than what I had encountered in my Iraq deployment. My platoon uncovered forty-two IEDs on one stretch of road alone. But one day we found out the hard way that we had missed one.

It was toward the end of my tour. I stood in front of a pickup truck piled with dead Afghan police. Their bodies had been blown to pieces by the explosion. I saw a torso, some legs, a few arms, and only a couple of intact bodies.

The other Afghan police stared, dumbfounded, at their dead comrades. "Don't just stand there, grab some body bags and let's help them out," my platoon commander said. Another Marine pushed a white body bag and rubber gloves into my chest. I knew instantly that picking up these limbs and corpses would haunt me for the rest of my life.

"Hold on!" our Afghan interpreter yelled. "The Afghan police do not want non-Muslims handling these bodies."

"Thank Christ," I thought with relief.

Suddenly, more Afghan police arrived to collect the remains of their comrades. I watched from a distance as two scrawny Afghan police attempted to load a torso into a body bag from the tailgate of the truck. They did not expect the unbalanced dead weight of the corpse. They lost their grip, and the body fell off the truck. As it slammed onto the pavement, the body released a disturbing sound unlike any I had heard before, causing me to turn away and avert my eyes in disgust.

The haunting scene would return to me in the most unexpected circumstances. My tour in Afghanistan came to a close soon after the incident. After completing two tours of duty, I left the Marine Corps. I never thought about the incident in Afghanistan again until two years later, when I was in a grocery store. As they do for most people, packed grocery stores make a real test of my patience. When I was at my wits' end, an elderly woman dropped a large melon from her shopping cart. The sound of the fruit slamming onto the floor was the exact sound of the dead Afghan hitting the cement that day. The noise made me sick. All I could see in my head was the Afghan corpse slamming into the pavement over and over again. I couldn't get out of the store fast enough. I left my cart full of food and made my way to the parking lot at a frantic pace.

On the drive back home, I stopped at the same red light where my dad and I had been eight years earlier. The same sign still stood there, as it had done for more than seventy years. "Andrew Biggio Square"—a dedication of metal and plastic to a young nineteen-year-old, killed while fighting the German Army on some unknown hill in Italy in 1944.

I had been clenching the steering wheel on the entire drive home from the grocery store. Only on seeing his name on that sign did my grip loosen up. Questions shot through my head. I wondered about the Andrew Biggio who had died in Italy as I asked myself why I had made it back home unscathed. Abstract questions about a deceased relative I had never met became personal. All of a sudden, I wanted to know one thing: What happened to the first Andrew Biggio on that damn hill in Italy?

The next morning I drove to my grandmother's house.

"Nana, do you still have Uncle Andrew's last letters home?" I asked.

She brought down a shoe box filled with deteriorating envelopes. "What do you want those for?" my grandfather asked. He was very protective of his brother's war mail.

"I just want to see something, Papa," I answered. I couldn't begin to explain the thoughts racing through my mind. Truth be told, I probably didn't know myself what I wanted to find. I just knew I needed to find information on my great-uncle Andrew and his time in the war.

The letters were mixed up. Some were from basic training, while others were from the hellish fighting up the coast of Italy. I pulled names, locations, and places from the letters. I attempted to find and reach out to survivors on the internet and social media. I struck out—and felt further disconnected from this long-lost relative who had the same name as me.

The next day, I read a letter on how much my great-uncle enjoyed shooting the "M1." At the time he had been writing, the M1 Garand was the U.S. Army's new rifle. Reading that letter, it hit me: I needed to go buy a Winchester M1 Garand rifle. I wanted to feel what he had felt. I wanted my family to own a piece of history.

The next day I purchased my very own M1. At home, I held it, aiming at the wall. *Now what?* I thought.

Even if I showed the rifle to the rest of my family, would they understand? They were not veterans and might miss the point. Who would get it?

I remembered my neighbor, a ninety-two-year-old Marine who had fought and been wounded in the Battle of Okinawa. He would understand the feeling coursing through my veins as I held the rifle, perhaps better than I did. I knocked on his door and let myself in.

Joe was an old man, in a similar condition to thousands of other World War II veterans across the country. Bound to the recliner in his living room, he was barely mobile anymore.

"Check out what I bought," I announced proudly as I showed off my new purchase. I placed the rifle into his hands. I was nervous the old man might drop it, unable to bear the rifle's serious weight. But suddenly a burst of energy soared through his body. He swung the rifle around his living room, aiming and pointing as if he were eighteen years old again. The weak and crouched-over old man was, for a few seconds, made young and strong.

My elderly neighbor was behaving in a fashion I had never seen. When I was growing up, my family had always considered Joe reserved and private, but all of a sudden he was happy and couldn't stop talking. "I had to live every day with this thing!" he yelled, shaking the rifle.

That's when I realized that I was holding something special.

As my neighbor brandished his old weapon, another idea came to me.

"Sign your name on the rifle!" I blurted out. I knew I might never get a chance like this again. I wanted to preserve his legacy.

As I left his house, I looked down at his name. My purpose became clear. I wanted to get as many signatures of World War II veterans as I could on that rifle and document their different stories. The battles in which they fought range from the Battle of the Bulge to Iwo Jima, from Leyte Gulf to the hills of Italy to the fleets at Pearl Harbor—and so many others that are often overlooked.

After talking to Joe, I knew that I could prove that veterans can live long, successful lives after near-death military experiences. I considered it a bonus if I could also unearth the story of my great-uncle Andy's last days fighting in Italy before his death. My mission began, and I knew that I was in a race against time.

CHAPTER ONE

"No Such Thing as a War Crime"

Joe Drago
U.S. Marine Corps, Sixth Marine Division

Corporal Joe Drago was involved in some of the most storied action in World War II history, and he just happened to live next door. My whole life I thought I knew Drago. He was a grouch. Whenever the kids in the neighborhood played baseball in the street and a foul ball landed in his yard, he was always short with us—the stereotypical mean old neighbor that most have pity on, but also steer away from. It wasn't until I became a Marine that Drago ever really warmed up to me, and by warmed up I mean that he waved to me occasionally from his porch. Ever the consummate grouch. Now I know that it was more complex than that.

Drago served alongside Corporal James Day, whose heroic actions were recognized by the United States government when President Bill Clinton awarded him the Congressional Medal of Honor.

Corporal Joe Drago. *Photo courtesy of Joe Drago*

Day and Drago served in the same division, the Sixth Marine Division. They participated in the Second World War's most ferocious battles. They sometimes spoke of their guilt and deep remorse for the civilians that were killed during the Battle of Okinawa on the tiny Japanese island. Some 100,000 civilians died, caught in the middle of the eighty-two-day battle.

Day was credited with killing over a hundred Japanese soldiers with a light machine gun during the battle. Some civilians were interspersed among the enemy army, some there on purpose, some by accident, and others forcibly conscripted by the Imperial Japanese Army.

Drago and Day didn't care whether civilians or professional soldiers came into their sights, and neither did the Marines. After the slaughter the Marines had faced on the Guadalcanal, Tarawa, and Peleliu islands, a general consensus surfaced among them. They had to fight their way through their opponent or risk being slaughtered.

"On Okinawa, there was no such thing as a war crime! Kill anything that moves," Drago explained. "Those were our orders, and that's what we had to do to stay alive."

As the two men sat at a fifty-year Sixth Marine Division reunion in New Mexico, Day asked Drago a simple question: "If you didn't feel guilty then, why should you feel guilty now?"

When I interviewed Joe Drago, he was ninety-two years old and still had plenty of Marine in him. While he sat in his recliner, toying with my new rifle, he barked an order at me from across the room.

"Open that drawer over there!" he shouted.

His home was filled with pictures of him attending reunions from over the years, going to veteran events, and hanging out with the former mayor of Boston. But Drago didn't want to show me memorabilia from his days as a veteran—he was thinking about his time on the front lines. I made my way to the drawer and did as I was instructed. I pulled out a purple, crushed-velvet Crown Royal liquor bag.

As I moved the bag around in my hands, I could feel tiny pieces of something clinking around inside—maybe a collection of pebbles from the beaches he'd landed on during the war. I loosened the strings on the bag and carefully reached my hand inside to feel the treasure he'd kept tucked away for almost half of his life. My eyes widened as I felt the bottom.

"These aren't…?" I asked.

"You bet your ass they are," he shot back. "Go ahead, open it up. They're yours now."

I held the gold teeth that had once been in the mouth of a Japanese soldier. Corporal Drago had knocked them out with his Marine-issued KA-BAR fighting knife. It was a macabre battlefield ritual practiced by many during the fight to control the island. On Okinawa, both armies celebrated victory with the gory rites that belong to the battlefield. The Japanese had their own rituals with American bodies. The old tradition made it hard for Drago to believe that Marines had gotten in trouble for urinating on Taliban corpses in Afghanistan in 2011.

"That's nothing compared to what we used to do," he said. "Ya know, U.S. Customs always asked GIs at the airport if we were carrying human trophies in our sea bags," he continued. "Something like 40 percent of the Japanese bodies in the South Pacific were missing skulls and teeth."

I looked down at the teeth and realized he had been carrying the weight of war on his chest for all these years. My childhood impressions of a grumpy old man had been motivated by something deeper. I wished that I had known sooner.

As I stood and pondered how humans could do this to one another, Drago interrupted my chain of thought.

"You really want me to write on this?" he asked.

He gave me an odd stare from his recliner with the white paint-pen in his hand and the rifle on his lap. Marking up such a beautiful firearm didn't feel right, and he didn't entirely understand the concept I had in mind. Since he was the first person to sign his name to it, I was asking him to imagine something that wasn't quite developed yet.

"Mamma mia," he whispered as he wrote his name on the rifle. He was loath to paint his signature on the polished wood, as if defacing such a remarkable weapon were a form of sacrilege. He hunched over as he wrote his name. The rifle pressed down onto his frail legs that had atrophied over the years from his inability to walk.

Just as he finished, I asked, "Do you ever have nightmares?"

"Oh yeah," he replied, staring at his name written in wet paint.

"Do they ever go away?" I asked.

"No!" he shot back quickly.

This was more than just a history lesson. It was a bond between two veterans, Marine to Marine. Drago began to take me back seventy-four years—back to Easter Sunday 1945.

■ ■ ■

The men of the Third Battalion, Twenty-Second Marines transferred from a troop transport ship into smaller landing crafts on the northern side of Okinawa, Japan. Okinawa was the last in the chain of islands that led to mainland Japan. It was the closest to the mainland—390 miles away, to be exact.

Drago's commanders and peers warned one another that the Japanese would fight harder and more desperately than they had ever fought. The Marines were close to their homeland; it was late in the war and U.S. forces were knocking on Japan's front door. Drago's command openly admitted to the young Marines that they expected 100,000 casualties on the first day of the invasion. Even with these facts drilled into his head, Drago wasn't nervous. But those feelings of youthful confidence would quickly disappear.

While Drago and the other Marines stood on the decks of their landing craft, the USS *Bunker Hill*, a massive aircraft carrier and magnificent symbol of American strength, sailed past. It had been struck by multiple kamikaze planes and was on fire.

"Suddenly we all became nervous," Drago confessed. "It was now real."

The Marines had just traveled two days since their formation on Guadalcanal. No one had bothered to tell them that they were on their way to Okinawa. The young Marines didn't know what was going on, and the sight of the aircraft carrier limping by sowed the first seeds of doubt into the confident ranks.

Drago's transport ship linked up with the Sixth Marine Division at a rally point in the Caroline Islands. There they were to join with the Tenth Army and First Marine Division for what would be the largest naval invasion of World War II. The invasion was twice as large as the historic D-Day landings in France.

Drago recalled, "There were thousands of ships and planes as far as the eye could see. It felt like every ship in the world was there."

The time came for the Marines to go below and load up in AMTRACs—amphibious tractor vehicles that would carry the infantry into battle. The vehicles were launched out of the bellies of the transport ships into the rough surf toward the enemy-occupied beaches.

The Marines were ordered to deploy from the stern of the AMTRACs upon reaching the beaches. Leaving from the back of the vehicle was the only way to avoid being shot immediately by machine gun fire. The tactic might give them a few more minutes to live.

Drago's division was made up of replacements—new guys with little to no combat experience. They were lucky, however, to have a few combat veterans of the Mariana and Solomon Island campaigns. Before preparing to invade Okinawa, Drago trained on Guadalcanal for nearly six months with Corporal James Day, who lived in the tent across from him. Drago and Day, like thousands of their fellow Marines, had no idea what lay in store for them. They were wracked with constant uncertainty.

While on the ship they would occasionally get updates from Tokyo Rose, a radio host from mainland Japan whose transmissions could be picked up on a GI's radio. Tokyo Rose was not just one woman. Different women spoke under the title, filling the airwaves with Japanese. The media tactic was used to scare and threaten U.S. military personnel serving in the Pacific. The steady stream of stories of Marines being "butchered alive on Iwo Jima" struck fear in hundreds of Marine hearts.

"None of the guys had even heard of Iwo Jima before, yet the Fifth Marines were there spilling their guts," Drago said.

They waited for naval bombardment to cease pounding the beaches and the suspected Japanese positions. When the bombing stopped, Drago's amphibious vehicle was sent straight for Hagushi Beach, in the northwest part of Okinawa. Drago jumped off the rear of the AMTRAC as it hit the beach and dug its metal tracks into the sand. Drago, a machine gunner with Item Company (also known as I Company), was in the first wave of Marines to hit the beach. "In other words, I thought I wasn't going to last long," Drago recalled. He carried the tripod of his machine gun and rushed ashore.

And yet, despite the expectations of slaughter, Drago and his fellow Marines took the beach without conflict. There was no enemy, no gunfire, no explosions, and no Japanese. Minor opposition and pop shots were few and far between—nothing like the murderous rain of gunfire everyone had predicted.

The history books and documentaries tell the same story: the U.S. Marines of the Sixth Division met little to no opposition during the first hours of their initial invasion, a tactic deliberately planned by the Japanese military. The objective was to lure as much of the American military onto the island as possible, then attack at full force. The plan was to tear them apart with intricate defense lines and intersecting fields of fire.

Upon taking the beach, Drago and the rest of Item Company were ordered to push forward to their first objective, the Yontan Airfield. They reached the airfield within thirty minutes of landing on Okinawa. As they stepped foot on the strategically valuable airstrip, the Marines caught sight of a Japanese fighter plane descending towards the runway. Nearly every Marine in the regiment opened fire on the Japanese pilot as he tried to land. The plane was shredded to pieces—along with the pilot's body. Drago wondered why the pilot had been trying to land on a hostile airstrip, but the strange behavior would remain a mystery.

Item Company continued to advance at a rapid pace. Just beyond the airfield, the company of one hundred Marines faced a deadly ambush.

Around dusk, Drago and his fellow Marines engaged the enemy. The riflemen ahead of Drago's squad took cover and dove for the ground as bullets popped around them. Drago set down his tripod and waited for his assistant gunner to snap the Browning air-cooled machine gun into place. Once he heard the clicks of both pins latching onto his tripod, he got behind the trigger and began to shoot.

"I don't even remember breathing," he said to me, with a look on his face I'd never seen before.

With a rush of adrenaline, Drago began aiming bursts of machine gun fire into the tree line and at locations where he thought someone could be shooting from. Suddenly, to his right, he saw enemy combatants running in and out of blast holes and trenches, the aftermath of the naval artillery fire. The enemy ran back and forth between the makeshift trenches, carrying ammo and rifles to different positions.

Drago held the trigger down on his Browning machine gun and watched a running figure in the distance fall facedown. He never confirmed that he had killed the man, but by nightfall Drago knew one thing for sure: he had survived his first day.

■ ■ ■

Drago suddenly stopped talking, looked down, and took deep breaths. Recounting the story was taking its toll. "Just give me a second," he said as he began to huff and groan. I suggested that we continue at another time.

"No!" he barked, yanking his head up to look me dead in the eyes. He was adamant that we carry on, and he jumped right back into the front lines.

"The first night on Okinawa my assistant gunner and I did not sleep," he started. "Japanese flares were frequent and many of the Marines were trigger-happy, shooting at every noise and movement in front of them."

At dawn they moved out again with the rest of the regiment. The Sixth Marines would go left and secure the north end of Okinawa while the U.S. Army hooked right and advanced south. After sweeping the northern part of the island, Drago's I Company was twelve days ahead of schedule. They began to hit heavy opposition when they started heading back south, assigned to protect the left flank of the Fifteenth Marine Artillery—the artillery unit tasked with providing support and cover fire for the Sixth Marine Division.

The Fifteenth Marine Artillery was engaged in a shoot-out with Japanese artillery. The Japanese counterbattery had the Fifteenth Marines zeroed in and was delivering precise, deadly barrages. The more losses the Fifteenth Marines took, the less coverage and support they could give the Sixth Marine Division when they went on the offensive. Protecting the Fifteenth Marines was necessary for the success of future Sixth Marine missions.

"They were being decimated as we watched from a hillside," Drago recalled.

But from that same hillside, Drago's Sixth Division could see a small village. Civilians were standing on some of the rooftops, looking out towards the American positions. Could these civilians be spotters for the artillery? The Marines inched closer, hoping to gather more information. Shooting the civilians from afar would only bring the artillery on their own position, and they did not want to kill innocent people.

After creeping forward some more, I Company made a push towards the village. The civilians from the rooftops scattered when the Marines showed up. One of them must have been a spotter for the Japanese artillery.

Drago and his squad entered a suspicious home that overlooked the Fifteenth Marines' position. As soon as they walked in, they heard noises coming from the building's crawl space.

"We asked—in Japanese—for them to come out," Drago said. After receiving no reply, Drago and his fellow Marines drew their .45 caliber pistols and began to fire through the walls and into the ceiling. One of the Marines climbed onto the roof to find a bleeding Japanese civilian with binoculars and a radio. The man was indeed a spotter, calling out targets for the heavy guns a few miles away. The radio was rushed back to regiment headquarters. The incident proved that the Okinawa citizens could not be trusted.

That night the Japanese tried to overrun several American platoons, including Drago's. The Marines were ambushed while they slept in their foxholes. The Japanese had crawled towards their positions with bamboo rods, which had long bayonets attached to them. They thrust the javelin-type weapons into American foxholes, and Drago was woken up by a piercing scream; the Marine next to him was being stabbed to death by a bayonet. As Drago scrambled to defend himself, a flare went up and lit the night sky.

Drago and his assistant machine gunner began to shoot at the Japanese soldiers from their prone position. Unsure what to do after being spotted, the Japanese started to stand up and move about, only to be gunned down by Drago's machine gun fire. Some ran into nearby homes as civilians ran out. In the nighttime confusion, all Joe and his assistant gunner could see were shadows. They shot at them, not knowing whether they had hit their marks.

The next morning, several Japanese soldiers lay dead or wounded. Civilian bodies were strewn among the maimed corpses—innocent men, women, and children caught in the nighttime crossfire, without a chance to survive. The sight of the civilians' dead bodies would haunt Drago forever.

But Drago didn't regret killing the rest of the attempted infiltrators. The wounded Japanese soldiers who had survived the previous night did not lie wounded for long.

"We walked right up to them and shot them right in the face," Drago told me. "We smiled when we did it, and even gave some of them cigarettes first."

That day, Drago collected his first set of gold teeth.

News came down from the surviving Marine artillery members of the Fifteenth Marine Regiment. A nineteen-year-old Marine from California named Harold Gonsalves was among the dozens of Marines who had been killed. The young warrior was eventually awarded the Medal of Honor for jumping on an enemy hand grenade.

Despite these occasional obstacles, the Sixth Marines continued their sweep through northern Okinawa at a rapid pace. Things were not going so well for the Army in the south. There, American troops were hit with three times as much opposition. By April 14, 1945, Drago's Sixth Division, along with the Twenty-Second Marine Regiment, had pushed south to link up with the Army and the First Marine Division along the famed Japanese Shuri Defense Line.

The Shuri Line was a series of complex defense systems which included caves, hills, catacombs, trenches, and machine gun and artillery emplacements. Constructed by the Japanese Thirty-Second Army, it had taken years of work to build.

On their way south to support the Army troops, commanders told the Marines not to dare laugh, call out, or humiliate the U.S. Army's Twenty-Seventh Infantry Division. The division had taken heavy losses and was falling back in defeat. It wouldn't take long for I Company to get a taste of the brutal action that was happening on the other side of the island.

As Drago's platoon came up on a marshland known as the Asukawa Estuary, they had to cross a man-made footbridge. Just as they made it to the other side, Japanese suicide squads hidden in the grass detonated themselves with high explosives. The explosion penetrated the foundation of the bridge, causing it to collapse. Drago and his platoon were stuck on one side of the bay, cut off from the rest of the company.

When Drago turned around to watch the bridge fall, mortar fire and small arms fire began to rain down on him. He ran through a rice paddy to find cover, but his left foot got caught in the thick mud.

"I was stuck like a mouse in a mousetrap and trying not to get killed," Drago recalled. "It's scary to take incoming fire, but it's even more frightening to be shot at and not be able to hide."

The heavy machine gun tripod Joe carried only made the situation worse. The tripod weighed him down and trapped both his feet in the quicksand-like mud. Unable to move, Drago heard soldiers speaking Japanese through the high grass. He dropped his tripod and removed his .45 caliber pistol. As soon as the voices got closer, he fired the pistol into the tall grass, emptying the clip. While attempting to reload, an explosion ripped through the grass, knocking him back. Japanese mortars began to land around him and the other cut-off Marines. Without an entrenching tool, Drago desperately tried to dig a foxhole with his bayonet, in fear of being hit a second time by shrapnel. He suffered only cuts and scratches from flying debris.

Luckily, the blast had freed both his legs from the mud. He began to crawl through the elephant grass, passing a Japanese body that lay in front of him. Later, Drago would wonder if the man had been killed by the pistol rounds he had fired into the grass, but there was no time to think about that now. His squad was able to make a dash to take cover behind a retaining wall, which gave them temporary protection from harassing gunfire.

The enemy fire was coming from a series of sugar mills—blown out buildings that gave snipers and mortar teams a place to hide. Drago and his assistant gunner set up his machine gun and began to strafe the buildings. Their tracers marked the skeleton buildings for the platoon's mortar squad to return fire on the other side of the estuary. The Marine mortar team began to drop high explosive rounds on the buildings, breaking them down almost completely, killing the snipers and spotters inside.

The rest of the company finally advanced through the neck-high waters. Soon, engineers built a makeshift pontoon bridge to reunite the company of Marines. The Marines won the short battle, but after the smoke cleared Drago saw that some of his buddies had not suffered only the minor wounds that he had. They lay dead in the same rice paddies he had gotten stuck in.

"I give those guys who fought in Vietnam credit," Drago said. "The rice paddies were some of the worst places to get stuck in during a firefight."

The day at the Asukawa Estuary would be I Company's first beat-down on Okinawa. The loss of life demotivated the Marines. Unfortunately, the enemy engagement was a mere glimpse of what was to come at the Shuri Defense Line in the next days. Soon the entire regiment would be in the biggest fight for its life.

With the First Marine Division in the middle and the U.S. Army on the far right, the Sixth Marine Division took the left side of the Shuri Line. It was a solid plan—until the Marine regiments were stopped dead at Sugar Loaf Hill.

■ ■ ■

Sugar Loaf was not so much a hill as an elevated mound. The unassuming terrain didn't look like it would pose much of an obstacle to the American forces' southward march. But the Japanese had set up for a bloody engagement. They had their tremendous artillery dialed in on Sugar Loaf. Caves containing both enemy soldiers and civilians who had fled the northern part of Okinawa pockmarked the terrain. Sugar Loaf needed to be secured in order for the American forces to push for the city of Naha, the campaign's objective. This was ultimately the Sixth Marine Division's last mission of World War II. This is where the division took the brunt of its casualties.

On May 12, I Company advanced towards Sugar Loaf. Gunfire and artillery fire were constant, but not a single Marine could see an enemy soldier. "They were like ghosts. You couldn't even get one of them in your sights," Drago recalled. Sometimes enemy soldiers posed as civilians—a common tactic in urban areas.

There was only one option: everyone had to be considered the enemy. "There was the threat that civilians wanted to kill you," Drago told me. "We killed anything that moved at that point. There wasn't even a second thought of it."

At Sugar Loaf Hill, the Marines had to kill the enemy both from a distance and up close and personal. Only one thing was consistent: no prisoners would be taken.

Six heavily armored tanks led the charge. Artillery fire, mines, and suicide squads descended on the tanks. Infantry protection provided little respite as Marines hugged the ground to avoid exploding shells. Japanese soldiers strapped anti-tank mines to their chests and sprinted towards the tanks. Some were gunned down by the tanks' machine guns before they reached their targets, but there were too many suicide bombers to stop them all. Counter-artillery continued to keep the American grunts ducking and seeking cover. The suicide squads crawled underneath the tanks and then detonated themselves.

"The explosions were so powerful, they would flip the tanks completely over, and the crews would burn inside, still alive," Drago said. Of the six tanks, only one made it through the opening salvoes. A Japanese suicide bomber had made it under the tank but failed to detonate his mine. He crawled with the tank as it moved forward, trying to avoid detection. A Marine who witnessed the sneaky action ran toward the U.S. tank through enemy artillery fire. Once at the rear belly of the tank, he knelt down and emptied his Thompson submachine gun into the Japanese soldier. On his way back for cover, the brave Marine was shot by an enemy sniper. Drago still doesn't know that heroic Marine's name or whether he was awarded for his courageous action.

The next day, Drago's platoon advanced past the destroyed tanks to the bottom of a ridge. The enemy attack was unrelenting: after making an advance, the Japanese would run back into caves and come out on another side of the hill to shoot again. The tunnels were difficult to figure out, and the American soldiers had to throw smoke grenades into the caves to see where the fog would come out on the other side.

While stuck in this quagmire, a squad of Marines passed Drago's machine gun emplacement to summit the hill. He recognized a Captain Marston leading the charge. As the brave Marines ran towards the peak, a friendly naval shell landed in their midst. It exploded and completely disintegrated their bodies. Captain Marston's squad wasn't the only one to be hit by friendly fire. "We don't know how many Marines were killed by American guns, but the number was high enough for us to to hold any further advances that day," Drago said.

At night Drago and his machine gun team slept in their foxhole. As they tried to get some rest, they heard the report: A few foxholes down, two Marines had partnered up to sleep. While one slept, the other got up to retrieve medicine from a foxhole he had dug earlier that day. On his way back, his sleeping partner awoke, startled, and fired at what he thought was an enemy soldier sneaking up on his foxhole. Instead, he had just killed his best friend.

"A few Marines cracked up after that," Drago barked at me, remembering the event as if it had happened yesterday. "You're never supposed to leave your foxhole at night! Those two Marines were like twins. The other Marine was never the same."

In the span of a week, Sugar Loaf Hill exchanged hands between the enemy and the Marines eleven different times. The Twenty-Second Marine Regiment suffered so many casualities that entire companies had to be reorganized into platoon-sized elements, which typically consisted of thirty to forty men. Thousands of American soldiers suffered from battle fatigue and were physically wounded.

May 21, 1945, was Drago's last day on Sugar Loaf Hill. Since the other Marines seemed to be gaining more territory, Drago and his assistant gunner broke down their machine gun and headed out with them. Drago remembers switching positions and passing dozens of bloated corpses, both American and Japanese, often stacked next to one another.

When they got to their new position, Drago went to set up his gun. Before he could reset the tripod, he heard the distant whistle of another artillery bombardment. An enemy shell hit, and with nowhere to take cover, Drago was launched into the air by the explosion. His body hit the ground like a bag of wet sand. He could not move, and with a mouth full of dust and rock, he struggled to breathe. His ears rang—he could only hear a faint popping sound and distant cries. As his vision went black, Drago thought he was about to die.

When Drago woke up, he was already on a stretcher. Two U.S. Army soldiers were carrying him across the field. "How or why the Army got to me, I don't know," Drago said. "I had no idea what happened to the other Marines in my squad. I didn't think anyone was left alive."

But as the Army soldiers carried Drago away, more Japanese artillery rounds impacted the area. The Army medics fled, leaving Drago in the middle of the battlefield. "They dropped me and ran for cover," Drago told me. "I never felt so vulnerable and scared in all my life."

Drago lay helpless on the stretcher as shells landed around him, burying him in dirt and rock. "The next time I woke I was inside a tent in a field hospital. The doctors informed me I had internal bleeding and other broken blood vessels. I was puking and pissing blood."

After twelve days of relentless fighting, the division took Sugar Loaf Hill. Sixteen hundred Marines were killed in action. Reporters from *Time* magazine walked through the hospital tents and tried to interview the wounded Marines. Most told them, respectfully, to "fuck off."

Drago was one of almost eight thousand Marines wounded and evacuated from the battle. His buddy, Corporal James Day, earned the Medal of Honor for his actions during that battle.

However, the American position wasn't yet secured. Although they were evacuated from the front lines, the U.S. Navy was still being attacked by Japanese kamikazes. Flak and other ammunition was pumped into the sky to strike enemy planes. However, shrapnel and bullets would rain down on the field hospitals along the beach, wounding patients as they lay on their stretchers. "Marines were earning their second Purple Hearts simply lying in hospital beds," Drago told me. "No place was safe."

Drago drifted in and out of consciousness and was eventually placed aboard a hospital ship heading back to Guam and then California. During the voyage, a man stricken with what was then called combat fatigue (now known as post-traumatic stress disorder) attempted to jump off the ship. Drago grabbed the distraught Marine before others helped restrain him.

Drago didn't reach his breaking point until he returned to the States. While getting ready for his first liberty, he witnessed a well-known boxer from Sixth Marine Division wearing his uniform with ribbons, as if he had been in front-line combat. "He was always in the rear. He was an entertainer. It was bullshit."

Drago was irate. Dozens of his friends had died for the same medals and ribbons that some entertainer was now showing off to the public. His anger got the best of him. He attacked the boxer, ripping the ribbons off his chest, an action he still doesn't regret. In response, the Marine Corps placed Drago in a psychiatric ward for a short period of time.

Drago finished his healing process at the Chelsea Naval Hospital in his home state of Massachusetts. There he watched the news broadcast announcing that atomic bombs had been dropped on Nagasaki and Hiroshima and that the Japanese had surrendered.

"Everyone in the entire hospital celebrated," Drago recalled fondly. "They waved their crutches and spun circles in their wheelchairs. It was the happiest day alive."

Nearly every service member in the Chelsea Naval Hospital put their uniforms on and hitchhiked into downtown Boston. Everyone wanted to be in the center of town for the celebrations.

Life moved on. In 1947, the government gave families who had lost loved ones in the war the option to have them exhumed. Their bodies would be dug up from the foreign battlefields on which they were killed and shipped back to the United States at Uncle Sam's expense. Some families decided to let their sons lie where they were buried, undisturbed. Others wanted them back home.

Drago found out that the family of one of his fallen comrades, Michael Pietrusiewicz, had decided to have his remains shipped home. Drago escorted Michael's body back to Methuen, Massachusetts, and met the entire family. As they celebrated their loss in Polish tradition, unsettling memories of the war came back to Drago. The experience made him uncomfortable enough to leave and hitchhike back home to Boston.

Nearly seventy-five years later, Joe Drago still finds it difficult to talk about the war. The Sixth Marine Division left the best part of itself on Okinawa, sacrificing men's bodies, minds, and souls to capture the strategic territory. In this last battle of World War II, nearly twenty-three thousand Japanese soldiers were killed. A couple thousand were taken prisoner. Drago lost twelve personal friends on the island. They won the last battle thanks to great sacrifice.

Drago lived his post-military life as a court officer, while also running a successful side business making awards, trophies, and plaques. He married and had a fulfilling life with his wife, sons, daughters, and six grandkids. Yet nightmares and survivor's guilt still haunt him.

"One day you will say to yourself, 'Was that real? Did that actually happen?'" he said. As Drago finished his two-hour-long story, he could hardly keep his head up. Physically exhausted, the energy from holding the rifle had faded.

I bid him goodbye and buckled the rifle back up in its case. He made sure I took the gold teeth and an ammunition cartridge belt he had worn during the battle. "I know you'll bring more attention to this stuff than I can now," he told me. I nodded my head in agreement but didn't want to. I knew he was at the end of his life, and it made me sad.

Joe Drago with the rifle. *Photo courtesy of the author*

As I thanked him again and closed the door, he called out weakly, "Semper Fi."

CHAPTER TWO

The Golden Acorn

Ernie Roberts
U.S. Army, Eighty-Seventh Infantry Division

Worcester, Massachusetts

The experience with Joe left me hungry to talk to more World War II veterans. I promised myself that I would fill the whole rifle with different names and battles, and after seeing the reaction that holding an M1 provoked in Joe, I was sure that I could bring some of America's forgotten heroes back to their days of adventure. I knew the vets would be hard to find, but I resolved to ferret them out wherever I could.

Since Joe had seen action in the Pacific, I wanted someone who had fought in Europe to sign the rifle next. Through some research I was amazed to discover that the president of the Massachusetts Veterans of the Battle of the Bulge Chapter was still alive.

In the fall of 2018, ninety-five-year-old John McAuliffe allowed me to pay him a visit at his home in Worcester, Massachusetts. I entered John's high-rise apartment and took the elevator to the fourteenth floor. He was, without a doubt, the oldest person living in that public housing complex—and he was living on his own.

Hanging on the door of his apartment was the Battle of the Bulge veterans' official seal—a helmet, rifle, and pine trees. When the old man

let me in, an eerie feeling came
over me. I felt like I was looking
at my future self. Documents,
reading material, and historical
information were stacked from
floor to ceiling. He had kept all
the minutes from the Battle of the
Bulge Association meetings since
the 1980s.

"Holy cow," I exclaimed,
as John brought out a huge
Rolodex.

"Some of these guys I know
are still alive," he assured me. He
pulled out names and phone
numbers. "I'm sure they would

Ernie Roberts. *Photo courtesy of Ernie
Roberts*

be glad to sign your rifle. As a matter of fact, you should call this man;
he was in the same division as me."

Grateful for the connection, I had John sign the rifle. The man was
clearly the glue that had been holding these World War II veterans
together over the years, and I was proud to have his legacy decaled on
the weapon. Before I left, John handed me a Nazi dagger. Etched on the
inside, in German, were the words "For the Fatherland."

"You can have this. We are lucky to have someone like you interested
in us," he said to me.

The immense honor I felt was second only to the responsibility I
felt to the task I had set myself. After a brief meeting, this man was
willing to hand over one of his prized wartime possessions. He thought
that the work I was doing was important enough to part ways with a
memento he had kept for decades. Gripping the dagger, I promised him
that I would let everyone know where it had come from. But John didn't
stop there. After rummaging around for a minute, John came back to
hand me his uniform. It was as if he had waited his whole life for me

to show up to his apartment. *Of all people, why am I the one to have the distinct honor of being given his wartime belongings?* I thought. Evidently, he knew he was at the end of his life, and trusted me to keep his legacy alive.

For the first time in ages, I drove home without the radio on. Thoughts—not music—raced through my brain. I couldn't make sense of what had transpired at this man's home. The Nazi dagger he had given me, his war trophy, was not just a piece of the war. It was a piece of him. I was grateful, but I felt as though I did not deserve it.

The next day, I took the list of phone numbers John had given me to work and began calling. I worked as a police officer Monday through Friday, but if one of the veterans could meet with me spontaneously, I had to be prepared. I brought the rifle and my research with me; that way I could leave my shift and go straight to their homes. My next stop would be Rhode Island to interview a vet from John's list whom I had contacted.

As I carried the M1 in its plastic case from my truck to the police cruiser, my partner asked with genuine curiosity, "New patrol rifle?"

"Not so much," I responded. I explained my ongoing project and that we would have to babysit the weapon in our cruiser. I was too scared to leave it in my personal truck alone all day. I placed the case on the tailgate of the truck and popped it open.

"This is the rifle that won the war," I told my partner.

The Golden Acorn

After work, I pulled up to the house of Ernie Roberts, the first vet I had successfully gotten a hold of through John's list. When I arrived, his wife greeted me at the door and led me inside to meet Ernie. I was amazed at how young they looked. Ernie showed me around his home. The garage was lined with years of remarkable paintings.

"I did this one a week before 9/11," Ernie told me, pointing to a painting of the Twin Towers in New York City, "then I did this a week after

9/11." The painting next to it showed both towers burning. "This is my therapy." He showed me more paintings of animals and lighthouses.

Ernie and I made our way back to the kitchen table, where I had left the rifle leaning up against the wall. His wife joined us. "What do you want to know?" he asked.

This wasn't my neighbor Joe I was talking to now. I realized I didn't have a list of questions to ask, so I winged it. "How old were you when you went in?" I blurted out.

He began telling his story without effort, as if he had been waiting for someone to ask. He wouldn't stop until he got to the end.

Ernie enlisted as a seventeen-year-old from North Providence, Rhode Island. Though young, he had three siblings in the military and wanted to join. However, he couldn't. In 1942 there was only one stipulation— Ernie was what the military considered "4F," incapable of military service. The status was usually given to recruits with hearing, visual, bone, or mental issues.

But Ernie had no physical problems. He was 4F because he was the only source of income for his ill mother. His father had died of cancer two years before the war, and all his siblings had entered the military.

His only way into the military was with written permission from his mother. She had made up her mind that she would not sign for Ernie. With three kids already in the military, she wanted her last son home. It wasn't until the family doctor told her that young Ernie would "never forgive you if you don't" that she began to think otherwise.

The fact was, in the 1940s, men sometimes committed suicide after being denied military duty. No one wanted to be the boy from the neighborhood who did not go fight, marked as a coward. Everyone wanted to take part in history.

Ernie eventually succeeded in getting his mother to sign for him. He could send her more money by being in the military anyway, so he chose the war and promised to send half his pay each month.

After completing basic training at Fort Eustis, Virginia, he was sent to infantry school at Fort Jackson, South Carolina, and became a machine gunner. Ernie ended up with the Eighty-Seventh Infantry Division, a National Guard unit activated out of Mississippi. Like every Army unit during World War II, the Eighty-Seventh had its own insignia—a golden acorn—as its unit crest, which each and every soldier in the division wore on his shoulder. It was not the most intimidating design, but the men who wore it would eventually earn respect for the unassuming badge.

In the fall of 1944, the men of the Golden Acorn boarded the USS *Queen Elizabeth*, a troop transport ship that was setting sail for England. Upon arrival in Great Britain, the men trained for two more months, learning more and more about their German enemy. The D-Day landings in Normandy had already occurred in June, but as of November, France was still not completely liberated. Multiple German infantry divisions held strong in the northern part of the country.

The Eighty-Seventh joined the fight late in the game. Their first mission: oust the remaining fanatic Germans from France.

Ernie's M Company of the 347th Infantry Regiment first stepped foot on the war-torn continent in Le Havre, France, on November 28, 1944. Before long they were loaded into trucks and rushed 350 miles to the front lines. Their task was to advance northeast to relieve the 26th Infantry Division. The 26th, also known as the Yankee Division, was a Massachusetts National Guard unit that was already hooking and jabbing with the Nazis who refused to let go of France.

Just eleven days after arriving in France, Ernie's green regiment met the enemy outside the town of Metz, an area of France just shy of the German border.

One Yankee Division company, once 156 soldiers strong, was now down to 25 men. The division desperately needed a break, but it would not come easy. While attempting to relieve companies of the 26th Infantry Division, the 87th Division came under heavy artillery barrage, their first exposure to combat.

The German 88 mm artillery cannon was the most devastating weapon the enemy ground forces had. It was one of the most accurate cannons in modern military times, and the number one cause of death for Allied infantry. It destroyed bodies and equipment, but most of all it destroyed morale. Even hiding in a foxhole couldn't save you. The Germans had developed a new airburst shell that exploded before impact, just above the soldiers, to devastating effect. "It wasn't uncommon to find headless soldiers still sitting in their foxholes," Ernie told me.

Dozens of men who had just arrived in Europe in Ernie's Eighty-Seventh were wounded on the first day of combat, all stemming from a hillside-entrenched enemy outside of Metz. As the Eighty-Seventh and Twenty-Sixth Divisions switched out, the artillery fire grew worse. The 88s were leaving men in pieces. "Soldiers lay dead with intestines sprawled out some five and ten feet in front of them," Ernie told me with horror. "Screams for medics came from different directions."

From their elevated position, the Germans had the advantage. The only way to stop the carnage was to charge up the mountain and beat back the enemy guns with force. Every step forward M Company took was met with incoming shells. The artillery bombardment did not cease. This close to the border of their country, the Germans were even more aggressive. It would be an uphill battle. "I immediately wished I was home," Ernie confessed.

Ernie advanced with the tripod to his machine gun in hand. But without a clear shot for the machine gun, Ernie and his squad had to engage the Nazis in a grenade battle. The Germans threw grenades down on Ernie, and his men threw grenades back. The exchange went on for several minutes. While bogged down, the soldiers dug in, but German artillery readjusted to the Americans' new position. A German shell landed so close to Ernie that it blew him out of his foxhole, splintering the buttstock of his rifle.

Another soldier, forced to act as a "runner," was instructed to go between the foxholes to notify the company to prepare to advance. "While running to different positions to relay messages to the men, he was blown to pieces when an artillery round went completely through his body," Ernie wistfully recounted. "I don't remember his name, but he was only eighteen years old."

With no choice but to outrun the artillery, the men advanced farther up the hill. Several companies charged the Germans, but since they had no time to stop and aim in the midst of the ongoing barrage, they shot from the hip. Some soldiers earned their first kills hip-firing their M1 Garands.

With the division's first battle under way, the M1 Garand rifle had already proven itself superior to the Germans' bolt-action Mauser. With speed and accuracy on the Eighty-Seventh's side, the German soldiers fell back into the woods, just beyond the peak of the hill. The division was able to call in their own artillery fire on the wooded area. Before M Company advanced beyond the hill and into the woods where the Germans waited, friendly airpower was called in. An American P-47 fighter plane began to strafe the area, quieting the enemy infantry and artillery for a while.

At the top of the hill, Ernie spotted a half-destroyed signpost. "Welcome to France," it said on one side; "Welcome to Germany" on the other. Ernie put together that the regiment had just fought one of the first American battles on German soil. The high ground was part of the town Obergailbach, which was occupied by the 110th Panzer Grenadiers, with plenty of supporting armor according to reconnaissance reports and POW intelligence.

By mid-December of 1944, the division was eager to push on into Germany. However, they were told to stand down. The top generals had given them new instructions to fall back, the exact opposite of what the men wanted to hear. Unfortunately, there was more bad news. Reports began to pour in that some hundreds of thousands of Germans had broken through into Belgium, surrounding multiple U.S. Army units.

The Eighty-Seventh and several other U.S. Army divisions raced a hundred miles into Belgium to stop the advancement from taking place. The major fight would later be called the Battle of the Bulge.

The men were packed into trucks during blizzard-like conditions and moved quickly, without sleep, through day and night, occasionally being strafed by German planes. Although the Americans had their first victory under their belt, it was clear the Germans were not routed, as they had originally presumed. The real fighting was about to begin for the men of the Golden Acorn.

By December 29, M Company arrived at the front lines of the fight in Belgium, just outside the town of Saint-Hubert. After a long and cold haul to the area, temperatures still had not improved. "It was ten to twenty degrees the entire time during the Battle of the Bulge," Ernie told me. "All we had was field jackets and raincoats."

Ernie's squad was tired and hungry. They took up shelter in a few homes and maintained a defensive position. While the other men in his platoon searched a barn for food and milked some cows, Ernie set up his Browning water-cooled machine gun in a second-story window.

Daydreaming at his post, Ernie suddenly heard the distant sound of a vehicle's engine. Not knowing of any enemy in the immediate area, he assumed it to be a friendly vehicle. As it approached, Ernie did a double take. "There was a black Iron Cross painted on the vehicle. It was a half-track full of Germany infantry."

The Germans began to jump out of the troop carrier and advance towards the homes. Unable to notify the rest of the platoon, Ernie leaned into the machine gun and opened fire. "I hardly let them get out of the vehicle."

Some Germans were able to fan out in different directions, but most were cut down as Ernie and other soldiers began firing. A few of the Germans attempted to make it back to their mounted MG-42 machine gun on the vehicle, but they were instantly shot dead.

"One German made it really close," Ernie said. In a last desperate effort, a German soldier sprinted towards the houses with a stick grenade in his hand. As he pulled back to throw it in a window, Ernie shot him square in the chest with a machine gun burst. He fell over lifeless with the grenade still in his hand, the snow around him turning red.

"None of them made it to the houses," Ernie said in a more somber tone. "It was the first German I know for a fact I killed. It's the one that still bothers me."

On New Year's Day, the division advanced further into the Battle of the Bulge, against freezing temperatures. Just outside the vicinity of Jenneville, Belgium, M Company again set up defenses in a series of homes. Ernie and his assistant gunner set up their machine gun in the window facing the area from which the enemy would most likely approach.

Several hours passed. M Company awaited orders. Ernie began to rest, but not before scavenging the area for food.

When he returned to the room where his machine gun was positioned, his assistant gunner was gone. All that remained was the tripod. In fact, all the rooms in the home that his squad had once occupied were now empty.

"No one told me we were moving out," Ernie recalled. Confused, he peered out the window where his machine gun had been set up, and suddenly his heart dropped. Staring at him from the top of a hill in front of the house was a thirty-ton German Panzer tank.

Ernie froze as he realized that the tank's barrel faced the house he was standing in. With a quick flash, the tank shot a single shell into the home. The round went through both walls of the room he occupied. For whatever reason, the shell did not explode, but it still sent splintering plaster, wood, and concrete into Ernie's face.

"I immediately lost my hearing and could barely see." His teeth and jaw were loose and his mouth was bleeding. Ernie grabbed the tripod and jumped headfirst out the window, falling in front of the tank. He threw the tripod over his back and ran towards a ditch. "I couldn't hear anything but I could feel the tripod vibrate violently." Without his realizing it, enemy rounds ricocheted off the tripod he was carrying. He fled the enemy guns and sought cover in the tree line.

Separated from his unit, Ernie came across an African American tank battalion a few miles away. With blood, soot, and dirt covering his face and uniform, he was unrecognizable. An African American captain thought he was a German at first and challenged him with questions. After the brief encounter, he was allowed to enter friendly lines and directed towards the Eighty-Seventh Division's new position.

Finally, a medic instructed Ernie to lie down. He covered Ernie's face with snow and began to treat his wounds. The following morning, Ernie was given the option to go back to England, but he rejected the offer. "I came here to fight a war," he told the medic.

After a few days of recovery, his hearing began to come back. He was suited with a new uniform and sent back to M Company two weeks later.

The Battle of the Bulge took place during one of the harshest winters ever recorded in Europe up to that time. The U.S. military was outnumbered and had limited to no supplies. But the hoped-for miracle of an American victory was realized in late January 1945. American Army divisions repulsed Hitler's plan to recapture all of Belgium and at the same time rescued Americans in Bastogne.

The 87th Division advanced towards Germany for a second time. From February to March of 1945, M Company pushed towards the Siegfried Line, a 390-mile defense line built during World War I that ran along the German border. It consisted of 18,000 bunkers, tunnels, and tank traps. The line was composed of thousands of jagged concrete blocks known as "dragon teeth," which were able to hinder tanks and other vehicles. It was an intimidating obstacle, and Germany's last chance to halt the invading Allied forces.

Several enemy prisoners relayed to the Americans that scores of their fellow soldiers-in-arms would be willing to surrender if notified. The division brought in generator-run loudspeakers to communicate a message across the battle lines in German. Those who wanted to surrender would be given the right to surrender. However, none of the enemy soldiers complied.

It was later discovered that Hitler had purposely stationed his most dedicated SS officers along the Siegfried Line. They were instructed to shoot deserters in the back if they attempted to give themselves up to the Americans.

Reverting to the original plan, it was M Company's turn to start the offensive movement. Ernie and the other machine gunners were instructed to cover the company's advance. The riflemen took heavy machine gun and mortar fire as they began to advance. Dozens of American soldiers fell. The wounded lay bleeding out along the tree line and in the field. Medics could not tend to the wounded due to the immense wall of enemy fire coming from the Germans' position. Ernie and the other machine gunners grew frustrated. They were unable to lay the cover fire they wanted to protect the men.

The enemy proceeded to pin down M Company, and the machine gunners could not return fire without hitting their own men. Suddenly, an idea occurred to Ernie. He placed a fork-like tree branch under the barrel of his machine gun in order to elevate his bullets, hoping to shoot over the heads of his men in the field. The rounds looped up over the friendlies before descending onto the enemy's defensive position. Without his knowing, and by what he considers "luck," Ernie's rounds were spilling directly into the windows of enemy pillboxes. With the German machine guns now silenced, M Company's riflemen began moving forward at the rapid pace they needed.

Upon reaching the pillboxes, the men witnessed just how accurate Ernie's machine gun fire had been. Several Germans lay dead, and an additional thirty-five enemy soldiers surrendered. Ernie's actions along the Siegfried Line earned him a Silver Star.

By March 1945, the Eighty-Seventh Division had taken thousands of casualties. The government could not get draftees to Europe fast enough. Replacement soldiers were so badly needed that the United States Army Air Corps had to send men to replace the desperate infantry. "It was a scary feeling getting new guys. Some of them had never even seen a machine gun before; let alone fire one," Ernie remembered.

As a decorated veteran and now a staff sergeant, it was Ernie Roberts's responsibility to show replacements the ins and outs of the Browning machine gun. These inexperienced teenagers had to learn quickly, for soon they would be crossing the Rhine River.

Crossing the Rhine River into the heartland of Germany was no easy task. The river was 766 miles long and crossed by 22 bridges and 25 railroad bridges. All but one was purposely blown up by the retreating German Army. The bridge at a town named Remagen should have been blown, but the detonation failed.

The Ninth Armored Division used the failed detonation to their advantage. Ernie's division wasn't so lucky. The Army hauled boats across France and into Germany to prepare for the river crossing.

The riverbed was thickly occupied by the nearly defeated German Army. Hitler had instructed his troops to fight using delaying-style ambushes to try and save the failing fatherland. Army Corps engineers could not construct a major bridge for crossing while under constant fire from the embedded Germans on the other side. The Germans' artillery and anti-aircraft guns were burrowed deep in the draws of the cliffs, which made it difficult for airpower and counter-artillery to destroy them. The infantry had to take out each position individually.

On March 25 it was M Company's turn to cross the Rhine. Already out of luck without a bridge, they would also be cheated out of motorized landing crafts. When the trucks showed up to the regiment with a delivery, the men hauled out rubber crafts strapped with oars. The men paddled across the river with their weapons and ammo—and no real protection from what lay on the other side.

At one o'clock in the morning, the first companies crossed the Rhine. Almost immediately, German flares blasted into the night sky, revealing the assault by boat. The water-bound soldiers began to take machine gun fire. Despite the lack of solid defenses, only two boats of the first wave failed to cross the river.

Ernie's squad wasn't part of that first wave, but they could hear the sound of American rifles across the river, making it evident that the division was engaging the enemy forces embedded in the river bluffs. At 4:00 a.m., Ernie boarded his paltry rubber assault boat with five other men from his squad. He clenched the rifle they had given him in place of his machine gun as the boat started to make its way into the Rhine's powerful current.

With daybreak approaching, the German forces had a clearer view of the second wave of boats attempting to cross. The river's current had picked up significantly since nightfall, and boats were pushed away from their target landing areas and closer to German weapon emplacements. Enemy mortars began to dunk and explode into the river around the boats. "The Germans then started to fire on the boats with a 20 mm flak gun, shredding them to pieces," Ernie said. An unknown object, most likely a bullet or piece of flak, struck Ernie's helmet. "The shrapnel put a hole through it. I threw it right in the river."

Falling mortar shells honed in on his boat despite the men's attempts to paddle faster. Violent splashes of water soaked the men so much that they couldn't keep their eyes open to steer the boat. "Flak then ripped chunks out of our boat, and the next explosion flipped us right over."

Capsized, each man was left to fend for himself in the Rhine's strong current. Ernie's rifle, given to him for the crossing, fell to the bottom of the river, and the river carried Ernie farther and farther downstream. He was separated during the chaos from the others who had fallen in. After several hours of swimming, Ernie eventually made it to the other side of the river. He was a half mile down from where he had tried to cross, and now he was separated from the whole division for a second time. "I had to break ice with my hands in order to get to shore on the opposite bank."

Soaking wet, and with no weapon, Ernie started walking back upstream in the direction of his unit. He removed his clothes and twisted the water out of them. By the time the sun set, Ernie was still wet and cold. He found shelter in different bushes. "During the night I could hear soldiers passing by, speaking German," he told me. "I spent three days on my own until I reached the new lines of the Eighty-Seventh Infantry Division."

Again he was challenged with new passwords he did not know. After a brief encounter making sure he wasn't a German, he was taken in and issued dry clothes and a new weapon.

The regiment wasted no time after crossing the Rhine. They pushed farther into Germany. They faced scattered opposition and didn't come across any more unified German defenses. The men were captivated by the total destruction of neighborhoods, buildings, and farms that had been completely leveled from bombing raids. "The big cities did not exist anymore," Ernie said, as if he had been mulling over the destruction he had witnessed in the decades that had passed.

Scores of civilians lay dead along the roads alongside horses and other rotting livestock. M Company was swarmed by surviving civilians asking for food or anything else they could spare. German POWs marched past, taunting the Americans. One German prisoner told Ernie, "We surrender and get to go to America, but you have to stay here and fight."

The remark sent chills up his spine. The men of the Eighty-Seventh and other Americans did not enjoy the jeers, and they would beat or hit prisoners for cracking jokes. "Remarks like that got some prisoners shot!" Ernie exclaimed.

The 347th Regiment raced through Germany, rounding up thousands of prisoners. The Germans eagerly wanted to surrender to the Americans rather than to the Russians. By April, the division had reached the border of Czechoslovakia. Of the original 200 members of M Company, only 10 remained.

Ernie had been there from the beginning to the end. He received a Purple Heart, a Bronze Star, and a Silver Star for his service. Over the course of his service, he had nearly drowned in the Rhine River, had seen his friends get killed, and had killed for his country.

Division medics diagnosed him as having severe battle fatigue. After months of seeing extreme action, Ernie had reached the breaking point—as any human would. He was shaking constantly and plagued by nightmares. When the military told him to leave the front lines for a second time, he didn't have a say in the matter. He was shipped back to the United States—to Lake Placid, New York, where there was a brand new facility suited for veterans suffering from combat fatigue, or what we now call PTSD.

The program was intended to give freshly returned veterans the space to decompress and learn how to live after war. But in the peak of wartime action, the facility doubled as a place to get soldiers mentally composed enough to deploy on another tour of duty. Most of the methods were experimental. Therapy included hypnosis, medication, and reverse psychology. After several months, Ernie was deemed fit to return to service. This time he was told he would be sent to Japan.

The war came to a close before Ernie ever made it to the Pacific theater. He was stationed in Muskogee, Oklahoma, when the atomic bombs were dropped. A few days later, when they learned that the Japanese Empire had formally surrendered, the base was whipped into a frenzy. Ernie was scheduled to have liberty to travel into town to celebrate with his fellow soldiers and citizens. But Ernie learned that the sergeant who had duty was from Oklahoma and had family who lived close by. Ernie traded spots with him and took his duty so that the other man could celebrate with his family.

The U.S. Army was good to Staff Sergeant Ernie Roberts, so much so that he re-enlisted. Honorably discharged in 1947, Ernie returned home to Rhode Island, and for over sixty years he worked as a painter and local handyman in the neighborhood. Today, at the age of

Ernie Roberts with the rifle. *Photo courtesy of the author*

ninety-four, he can still tell you how to get the headspace and timing of a water-cooled Browning machine gun and how to change the barrel on air-cooled ones.

He can also tell you he'll never forget the Golden Acorn, his comrades who fought so valiantly beside him, and those who died heroes, both sung and unsung.

Ernie wouldn't let me leave the house unless I took some of his paintings. "Take these and raffle them off for your injured brothers." He piled up the artwork in my open arms. "Don't forget to take one for yourself."

When I got home, I hung a picture of a Rhode Island lighthouse in our bathroom. "Where did you get this?" my fiancée asked.

"It's a long story," I replied.

CHAPTER THREE

No Stalag

Clarence Cormier
U.S. Army, 106th Infantry Division

Gardner, Massachusetts

After visiting Ernie Roberts and hearing about how he evaded capture several times, I wanted to get a former POW's signature on the rifle. On Veterans Day, I read an article in a local paper about Clarence Cormier. I asked a friend who lived in his neighborhood to knock on his door. After he explained my story to Clarence, Clarence agreed to meet with me a few weeks later.

A few days before we met, Clarence Cormier pulled his Cadillac up to a gas station in Gardner, Massachusetts, and noticed a dirty-looking, long-haired man in his thirties holding a cardboard sign that read "VET WHO NEEDS HELP," written in messy black Sharpie. Clarence parked his car and retrieved his walker from his trunk. He closed his trunk and headed towards the gas station. His license plate read EX-POW.

"Help me with a few bucks, buddy?" the panhandler asked.

Clarence didn't look at him. Instead, he stared at the entrance to the gas station door. "Come in here with me and I'll buy you breakfast," he offered. "But I am not giving you cash."

"What the fuck's a matter with you?!" the man yelled in response. "You don't like veterans or something, pal?"

I sat in Clarence's apartment as he shared the story from a few days earlier. I couldn't imagine how anyone, let alone a veteran, could fail to notice Clarence's "Ex-Prisoner of War" license plate. I handed Clarence the rifle, but he admitted that he had never gotten the chance to fire an M1 during the war. He handled it with curiosity and caution. It was obvious that he hadn't touched a firearm since the war.

That December of 2017 marked the seventieth anniversary of his parents' receiving a telegram stating Clarence was "killed in action."

The Western Union telegram that Clarence Cormier's parents received in 1944 informed them their son was dead. "We regret to inform you that your son has been killed in action," the message read. It was false—despite the fact that, in Clarence's case, death would have been easier than surrender.

The six-foot-tall soldier weighed in at 200 pounds when he first enlisted. By the time he was rescued, he was just 130 pounds. For months, he wore filthy, worn-out Army fatigues and had long, dirty fingernails, with lice crawling through his beard and pubic hair. For almost five months under Nazi captivity, he ate grass, tree bark, rotted vegetables, and snow to survive.

"Surrender" is a forbidden word in the U.S. military, a topic avoided by veterans and proud historians. It isn't in America's vernacular. After all, there is this image in America that our armed forces win every battle of every war—the Revolution, World War I, World War II, and the Korean War.

Many people do not know that in World War II the United Sates had one of the biggest surrenders since the American Civil War. In December 1944, some seven thousand U.S. soldiers surrendered to the German Army just outside the town of St. Vith, Belgium. But that didn't mean that all seven thousand would come back home. "Surrender was only half the key to survival," Clarence explained.

In the fall of 1944, the U.S. government had to get men overseas at a rapid pace. Heavy casualties in France, North Africa, Italy, and countless other islands in the Pacific meant the Army had to generate entire divisions made of fresh officers from West Point, draftees, and volunteers with no combat experience whatsoever. The 106th Infantry Division was one of these units.

The division was as green as green could be. Based out of Indiana, the new unit was supposed to have airborne elements, ground forces, and gliders. But instead the division was rushed into Europe after just barely having finished scheduled training.

No one could judge the men of the 106th for surrendering to the Nazis. As one of 15,000 men poised to be overrun by some 300,000 Nazi troops in the Ardennes, Clarence had no choice but to give himself up to the Germans—or face total annihilation. Surrender wasn't easy, and the 106th paid dearly for the military brass's decision to rush them to the front lines.

Clarence's linebacker-size frame was enough to intimidate any man. He was the kind of guy that higher-ups always take an immediate liking to. He had good command presence and a booming voice. After basic training at Camp Atterbury, Indiana, he made the rank of sergeant during his anti-tank crewman course.

Like nearly every other unit preparing to enter combat, the division's first stop was England. The 106th spent most of the month of November training before they crossed the English Channel, learning the dos and don'ts from intelligence reports pouring in from France. Clarence was an official member of the 422nd Infantry Regiment's Headquarters Company Anti-Tank Platoon. He would master both self-propelled and towed guns used for knocking out enemy tanks.

In the first days of December, the 106th landed in France, entering the port in Le Havre. By the time Clarence stepped foot on the continent, France was completely Nazi-free. The Germans had been pushed back into Holland and Belgium.

The 106th moved over 300 miles into a small Ardennes village called St. Vith to meet and relieve the 2nd Infantry Division. They were told the area was known as the "honeymoon sector." It was so quiet and boring that each of the men of the anti-tank company was given only one clip of ammunition. "We were barely given any ammo moving into Belgium," Clarence recollected. "One clip for the M1 and one clip for the .45. We were told trucks would resupply us the next day."

On December 9, the 106th officially took over for the 2nd Infantry Division in the so-called "vacation land." Their resupply, however, never came.

At the crack of dawn on December 16, Clarence and the rest of the company were violently woken up by enemy artillery. The trees that provided them cover suddenly burst into flames. Pine cones, branches, and bark fell on their heads.

An artillery barrage of cannons, railway guns, and tanks tore into the woods east of St. Vith, turning "vacation land" into a living nightmare. Some soldiers did not have a chance to wake up before they were killed. The Germans had begun the offensive that would later be known as the Battle of the Bulge. Clarence's location was the exact spot where the battle broke out.

The cover of darkness, combined with nearly a week's worth of poor weather, had made it impossible for U.S. aviation to detect the movement of the German Army. More than 100,000 Germans with every weapon system imaginable moved in on three sides of St. Vith and circled the 15,000 Americans, cutting off multiple regiments. With less than two weeks in Europe, the 106th was introduced to combat in the most extreme circumstances. They were outnumbered 20 to 1.

In the woods east of St. Vith, Clarence prayed for his life. Artillery rained down on him and the rest of the anti-tank men of the regiment. As soon as Clarence had the courage to stand up and attempt to get a glimpse of the enemy, an artillery round landed in front of him. Dirt and rock collided with his body. Clarence went deaf. Both men in front of him were blown to pieces. The explosion was so close that it knocked him over. A piece of shrapnel snapped into his right shin. Clarence hugged the ground, figuring the next artillery shell would hit him directly.

After several minutes, he began to crawl towards another foxhole. Minutes turned to hours. The bombardment continued throughout the day with no break. Tree branches and body parts were strewn across the snow. The artillery finally ceased at dusk. Enemy soldiers began to appear in the distance, and the Americans expended what little ammunition they had. The one clip of ammunition they had been given did not last long as the German Army's 294th Volksgrenadier Regiment closed in on them.

Tanks, half-tracks, and infantry began to roll in closer on the same roads that intelligence had informed the regiment were impassable by vehicles. After all their ammo was gone, there was nothing they could do. With no tank support and no ammunition, they had to sit on their hands and wait. German infantry got closer and closer.

A desperate soldier ran over to Clarence with a white rag. The Army captain instructed the surviving anti-tank crewman to surrender himself to the first Germans he saw. Clarence began to tie an extra cloth liner from his jacket around the bleeding wound on his shin. When he looked up, he could hardly breathe. He was staring up at an enemy soldier, who was pointing a Mauser rifle in his face.

Clarence kept his hands raised as multiple Germans began to strip him of any extra clothing and gear. Frightened, he turned his eyes away from the faces of the enemy soldiers, only to accidentally focus on the dead Americans who lay around the wooded area—the soldiers who had not survived the day-long artillery siege. They lay where they had died. With no time to bury them or record their names, Clarence felt the agony of defeat.

Clarence and thirty others were placed in line and marched deeper into the woods. More and more Germans marched past them. German tanks spread out through the roads and trees. There were too many to count. "There's no way we could have won this," Clarence thought to himself.

Depressed and scared, he felt like he had been let down by his own military, starting with the lack of ammunition. How could they abandon them like this? Was the lack of planning going to end with his execution?

As he got closer to a road, hundreds of Germans occupied the area. One German soldier took a liking to Clarence's boots.The enemy soldier forced Clarence to remove his boots and hand them over. Another enemy soldier threw a worn-out pair of German shoes at Clarence. They did not fit. While struggling to put on the three-sizes-too-small shoes, he was forced to march off with the rest of the prisoners. Clarence continued to try to force the shoes onto his feet, falling behind. An irritated German soldier ran over to Clarence and slapped him. The enemy soldier took out his bayonet and cut a hole in each shoe. Clarence slipped his feet in, but his big toes hung out.

The American prisoners marched for two days without food and water. Another American handed Clarence a pair of socks. He tied them around the tops of each shoe to protect his toes from frostbite. The socks would slip off as he marched, and each time he tried to adjust them his German captors would hit him with the butts of their rifles.

The Americans, now prisoners of war, marched through the first night. The second night, the men huddled together to keep warm. "No one slept, we were so cold. We could also hear gunfire nearby," Clarence recalled.

The distant gunfire was not a rescue party, or at least not one coming for Clarence. The next morning Clarence faced a set of train tracks. The men watched as a large train with tall boxcars rolled in. The boxcars had originally been used for cattle—hay and feces were still on the floor. One by one, the men were forced into the train cars at gunpoint. The train car Clarence was placed in was packed so full that the men were unable to turn around. Once the captives were loaded onto the train, the Germans slammed the door shut and the boxcar turned black.

The train was in motion the entire day. Men were not let out even to relieve themselves. The soldiers squished body to body had to urinate on themselves. "It wasn't uncommon to feel someone pissing on you," Clarence admitted, embarrassed.

While riding like farm animals into the German heartland, the men could hear the engines of incoming planes in the distance. Although the sound of the clinking railway was loud, the American prisoners strained to listen as multiple planes nose-dived above them. Bullets began to tear into the train cars. The heavy-caliber aircraft bullets punctured the roofs of the train cars and some of the men's skulls inside them, killing dozens of them. The high-velocity rounds often hit multiple soldiers at once.

The train halted. The men in the cars were in a frenzy. They heard the airplanes making a U-turn and braced themselves for a second attack on the train. They began to climb over each other to make it to the doors and break them down. A second strafing occurred, putting more holes in the walls. The American pilots had no idea they were killing their own men. For all they knew, they were carrying out a successful attack on a German cargo train.

Suddenly there was a glimpse of hope as the men began to break out of the boxcar. A German soldier attempted to keep them in the train but was overwhelmed by the groundswell of Americans trying to burst free. The prisoners who escaped ran up a tiny hillside. The American planes began to make another roundabout. With no hope of communicating to the friendly pilots, an idea occurred to them out of nowhere. The men on the hill lay down and formed letters with their bodies.

"Just as the planes came around again, we all got on the ground and formed the letters POW," Clarence told me. "We clenched each other's hands, praying the pilots would recognize us as we heard them soaring in again."

The planes did come around again, but this time without guns blazing. "The pilot flew so close to us, I felt like I could touch the plane. He was waving his kerchief to acknowledge he saw us."

As soon as a sense of safety swept the men, they were forced back into the train cars. Dozens of dead Americans lay both inside and outside the damaged boxcar, victims of friendly fire. The dead were dragged off the train cars and left on the side of the railway as the train departed. Clarence and the rest of the prisoners had to stand in their friends' blood and brain matter in the boxcar. He couldn't stop thinking with envy about the pilot who had opened his cockpit and waved: that man was free to fly away, while Clarence was stuck in a hellscape.

After another day of chugging along, the train finally halted. The men were taken out and placed into trucks, which took them to a stalag, a German prison camp for POWs. Before they left, the Germans separated the men and placed them into different rooms. They put Clarence in a room as small as a closet, sitting him at a table across from what appeared to be an interrogator. Another German cocked his Mauser rifle and put it to Clarence's temple. "They asked me what unit I was in, what my objective was, and how many of us there were. As a brand new unit, I had no information to give them."

Since he was a non-commissioned officer, the Germans figured Clarence was playing stupid. "The Germans considered NCOs to be more combat-knowledgeable than officers," Clarence noted. Fed up with him, they loaded him back on the train and separated him into a group with a handful of others. This would be the first and last time Clarence would ever see the inside of a prison camp during the war. The train went back into motion, stopping only for refueling, without letting the men out. Another several days passed without food, water, or breaks to relieve themselves.

The train finally made a stop and the Germans opened the car doors. The Americans were pulled off the trains and lined up on a road. Parallel to the road was a small brook. Hundreds of men dashed to the stream and began to drink the water. "It felt like pins and needles going down your throat," Clarence remembered, "but we were so thirsty."

The prisoners weren't allowed to roam far, so the men farther up the stream were defecating into the water and washing themselves, while others downstream were drinking it. "There was no option. It was mass confusion, no coordination whatsoever, and we were desperate."

It was the last stop for the train. The prisoners were marched into another stalag. It was unclear why, but again Clarence was not left at this prison camp. They continued to march him and fifty others farther into Germany. "It felt as though I was on a death march," Clarence told me.

Days turned into weeks. Clarence and his fellow prisoners were surviving on a diet of snow, grass, and rotting vegetables they found in fields or ditches. The winter nights grew colder. The Germans took up shelter in different homes, leaving the American prisoners outside. "They warned that they would be watching us," he said. One German was assigned to watch the prisoners from inside the home.

The Americans went several months without having a roof over their heads. To sleep, they formed a "pig pile" in order to keep warm with each other's body heat. It got so cold at night that they had to take turns sleeping at the bottom. Their sleeping techniques did not prevent men from getting sick from the constant exposure to the elements. Frostbite, infection, and hunger were slowly killing the men one by one. It wasn't uncommon for Clarence to wake up some mornings and discover that one of his buddies had not made it through the night, succumbing to whatever illness he had contracted.

Clarence and his fellow captives become cleverer at night, sneaking into the fields to pilfer rotting crops or chicken eggs. Their hunger grew worse. One night they came across a field that had once been occupied by livestock. There were no crops whatsoever; the only thing left behind was cow manure. With no other choice but to starve to death, the men ate the cow dung. "I'll always tell people, cow dung is very sweet," Clarence said, with a trace of humor still intact.

Those who didn't give in to the disgusting diet continued to die. Every day was a challenge. "We woke up in the mornings and said, 'How can we beat the guards?' That's what kept some of us alive."

Clarence and the others had accepted that they were prisoners of war from the day they raised their hands above their heads back in Belgium. After a few months of the same routine of marching and eating snow, tree bark, cow dung, and rotted vegetables, it was evident they weren't just prisoners; they were on some sort of death march. After all, the Germans had refused to put these fifty men in a stalag prison camp.

As much as Clarence tried to stay hopeful, more men died. Their numbers dwindled down to fourteen. They weren't allowed to talk to one another and were kept separate for most of the day. "We lost track of time, days and the months," he told me. By the end of winter, he had long hair, a long beard, long fingernails, and rot and rashes around his body.

He fell violently sick from the things he attempted to eat along the ditches of what he later found out was southern Germany. When civilians approached the captured men and attempted to give them food, the German guards turned them away. By late March 1945, Clarence was close to giving up.

But then early one morning, the dying men heard small arms fire ring out in the distance. It was the closest small arms gunfire they had heard since being captured. Something was up. The guards, who had occupied a farmhouse the night before, were nowhere to be found. They had probably fled while Clarence and the others were sleeping. Unsure what to do, they stayed put.

The sounds of vehicles got closer to the farmhouse. Fifteen infantrymen appeared, accompanying a tank with a large white star on it. It was the U.S. Army. "They told us not to be alarmed and that we would be OK," he remembered. Clarence and the others cried. When he asked what month it was, the GIs told him April.

A truck was called up from the rear, and the surviving American prisoners were brought back into a wooded area. An officer informed the fourteen surviving men that someone wanted to speak to them. Clarence and the other filthy, bearded soldiers, all wearing rags, stood in formation and waited. They were joined by more rescued American prisoners from other locations.

Suddenly a vehicle pulled up and, lo and behold, there was General George S. Patton. Patton jumped out of the jeep and stood in front of the men. "I want you men to know there isn't a fucking politician or military officer who can hold you here any longer," he yelled. "You will all be home in thirty days!"

Clarence and the men broke down and cried again. "He didn't lie. We were home in the United States in less than thirty days."

Before they could be sent home, they needed immediate medical treatment. The former prisoners were brought back to Camp Lucky Strike in France. They needed to be quarantined, as their bodies and hair were infested with bugs.

A cook offered them any meal they wanted. Clarence asked for a steak. The cook prepared the best hunk of meat he could find, but Clarence's stomach had shrunk so much that he could eat only a few bites of it. His cow manure, grass, snow, and rainwater diet had made him weak and sickly, causing him to lose seventy pounds. He was cleaned, given new clothes, and shaved. From France, Clarence was sent to England for further evaluation.

The men were put through psychiatric screening and received more medical care. Two doctors had different opinions on his feet. One wanted to amputate Clarence's toes because parts of them were black. They ultimately decided to see if they would recover with time. It would take years, but Clarence's toes would regain part of their normal color and feeling.

Back in the United States, Clarence found out that his family had been told he was killed in action. His parents had been holding Masses and vigils for him since December. In April they received a new telegram stating he was alive. However, his reunion with his family was postponed. He had to complete more therapy and reintegration training in Lake Placid, New York, at the same facility where many other veterans with battle fatigue went.

Even after spending nearly five months as a prisoner of war and completing the mandatory screenings, Clarence's military obligations were not over. Upon seeing his family, Clarence was given new orders.

He was sent, ironically, to Greenville, Maine, to monitor a German POW camp. The German prisoners were responsible for cutting timber and stacking wood. Clarence could have gotten any kind of revenge he wanted, but he didn't. He never held a grudge or bitterness towards the German prisoners.

By 1946, Clarence's time in the Army was over. His proudest, most emotional moment was being addressed by General Patton. After attending his first and only regiment reunion in the 1970s, he decided it wasn't for him. Nearly every veteran of the regiment was an ex-POW—except they had gotten to live in stalags. Clarence hadn't. He watched as the men laughed and reminisced about being in prison camps. Clarence couldn't relate, and he never took part in another reunion.

Further research was done after the war to learn why Clarence was never put in a stalag. It was determined that he and other American prisoners had been on their way to a stalag that got overrun by the Russians on the east side of Germany. With nowhere to put the Americans, the Germans continuously marched them around looking for a camp to place them in. The advancing armies on each side of the country delayed the men's ever being placed in one spot.

Clarence dealt with his nightmares over the years. He retired as a nuclear engineer in the 1990s, was married for sixty years, and had six kids. He took grace in attending his monthly Veterans of Foreign Wars meetings in Gardner, and he played golf until he was ninety-two. In 2018, the ninety-three-year-old still stood six feet tall with the help of a walker. How the body heals.

He was offered the chance to return to Belgium or Germany several times. He declined every offer.

Clarence Cormier with the rifle. *Photo courtesy of the author*

CHAPTER FOUR

"A Different Composition"

Bernard Ruchin
U.S. Marine Corps, Second Marine Division

Bernard "Bernie" Ruchin grew up on Long Island, New York, a first-generation son of Lithuanian immigrants. His parents didn't teach him their language because they wanted him to adapt to American culture. His dad was a cabinetmaker, and his mom was a cautious lady who refused to sign his enlistment papers when he was sixteen. He graduated high school in the spring of 1943, intent on joining the Navy until he saw a screening of the movie *Wake Island* at his local theater. In a particularly memorable scene of the movie, a group of surrounded Marines receive a telegram from the command asking what they need, and they reply, "Send more Japs!" Bernie fell in love with the Marines' warrior spirit. His mind was made up after that—he was going to be a Marine.

Bernard Ruchin.
Photo courtesy of Bernard Ruchin

When Bernie turned seventeen, he headed to Manhattan to enlist. On Church Street, Bernie and other hopeful teenagers boarded trains to

Washington, D.C., which was a major hub for recruits going to different bases. Bernie and the other New Yorkers then rode in an Atlantic Coast cattle train. Black smoke poured into the windows. Eventually the train pulled into Parris Island, South Carolina, the Marine Corps Recruit Depot.

The recruits boarded a bus headed for the base. At the main gates, a Marine dressed in khakis held a clipboard and boarded the bus. "He told us we were going to be fed, get new clothes, and get a good night's sleep," Bernie said. He was comforted by how nice this Marine was to them. A few minutes later, when they pulled up to a building, the kindness ended.

Another Marine, this time a corporal, boarded the bus and began to scream. "All you people have ten seconds to get off my fucking bus—now!"

The recruits jumped quickly off the bus. Except for one. "I think he was trying to fix his belt," Bernie remembered. The drill instructor reentered the bus, grabbed the boy by the hair, and kicked him off the bus. "When I say move out, I mean fuckin' move out!" the instructor barked.

The recruits had their hair cut and were put into showers. Drill instructors hit them with swagger sticks if they moved too slowly. They lined up the men. "Listen up, little shits. Even though your heart may belong to your sweetheart, your soul may belong to God, here your ass belongs to me. When I say move, you better fuckin' move!"

The next several months proved a brutal wake-up call for Bernie and the other schoolboys turned Marine recruits. Their whole lives had been school days, milkshakes, and bicycle rides. Now they were being taught how to march and kill at close quarters. But that didn't put Bernie or his fellow recruits off. In fact, it made them want to earn their stripes even more. "I didn't care how hard things might get," Bernie told me. "Nothing was stopping me from becoming a Marine."

In late summer of 1943, Bernie graduated from Parris Island and became a U.S. Marine. He attended infantry school in New River, North Carolina, which would later become part of Camp Lejeune. He became a master with his M1 Garand rifle and the Browning automatic rifle, and he had the distinction of being a trained infantryman. Soon Bernie joined the rest of the American Marines and soldiers in the "replacement system." He boarded another train; this one was headed to California.

Bernie's stay in California was short. He received more weapons training, this time being introduced to mortars, machine guns, and bazookas. After a couple of months, a troop transport ship took him to Hawaii. Upon reaching Oahu, Bernie joined the Second Marine Division, a storied division that was already established and battle-proven. They had fought on the island of Tarawa, taking heavy casualties but defeating the Japanese. One thousand Marines had been killed in action, and over two thousand were wounded. Bernie would be a replacement Marine for the Easy Company Second Battalion, Second Marine Division.

The veteran Marines of the Battle of Tarawa did not warm up to the replacements right away. "They didn't mistreat us, but they politely ignored us," Bernie recalled. "The men who'd fought on Tarawa were very tight, and when they lost a buddy, it was a shock. When a new face came in, the green kids could never replace the man they had fought with."

The division was on the Hawaiian Islands to train, not just recover. For weeks they practiced landings on Maui and Red Clay Beach. The soldiers wanted to make sure they didn't make the same mistakes they had made on Tarawa, where scores of Marines had lost their lives after the landing crafts got stuck on coral reefs. They had been caught in the open, sitting ducks for wave after wave of Japanese artillery fire.

After almost a year of serving as a Marine, Bernie's time to deploy abroad finally came. The order came down for the Second Marine Division, the Fourth Marine Division, and the U.S. Army's Twenty-Seventh Infantry Division to rendezvous at Ulithi Atoll, a small island in the Pacific, south of the Philippines and Mariana Islands. The Marines and the Navy used Ulithi to dock ships, fix aircraft, and resupply. With thousands of ships surrounding the islands, the men of Bernie's company knew the day for which they had been training was fast approaching.

While ships moved out for their next mission in the Pacific, the Normandy landings were taking place in France. "They came over the intercom on the ship and asked us to pray for the guys invading Europe," Bernie said. "'Who is praying for us?' I thought."

More serious communication wasn't transmitted by radio. Another ship pulled alongside Bernie's troop transport ship. After a wire was strung from deck to deck, the other ship slid a buoy over on the line containing orders for the Marine commanders—a safety measure to assure that the Japanese could not decode messages over radio. The documents contained orders to head for Saipan in the Mariana Islands— and invade it. The news spread. The new guys celebrated as the veterans brooded. The men were given steak and eggs with a shot of brandy. After all, it could be the last meal they ever had.

The Marines had never heard of Saipan. It was 12.5 miles long and 1,400 miles away from mainland Japan. This meant jack shit to the Marines but everything to the Army Air Corps. From Saipan, they could launch bombing raids against mainland Japan, which they hadn't been able to do before. Range was everything to the Air Corps.

In the early morning of June 15, 1944, Bernie and his fellow troops were ordered to climb down the nets set over the side of the ship to board Higgins boats. After the small landing crafts were loaded, they circled offshore for nearly two hours as naval artillery bombardment and air raids pounded the island. Japanese artillery was zeroed in on the beach, prepared to make mincemeat of the landing Marines. The enemy guns were located on the reverse slope of the hillside that the Marines later nicknamed "Mt. Tapioca."

Three hours after he had boarded the Higgins boat, Bernie's landing craft headed towards the beach. "The tide was very strong. I was in the sixth wave," he said. "Luckily, we didn't end up too far off course."

But despite seamlessly navigating the challenging conditions, Bernie's boat still faced a chaotic situation when it arrived at the beach. The beach master who was supposed to direct Bernie's assault wave was nowhere to be found, and as a result the men didn't have instructions about how they were supposed to storm the island. The confusion didn't last long: the Marines had no choice but to push forward without clear direction.

They dismounted safely and made their way towards the sandy beach, with fires raging in the jungle tree line just beyond it. Multiple pillboxes were destroyed, containing what Bernie recognized as his first dead Japanese soldiers. "Their blood covered the cinderblocks that were once their bunker," he told me.

Friendlies were also dead. Lifeless Marines—most likely from the first wave—and blown-up landing crafts were scattered along the beach. Bernie carried his M1 Garand rifle and took cover along a berm, awaiting orders. He had no targets and no Japanese to engage his first day on Saipan. The Marines advanced beyond the beach, but not far. They dug in for their first night on the island.

The next day, the Second Marine Division pushed up the coastline. The division waited until its adjacent units aligned with it. They picked up the left flank, with the U.S Army Twenty-Seventh Infantry Division in the center and the Fourth Marine Division on the right. When all the divisions were in formation, they would begin their push north. The Navy provided auxiliary support along the coastline. At night they would shoot white star illumination rounds in the air to give the infantrymen some visibility.

During the second night on Saipan, the Marines could hear the sound of tracked vehicles in the distance. All of a sudden, explosion after explosion landed close to their foxholes. A white illumination round went screaming into the sky, bursting to create a temporary daylight effect. The bright flash of light gave the Marines a sight line across the plain in front of them: six Japanese tanks were advancing on their position.

Bazooka men were frantically called up to the front. Brand new to combat, they juggled the rocket launchers nervously at the first sighting of the enemy. Some men dropped the explosive shells in the mud. Men began to fire on the tanks, with some missing and others scoring hits on the tracked vehicles. Bernie and the other Marines engaged the advancing infantry. Without the help of the illumination round, they couldn't make out the enemy soldiers clearly and aimed their gunfire at the advancing tanks.

Half-track howitzers and their 75 mm cannons were the most essential weapon in the battle. The half-track howitzers knocked out the tanks one after another. The Marines manning .50 caliber machine guns continued to create a wall of fire with assistance from the Navy's flares.

After almost an hour, the Japanese tanks stopped moving. They were on fire or destroyed. The Japanese infantry—nearly one thousand men—lay dead or had retreated. The glow from the burning enemy tanks provided small pockets of light throughout the night. Wounded Japanese soldiers could be seen crawling for safety, but Marines picked them off before they could reach cover.

The next morning, the Marines of Bernie's company couldn't advance. They were ordered to wait for the Fourth Marines and the U.S. Army to pivot in their direction. Marines walked through the destroyed Japanese tanks, some still smoking. "The half-track howitzers and U.S. medium tanks were so accurate," Bernie recalled when describing the wreckage. "We later heard that this was the biggest tank battle of the Pacific War."

The American forces had destroyed thirty-one Japanese tanks. But despite such an impressive showing, the victory celebration was short. The push north was about to begin.

By June 20, five days after landing on the beach, all three divisions started to make their way deeper into Saipan. It wasn't long before inter-military branch communication became difficult. The Marines and the Army followed different procedures, which quickly became confused in their forward push. The Army's Twenty-Seventh Infantry Division became bogged down in the center of the island. "They seemed to move slower than us. They would really drag when opening up a flank," Bernie explained.

The brass wasn't happy with the Army's lack of progress. General Holland Smith, commander of the Saipan operation, relieved Army general Ralph Smith, accusing him of moving too slowly and not protecting the Marine flanks. The decision would remain controversial for decades.

Whether the reason was a different caliber of training or stiffer resistance, it was no secret that the Army was having trouble in the center of the island. The Army faced more valleys and hills with strong defenses, which inflicted heavy casualties on the Army men in what they called "Death Valley." Intense fire rained on them, whereas the Second and Fourth Marine Divisions often moved unopposed.

After overcoming the enemy encampments, the Army's 27th Infantry Division began to move steadily again. Aggravated by the rivalry with the Marines and embarrassed that his commander had been relieved, the regimental commander of the 105th Infantry, Colonel O'Brien, led his soldiers to outflank Japanese positions on a ridge. Colonel O'Brien darted across an open field armed with only a pistol, leading his soldiers to win multiple firefights against the enemy. The attack was fierce enough to surprise a company of Japanese soldiers positioned in a valley. The Army captured multiple artillery pieces and killed scores of Japanese, restoring their confidence.

"We were impressed with the rumors we heard," Bernie said. "The average Army soldier performed well; it was their leadership that originally failed them. Some would have made damn good Marines."

Advancing farther up the west coast, Bernie's battalion reached the valleys of Mount Tapochau by late June. "Tapioca," as the Marines called it, was lined with Japanese artillery. The Marines had been dreading this moment, which promised to be their own Death Valley. But the Army had pulled its weight; now it was their turn. They even gave the valley through which they advanced its own nickname—Harakiri Gulch, due to the fact that the Marines were exposed on all sides.

As they advanced through the gulch, the Japanese attacked the Marines with mortars and sniper fire. After ambushing the Marines, the Japanese would retreat into tunnels they had excavated and then attack again from different openings. The Marines never knew where an attack would come from, and many succumbed to the waves of enemy fire. In response, the infantrymen escorted what they referred to as "Zippo" tanks toward the tunnel and cave entrances. The Zippo tank was a Sherman tank equipped with a giant flamethrower instead of a cannon.

The idea was to burn out the Japanese soldiers in the cave and tunnel networks. As the Zippo released a massive plume of flame into the entrance of a particular cave, Japanese soldiers, set on fire by the flamethrowers, would emerge from different spider holes in search of safety. The Marines would then fire at them, leaving their burning corpses where they lay.

Once they made it through Harakiri Gulch, Bernie's unit was tasked with advancing through a field just past Tapioca to help secure the mountain. As they pushed forward, a firefight broke out. Enemy rounds began to snap and crack around Bernie, forcing him and his fellow Marines to seek cover in the field. He knelt in some brush and called out to his fellow Marines, asking if they could make out the enemy's location. After emptying eight rounds of his M1 Garand in the enemy's general direction, he moved to take up a better defensive position.

As he scrambled in search of a natural depression that could provide some cover, Bernie saw an object land to his left in his peripheral vision. Before he could make out exactly what it was, the Japanese hand grenade detonated, sending shrapnel into his leg and face. Bernie fell to the ground in shock. He had finally been hit. "I knew it was going to happen sooner or later," he told me. "My hearing was also gone."

He crawled to safety, and the Navy corpsmen carried him away. Despite the fact that he didn't know where the Japanese soldier who had thrown the grenade was, Bernie was confident that he was not alive. The Marines had shot up everything and anything in the area. The Marines had taken heavy losses; tragically, Bernie lost two of his good friends, Dutch and Brad.

Back at the aid station on the beach, medics had to remove the shrapnel from Bernie's body. Shrapnel had just missed Bernie's eyeball, but was lodged in the corner of his eye socket. The doctor told him to sit still. "The doctor came at me with this thing that looked like a small pitchfork to remove the metal," Bernie said. "Naturally it was hard for me not to move my eye around." The doctor became frustrated as the injured Bernie instinctively averted his eye, but he was able to extract the shrapnel after some struggle. After just one day of healing, Bernie was ready to go back with his Marines. "You don't want to leave your guys. That's your security," Bernie reflected. "I wanted to stay with the Tarawa Marines so they could tell me how to survive through this."

It was now July, and the Second Marine Division was ascending northern Saipan. The Japanese had seaplanes and airplane hangars in one of the northern harbors, Tanapag Harbor, where they were storing the rest of their tanks and equipment. Bernie and the Marines met stiffer resistance in this area, forced to take on whatever the Naval airpower wasn't able to eliminate.

Advancing with tank and friendly artillery cover, the Marines swarmed Tanapag. A straight line of U.S. Armed Forces stretched across Saipan—the Second Marine Division on the left, the U.S. Army in the middle, and the Fourth Marine Division on the right. All units were caught up after the heavy losses at Garapan, Death Valley, Purple Heart Ridge, Mount Tapioca, and Tanapag Plain.

The interservice trash talk and rivalry ceased between the Army and the Marines once the situation on Saipan got more violent than ever. The Americans knew they had all sacrificed something. The blood of fallen soldiers turned competition into a mature spirit of cooperation. They would soon have the Japanese soldiers pinned against the ocean in northern Saipan. Resupply was not an option for the enemy, as the Battle of the Philippine Sea had destroyed any chance of their ships making it to Saipan for rescue or reinforcement.

The Japanese troops on Saipan had nothing left. After less than a month of fighting, the survivors had been pushed all the way to the tip of Saipan, known as Marpi Point. Their artillery was destroyed or captured by the Americans. Their tanks had all been knocked out in earlier battles. The desperate Japanese soldiers had little to no personal ammo.

On July 6, 1944, Bernie's battalion pushed out of Tanapag toward Marpi Point. The day was uneventful. At night the companies dug in.

Bernie shared a shell hole with another Marine whose name he would not remember. At around three o'clock in the morning, Bernie heard wrestling and movement ahead of him. "All of a sudden you could hear Japs hollering and hooting," he recalled.

Bernie's squad leader ran from foxhole to foxhole. "He told us to maintain fire discipline, to fix our bayonets, and not to give away our positions." This far into the Saipan campaign, the Marines were aware of the Japanese tactic of making noises to get trigger-happy Americans to shoot, giving away their position. Wise to the trick this time, Bernie and his company did not fire a single shot. They held tight to their rifles fixed with bayonets and waited. "It was nerve-racking. At nighttime, your eyes play tricks on you, too—shadows, the wind. It all creates paranoia."

As the company of Marines fought through their anxiety with much patience, they heard broken English in the distance. Bernie heard a Japanese soldier yelling, "Tonight we drink Marine brud! Tonight we drink Marine brud!" The Americans noticed that the Japanese had trouble pronouncing Ls, which led them to a clever idea of their own. "That's why all our nighttime passwords were like 'lollapalooza' and 'lollipops,'" Bernie explained.

The noises got closer and turned into rapid footsteps. Screaming Japanese soldiers began to assault Bernie's company. "I had three grenades and I lined them up on the ridge of my foxhole. Four Japanese soldiers advanced on us. I had an M1 Garand and fired all my rounds towards the Jap soldiers. I know I hit the closest one, but he still kept running towards me." With no time to reload, Bernie prepared for hand-to-hand combat. "He ran directly into my bayonet!"

The Japanese soldier plunged into Bernie's bayonet, which was attached to his rifle. "It was either a lucky hand-to-hand combat maneuver, or he fell into it as he was dying," Bernie said, mulling over the scene from more than a half century prior. "I'm not sure," he concluded, "but the threat wasn't over. My bayonet entered his chest and I couldn't get it out. I was trying to pull it out when another Japanese soldier ran up on me and hit me in the head with some sort of sword."

The sword hit Bernie's helmet and slid off without injuring him. With his rifle still stuck inside the enemy soldier's chest cavity, he went right for his Marine-issued KA-BAR knife and plunged it several times into the Japanese soldier. "I grabbed him, brought him into my body, and stabbed him in the neck and chest." The other Marine in the foxhole had his own enemies to fight and couldn't help Bernie. While Bernie was engaged in hand-to-hand combat, his partner kept shooting out of the foxhole at the charging Japanese. He managed to kill another Japanese soldier entering the foxhole while Bernie was locked in his struggle with the second Japanese attacker. After dispatching the second invader, Bernie used all his might to pull his M1-Garand out of the first enemy soldier. Visibly shaking, he reloaded eight new rounds and opened fire on the advancing enemy until sunrise.

The carnage of that night was like no other. The next morning, the field was strewn with Japanese corpses. Foxholes were filled with dead Japanese next to dead Marines, who had fought until they were overwhelmed. The Americans later learned that they had fought through the largest banzai attack of World War II, a suicide charge the Japanese often engaged in when they were severely outnumbered. Some three thousand Japanese soldiers charged three different front lines, ordered by General Saitō to fight to the death—and bring as many enemies down with them as they could.

This banzai attack was carried out by desperate Japanese soldiers with little to no ammunition. Their own wounded and civilians charged in their ranks, carrying sharp bamboo sticks. While all were ultimately killed, the attack managed to do some damage. Some of the charging horde had penetrated the front lines, making their way to the artillery units in the rear. Facing point-blank cannon fire, some Japanese still managed to overrun the artillery positions, hoping to use Marine howitzers against American forces. Marines manning howitzers were forced to fire on their own artillery pieces, which had been taken over by Japanese infiltrators. Some Marines were forced to retreat, destroying their howitzers with grenades to prevent them from falling into enemy hands.

But in the end, even the most successful enemy waves were repulsed. The massive banzai attack was successfully warded off.

"Attacks continued throughout the days, but nothing like that night," Bernie told me. For the next two days, the men pushed farther towards Marpi Point. On July 9, Japanese general Saitō committed suicide with the other Japanese commanders. His last orders were that no one—including civilians—was to surrender to the Americans. "The Japanese Army told the civilians on Saipan that the Marines would murder and rape you, and that in order to be a Marine, you had to kill one of your own parents." Scores of civilians committed suicide. Some asked Japanese soldiers to kill them. Others, including numerous families holding their children, began to jump off cliffs at Marpi Point, crashing on the jagged rocks below. "Their bodies would sit at the bottoms of the cliffs all day until a tide strong enough would take them out." The U.S. military brought in loudspeakers along with translators to plead with the civilians. Some of the Japanese civilians who considered surrendering but hesitated to exit were shot by Japanese soldiers hiding in caves.

The U.S. military labeled Saipan secure by early July. The U.S. forces on the island had suffered some 3,500 deaths and 13,000 wounded. Nearly 27,000 Japanese soldiers died on Saipan, but only a few hundred prisoners were taken. Although announced "secured," approximately 2,000 more Japanese soldiers and civilians still hid throughout the island. For the next twelve months, U.S. Marines would lead different missions to kill or capture them.

Bernie and the Second Marine Division were given a two-week break once Saipan was officially secured. The break flew by; soon enough they had to load onto landing crafts at Tanapag Bay to assault the next island, Tinian, seven miles away from southern Saipan. The next assault was left solely in the hands of the Marines; no Army this time.

Tinian proved to be much easier than Saipan, as the Japanese resistance was far outnumbered by the Americans. The two Marine divisions overwhelmed the eight thousand Japanese soldiers. The island was only a support island for the Japanese Army and not heavily defended. The Marines took the island in just eight days.

As the Marines pushed their way through the first airfield and multiple sugarcane fields, the Naval airpower had any Japanese on the run. "The Navy planes flew overhead with these big torpedo-looking things and dropped them, and entire buildings and fields exploded into fireballs," Bernie said of the scene on Tinian. At the time, he didn't know that he had just witnessed the first time napalm was ever used in World War II. "It burned out everything and was the best weapon against the Japanese, who were always burrowed away in defensive positions."

Once Tinian fell, Bernie was sent back to Saipan until the war's end as part of clean-up operations. "Tinian was nothing compared to Saipan. Nothing will ever be the equivalent to that last banzai charge," Bernie remembered. "The human thrust that came at us that night was horrifying. We fought within arm's length. It's nothing compared to a long-range firefight; its personal."

Bernie stayed on Saipan until the dropping of the atomic bombs. At the end of the war, in 1946, Bernie arrived at Penn Station in New York City. "I had a few sea bags, and this nice Marine recruiter gave me a ride all the way back to Long Island." In the car, the Marine persuaded Bernie to stay in the reserves. That way if there was another war he could keep his rank and same pay. "I couldn't say no. I felt bad for the guy giving me such a long ride and signed up as a favor," Bernie admitted to me.

In 1947, Bernie accepted a job with the New York state police. In the summer of 1949, Bernie was dispatched to a small town in upstate New York. One night, a caller reported that a man was running loose in the town square, swinging a machete. Speeding with lights and sirens, the state troopers reached the center of town. Bernie and a second state trooper circled the man. A bystander informed them that the man had fought in Europe and was "off his rocker."

Neither Bernie nor his partner wanted to shoot a fellow veteran. They distracted the crazed man, tackled him, and removed the blade from his hands. "The incident was the first time I realized that we, as veterans, are all built of a different composition," Bernie said.

But in 1950, Bernie's time as a trooper came to a brief close. His favor for the Marine recruiter came back to bite him in the ass. "The police dispatcher got on the radio and told me to call home," he told me. "I was about sixty miles away in my cruiser." When Bernie called home, his wife was crying. She began to read him a letter from the U.S. Marine Corps. "The letter said I had eight days to report for active duty, and that I was mobilized," Bernie said. "I couldn't fucking believe it."

Bernie, now a gunnery sergeant, was activated for the Korean War. A few months later, he was wounded for a second time when a mortar shell exploded near him. His Korean War experience lasted just a couple months before he was able to return home and work as a state trooper again, a position in which he served twenty-two years.

When he moved to New Hampshire after retirement in the 1980s, he remained actively involved in veteran affairs, especially with a group called Building Dreams for Marines. Working with vets grounded him. Not only was he able to give back and help fellow brothers rebuild their homes for better access, but he was reminded of how lucky he was. Even after being wounded in two wars, he had come home. And there he sat, grateful for a life after war.

Bernie Ruchin with the rifle. *Photo courtesy of the author*

CHAPTER FIVE

Uncle Rodney

Rodney Perkins
U.S. Army, Eighty-Seventh Infantry Division

Rodney had waited seventy-five years to do something with the letter he now held out to me. It was placed neatly in a binder that contained a brief history of B Company in the 345th Infantry Regiment, 87th Division. Rodney and I were in Saint-Hubert, Belgium, standing in a farmhouse that had been converted into a museum dedicated to Rodney's old division, the 87th, which had been responsible for liberating the area. When Rodney walked in, he was treated like the pope walking into the Vatican.

With the letter in hand, I got everyone's attention in the room. "This is a letter written by the mother of Leo Luxemburg," I told them. "Leo was killed in action here in Belgium. This letter was written to Rodney from Leo's

Rodney Perkins. *Photo courtesy of Rodney Perkins*

mother. He would like to dedicate it to your museum. He thinks it deserves to be here."

As a translator repeated what I had said in French, I could see the museum owner begin to get emotional. He looked more like a farmer than a philanthropist. He had missing teeth, dirty boots, and old clothes on. He wasn't in it for the money; he truly believed that the Americans who had liberated his small town seventy-five years ago were heroes.

Rodney looked satisfied, but not overly enthused. He had wanted to leave the letter in the town that Private Leo Luxembourg gave his life in, Moircy. The town was just ten minutes away, and it's where Company B made its sacrifices during the winter of 1944–1945. But Moircy had forgotten the warriors who had liberated her. Any representation of the United States and its battles no longer existed. The pub Rodney had visited in 1996 that had taken his 87th Division hat and hung it up was gone, which visibly upset Rodney. "They told me it would be there forever," he muttered with a shrug.

Moircy was more than just a town. It was a name Rodney's kids and grandkids learned at a young age. It was the town in which Rodney was wounded, the town in which he survived the Battle of the Bulge, and the town in which he lost friends. And at this very moment, it was the town to which I had convinced him to return seventy-five years later.

I had met Rodney just six months before. He lived in a town in Massachusetts called Warren that I hadn't heard of before. Rodney was referred to me by John McAuliffe, the veteran who connected me to so many men, including Ernie Roberts, during my visits to Worcester. John was supposed to join us on the return trip to Belgium, but he had started dialysis. He gave his seat to Rodney. John died at the age of ninety-six on the day we left for the trip. To me, it was a sign that I was supposed to meet Rodney.

Hundreds of family photos were hung from the floor to the ceiling on the walls of Rodney's home. There were photos of kids, grandkids, and great-grandkids as far as the eye could see. They had massive family reunions, and they proudly displayed the evidence. I couldn't help but call him "Uncle Rodney." He was obviously a family man who brought people together.

Rodney was short and looked like he was in his mid-seventies, not ninety-four. He was the kind of guy you could look at and still see the nineteen-year-old he once was. After he showed me his family photos, we sat down at the dining room table. I broke out the rifle and laid it in front of him; he smiled from ear to ear. He picked up the rifle without asking and slapped it against his palms several times. The man was still an infantryman at heart.

Rodney grew up in Leominster, Massachusetts, and was drafted in 1943. After completing basic training at Fort Jackson, South Carolina, Rodney went on to become a member of the Eighty-Seventh Division. The division landed in Le Havre, France, in November of 1944, seeing its first action not long after.

I had already recorded the division's combat in France with Ernie Roberts, so I asked Rodney, "What was worse, France or Belgium?"

Without hesitation, he replied, "Oh Moircy, Belgium—it was such a small town, the fighting raged for days and it was really close quarters."

I had Rodney take me in his memory right into the town of Moircy. "I was the first scout of the company; the first man in. I had to recon it and report back to the company what I observed. The homes in the town were made of stone; there was a brook that ran past the village and under a wooden bridge." Rodney gestured with his hands as if he were creating a model of the town on the dining room table. It was unbelievable that he could remember so many details so long after he had been there.

"When I went back to give my report to my commanding officer, I told them I didn't think we should cross the bridge," he recalled. "I told him I was afraid we would be zeroed in on by indirect fire." Taking his advice, Rodney's company decided to cross through a shallow brook on foot. It was the first time the men's feet got wet, and they would stay that way all winter. Frostbite and trench foot became serious issues later on, but the men had to risk crossing the brook to avoid getting blown apart by artillery.

Rodney again took the lead back into town. "As I entered a field upon crossing the brook, a machine gun opened fire. The fire was coming from inside a house on a hill," he remembered. Rodney hit the ground as dirt flew up all around him. As he attempted to get up to run, Rodney felt a burning sensation in his butt cheek. He had been hit.

"Every third round was a tracer, and I knew that's what must have hit me. It burned so bad, and I fell back on the ground and just lay there," he said. More machine gun bullets hit the ground around him. Rodney lay there for a while, knowing he was a dead man if tried to make an escape. "I figured the Germans would exit the home and come capture me, but they didn't," he told me.

Instead, firefights broke out from the town and into the tree line where Company B was. Snipers were scoring kills on American officers, leaving leadership to the sergeants, who then found themselves in deadly crosshairs. Rodney's sergeant, Sergeant Teel, was soon killed. As several squads made their way past Rodney, they helped him up. Once the enemy machine guns had been silenced, they approached the town. The Americans stormed a house, taking several German prisoners.

"The sergeants had anyone that was wounded take the Germans back to the rear," Rodney remembered. "I didn't think my wound was bad enough, so I stayed with the company. I just had a combat medic patch me up, and I limped around afterwards." Rodney and anyone who wasn't wounded badly began to take shelter in the homes in Moircy. "The bridge that I didn't want the company to cross had an MG 42 on it, and it was smoking. The Germans left it when we got closer," he said.

Rodney's squad found a Belgian family inside the first house that they entered. The family was very shaken up from the fighting. "There was an older couple in the home. The woman seemed nervous, but an American soldier put his arm around her and said, 'Don't worry, the Americans are here now, we will take care of you,'" Rodney remembered. "No sooner had he said that than a bullet entered the window of the home and struck the soldier across the nose." The woman fainted instantly.

The six Americans, including Rodney, rendered aid to both the civilian and the soldier bleeding from the face. As things quieted down, the local family shared what little food they had with the men. The soldiers had toast with jam and a warm cup of milk, straight from the cows in the barn.

Just as Rodney and his squad were getting somewhat comfortable, the Germans began to move back into Moircy. "Our company decided to fall back into the woods, but my squad was never told. We didn't have communication wires set up yet, so we did everything with runners," he said. As gunfire and artillery landed all over town, Rodney peered out the window and saw a dead American soldier. Rodney later assumed that the dead man had been a runner sent to inform his squad that the company was falling back.

Smoke from the burning homes of Moircy filled the streets. Rodney began to cough, thinking the smoke was pouring in from the nearby fires. But he soon realized that the smoke was too thick to be coming from the house next door; the house he was in must be burning too. The homeowner went upstairs and began to shriek. The roof of his home was ablaze.

"I went into the attic on a ladder and saw the flames. We started a bucket brigade to try to save the man's home, but the smoke became too much to bear," Rodney explained. As he and the others were overcome by smoke, they had to pull the Belgian man away from the flames. He was desperate to save his home, but he would die if he stayed any longer. "The old man didn't want to quit, I had to push him off the ladder," Rodney recalled.

In a last-ditch effort to save some of his property, the Belgian ran to the attached barn and released his cows. Watching the cows exit the barn and escape being burned alive was a small relief. At least the man's livestock had been saved. But as the cows wandered up the road, machine gun bullets tore into the innocent animals. A German Panzer tank was parked up the street, unleashing its MG 34 on the herd of cows, mowing them down. Rodney could hardly process the scene then, but seventy-five years later there was time to reflect, and he wept for the cows as he told me the story.

This was the second time I had seen a World War II veteran cry while discussing the death of animals during the war. In fact, veterans sometimes seemed to be more emotional over an animal's death than a human's. Perhaps the animals represented something innocent in war, while the humans knew what they were getting into. It was a question I couldn't get myself to ask Rodney or the other veterans. Seeing men in their nineties cry was one of the hardest parts of this journey.

After I gave Rodney a break, we dove right back into the story. "When we rejoined the company, orders came for us to move back into town the next morning," he said. Company B advanced back into Moircy to learn that the Germans had fallen back again. "They wanted us to dig in on the other side of the town to defend it from being retaken," Rodney explained.

As Company B pushed outside town, they noticed foxholes that had already been dug. "There were Americans occupying the holes, but they were all dead, every one of them. Some were stripped completely naked," he said.

"Were they Eighty-Seventh Division men?" I asked.

"No, I still to this day don't know who they were. All I know is some were naked, and the Germans had taken their uniforms to wear in order sneak into our lines," Rodney replied. "That kind of stuff was happening during the Battle of the Bulge."

The men soon came under enemy fire and were forced to jump into the foxholes already manned by the dead, naked American soldiers. "We tossed them out of the holes to make room for ourselves," Rodney remembered. "I'll never forget Sergeant Nowak hesitated to do so, and he got shot." Nowak died from his wounds. It was also during this time that Leo Luxemburg was killed, but Rodney didn't learn this until later. The Germans had opened up on the Americans using an anti-aircraft gun, a weapon meant for planes and vehicles. It decimated part of the company.

In the following days, the battle raged and the temperature dropped. "One guy in my company, he was a big fellow, took off his boots and his feet immediately puffed up," Rodney said. "He couldn't get his boots back on and I remember him walking around with his boots over his shoulder. Later on they had to amputate both of his feet due to frostbite."

The men of the 345th Infantry Regiment, although badly beaten, went on to survive the Battle of the Bulge and the German counterattacks. In February 1945, the 87th helped with clean-up operations around Belgium. It was during this time that the division began to receive replacements for those killed in the Ardennes offensive.

"One time I had to bring a few new guys out to the front lines to create an outpost. I walked them out in knee-deep snow with some communication wire so they could report their observations," Rodney said. He watched as the two new replacements struggled to dig a foxhole. The ground was covered in snow, frozen solid. "I know the ground was frozen, so that's why they were having a hard time. It was just funny that the veterans in our company, who knew what it was like to come under artillery fire, never seemed to have an issue digging a hole, no matter what the weather was." Rodney laughed as he reminisced. He ultimately grabbed a shovel from one of the men and began to help.

"While I was digging, I heard one of the new replacements say, 'Halt!'" Rodney recalled. He dropped his shovel and looked up. "The soldier then went on to say, 'Oh, sorry, I thought you were a German.'" Rodney glanced at the person who was walking up on them, and he immediately knew that the replacement was right: the approaching man was a German soldier. "I knew he was German because he was carrying a burp gun, and we didn't have any weapons like that. He was wearing white camouflage, too." Rodney screamed at the replacement, "Shoot, shoot, shoot!" Just as the German began taking his machine pistol off his shoulder, the American soldier fired eight rounds into him. "The German fell over, mumbled something, and died quickly," Rodney said. "It was then that I thought, I bet there are more coming now."

When the sun came up the next morning, Rodney and the replacements were lying in a half-dug fighting position, with the dead German just a few feet away. His once-white camouflage suit was now blood-red. "I could see a patrol of Germans heading our way," Rodney remembered. "I had one of the new guys radio back to the rear positions that we would be falling back." The replacement looked at Rodney and said, "The commanding officer says all outposts must stay put."

"If we stay, you are going to look like him really soon," Rodney fired back, pointing to the dead German. Rodney got on the communications phone himself and told the soldier on the other end that they were coming back and to hold their fire.

Rodney looked at the nervous soldiers and told them to follow his lead. They ditched the observation post and made a break for it. As soon as the men took off, they came under fire. "Rounds were snapping all around us; the enemy patrol had us in their sights," he said. The Americans began to crawl in two feet of snow. Periodically they got back up to run, but they had to dive into the snow to avoid being shot.

As Rodney and the replacements dove into random foxholes back at the American lines, they attempted to return fire. "My rifle was frozen solid; I couldn't shoot," Rodney remembered. The other American soldiers who occupied the foxholes were also hindered by frozen weapons. The Germans were able to get closer because of the lack of firepower coming from the Americans' position. "If it wasn't for our mortar men, we would have gotten overrun," Rodney said.

The company's mortar squad placed accurate high-explosive rounds on the German patrol, scattering them. Rodney was able to squeeze a round out of his M1 rifle, bursting the ice that was encasing it. He began to lay accurate rifle fire on the enemy, repelling them from friendly lines.

This last firefight marked the end of the Ardennes campaign for Company B of the 345th Regiment. By March of 1945, the 87th Division was finally making its way into Germany. Its first objective was to assault the Siegfried Line.

The Germans were no longer defending their territory from wooden houses that could be fired upon and easily destroyed. They were in bunkers and pillboxes with reinforced concrete walls. Their guns stuck out of small apertures, so that it was easy for them to fire on American soldiers and difficult for fire to be returned on them. It was a defense line that had been set up before World War I. It would not be easy to take.

After the 345th Regiment crossed the border into Germany, B Company was responsible for taking out some of the first fortified positions on the Siegfried Line. "They made three of us demolition men," Rodney recalled. "One soldier carried the primer cord, another the blasting caps, and I carried the TNT."

As Rodney's platoon fired on a pillbox, he and the two other men sprinted towards it. Rodney climbed on top of the concrete fortification, ready to prep his explosive and place it into the smokestack. "When I turned around for the guys to hand me what they were carrying, they weren't there; they chickened out," he said. Rodney was furious. He had been left by himself on top of an enemy pillbox with an unknown number of Germans inside it. Without the proper pieces of the bomb, he couldn't finish the job.

Rodney was forced to climb off the bunker and retreat. The men who had been assigned to him were new replacements. Once he found them, he stripped them of the primer cords and blasting caps. "I held on to all the equipment after that, so I wouldn't be left high and dry again," he said.

"If you took that pillbox on your own, you would have gotten a Medal of Honor," I said.

"Yeah, well, a lot of guys did heroic things in World War II and were never written up for it," he replied.

That night, the Eighty-Seventh Division set up loudspeakers. They made announcements in both German and English, demanding that the enemy soldiers surrender. "My captain, Captain Pike, came up to me and said, 'Rodney, we need to go grab some German prisoners from CP. There are some German foxholes up ahead, and we want to show the

Germans we aren't going to hurt them by using already captured prisoners as proof,'" Rodney remembered. The captain thought it would be a good idea to use German prisoners as bargaining tools.

As Rodney and his captain marched the Germans closer to the enemy positions, they took fire from a German soldier positioned in a tree. The men hit the ground, and their prisoners took off. The Americans returned fire, killing the German soldier in the tree. Dismayed that they had just lost all their original prisoners, Rodney and his captain approached the enemy foxholes.

"I laid my M1 rifle down on the ground, took out a grenade, and prepared to throw it in the hole. For some reason I could not do it. I threw the grenade in without pulling the pin," he admitted to me. I was surprised to hear Rodney say this, but maybe he had had enough of the killing by then.

The captain, however, did pull the pin, lobbing his grenade into a foxhole and killing a German soldier. Rodney rushed the foxholes with his M1 on his hip. Rodney and the captain captured two Germans, who happened to be medics. "Not only were they medics, but they had an American soldier with them," Rodney said. "The soldier told us to take care of these Germans because they had taken care of him." Rodney respected the wishes of the rescued American. The Germans and the American soldier were guided back to friendly lines.

"My regiment pushed through the Siegfried Line relatively easily after that," he recalled. After breaking the defenses, the Eighty-Seventh Division captured the capital of the Rhineland, the city of Koblenz. "I remember there was a great big statue of a general riding a horse in the city. General Patton ordered us to blow it up, so we did. The statue tumbled down into the river and sank to the bottom. I don't know why we did it—I think maybe Patton was jealous, but when I went back in 1996 it was standing back up again, where it was supposed to be."

By March 16, 1945, the 87th Division was set to cross the Rhine River and head deeper into German territory. "My company was one of the first across. It was six men to a boat, and we paddled our lives away,"

Rodney remembered. The company's heavy mortars shot smoke screen shells on the opposite bank to provide cover. "By the time we got across, engineers had finished a Bailey bridge. The first tanks were already making their way over, on the first day!"

Once across, the company raced towards a bridge that hadn't yet been blown. "They wanted us to secure any bridges possible. We were meters away from it when the Germans detonated it. I said to myself, 'Thank God I wasn't on that bridge when it went boom!' It was too bad the Germans blew all those beautiful bridges over there; it really didn't slow us down much," Rodney said.

The Eighty-Seventh Division blasted its way through Germany all through the month of April, town after town, capturing thousands of

Rodney Perkins with the rifle. *Photo courtesy of the author*

prisoners. The German soldiers were surrendering to the Americans en masse for fear of being forced to surrender to the Russians. On May 12, the Eighty-Seventh Division met the Red Army in Czechoslovakia.

"They had been through hell, just like us," Rodney said. He met a young Russian soldier in the street. "He gave me a big hug and a ruble. I still have it to this day." Rodney smiled; it was one of his fonder memories of the war. "I wish I got his address or something."

Rodney returned home and did what most central Massachusetts boys did in those days: he got a job at a factory. He worked making matchbooks, egg cartons, and other materials. For just $10,000, he purchased 200 acres of land on which he still lives today. With the land came 20 cows. Rodney wasn't a farmer. He didn't sell milk or make cheese. I often think he kept the cows around to make up for what had happened in Belgium to that farmer's cows. Seeing the cows and taking care of them brought him peace in his life.

CHAPTER SIX

Seventy-Two Seconds

Hershel "Woody" Williams
U.S. Marine Corps, Third Marine Division

Ona, West Virginia

Hershel "Woody" Williams was a living Marine legend. For Woody's valiant service with a trusty flamethrower, President Truman hung the Medal of Honor around his neck, changing his life forever. Seventy-five years later, Woody sat in his living room with some pathetic nerd from Boston asking him for an interview and to sign a rifle, forcing him to pretend like he hadn't done these interviews a million times by now.

Those were the thoughts running through my head as I drove down a West Virginia road to meet Woody at his home. The fact that he even gave me the time of day was due to other veterans who had signed the rifle before him. Their confidence in me, plus my efforts to help severely wounded veterans back in Boston, was enough to win over Woody's trust. His grandsons, Brent and Chad, had set up the meeting. They accompanied him all over the country for veteran events and Medal of Honor appearances. They were his caretakers, agents, and the best grandsons a man could ask for. They had just as much class as he did.

Woody had been doing interviews and speeches and making special appearances for the last seventy-four years. How could I think my interaction with the old war hero would be something special? Woody was a legend in the Marine Corps. Recruits were taught about him in boot camp. His photos hung in museums all over the country. Multiple documentaries had been produced about him. He had a bridge, an Armed Forces Reserve training center, a Virginia facility, a park, and a U.S. Navy ship named in his honor.

Woody was the most intimidating interview of my project yet—I would be interviewing the last living Marine Medal of Honor recipient of World War II. All I knew was that as a Marine myself, I'd better not royally screw this up.

As I sat in his driveway, I could see him writing at his kitchen table. I grabbed the rifle, still in its case, from the trunk and walked towards the porch. "Come on in, I'll be with you in a minute," he said as he saw me approaching. On his kitchen table lay a pile of fan mail from around the country, mostly requests for autographs. "I only hope they are doing the right things with these," he remarked, sliding an autographed photo of himself into a yellow envelope. "I don't want this stuff on eBay."

As I began to ask how much fan mail he receives, the UPS came to drop another package off at his door. Woody walked over and picked it up. "This one is from New Mexico," he said as he read the label. His posture, stance, and attitude were all those of a younger man, definitely not of someone in his mid-nineties. Despite his age, he was living alone, driving, and taking care of himself just fine. Sadly, his wife Ruby had passed away twelve years before.

Woody was gracious, but even his generous overtures intimidated me. "Set up whatever you need in the living room," he offered. I was embarrassed to tell him that I had no camera crew, no microphones.

"Well, it's not much," I responded with a nervous laugh. "Just recording you on my iPhone." He must have assumed a tripod and camera were in the case that held the rifle.

I unbuckled the latches and removed the rifle, now covered in signatures, and held it out to him. Just like that, the tone of our meeting changed. He peered quietly at the rifle I held out in my hands.

He looked pensively at the rifle. "Anytime I could, I would use the M1," he calmly told me. "I loved this rifle, and it far outweighed the carbine." Then, all of a sudden, Hershel snatched the rifle out of my hands and snapped, "Don't hand it to me like a boot!"

"Boot" was a Marine term for a newly enlisted soldier with no experience. I wasn't nervous anymore: I knew for sure my interview with Woody would be different from the eBay groupies sending him fan mail.

Seventy-Two Seconds: A Woody Williams Story

"That medal does not belong to you."

There was a pause. Silence. Hershel "Woody" Williams stood at attention with the Medal of Honor draped around his neck in the office of the eighteenth commandant of the U. S. Marine Corps. Woody was a corporal in the U.S. Marines, and he was more nervous now than when he had met President Truman to receive the medal.

The man with whom he was face-to-face was like a god to the Marines: commandant and four-star general Alexander Vandegrift.

"It belongs to all the Marines who didn't get to come home," the general continued. "Don't ever do anything that would tarnish that medal."

Without blinking, Hershel replied with a quick, "Yes, sir."

The commandant was also a recipient of the Medal of Honor for his actions early on in World War II during the Battle of Guadalcanal. Hershel took his words to heart.

Hershel, or Woody as his friends called him, had never even heard of the Medal of Honor when he first enlisted. A particular instrument of warfare helped him earn it and join the ranks of America's most vaunted heroes. Woody made his name thanks to his work with a flamethrower, a legendary weapon in American military history. It took seventy-two seconds for the flamethrower to completely empty the fluid strapped to its bearer's back. It had a seventy-two-second shelf life.

Woody wasted no time in taking me back to 1943. Back then, the first three words ever spoken to a young Hershel by a U.S. Marine were

"You're too short." The Marine recruiter shrugged his shoulders while Hershel stood there in disbelief. In 1943, there was a height requirement—five feet, eight inches minimum—in order to join the Marines. Woody stood at five feet, six inches. It was back to the farm in Quiet Dell, West Virginia, for the distraught wannabe Marine.

This was the second time Woody had struck out trying to join the military. The year before, his mother had refused to sign the enlistment papers for him because he was underage. After his dad had passed away when he was eleven, Woody had been raised by his mom.

A year after the Marines turned him down, a defeated Woody was mowing his lawn when a car pulled up. It was a Marine sergeant in dress blues, a familiar face. The recruiter exited the vehicle and called out to him. "Hey, son! You still have an interest in serving with the Marines? We changed the height requirement." To Woody's surprise, the recruiter kept a record of everyone he turned away for height issues, just in case the requirement should change. He personally went to the men he had once rejected, eager to get them to sign up.

After two years of waiting, a very excited Woody, now nineteen years old, was on his way to boot camp. The Parris Island Marine Recruit Depot was full. There were so many young men joining to fight the Japanese that Parris Island could not handle any more recruits. So the Marine Corps did the unusual. They sent recruits west to San Diego instead.

Despite the change in protocol, boot camp was the same nightmare of an experience that it had been for other Marines. It was a brutal wake-up call for the God-loving country boy, but it only made his love for his country grow stronger. After a few months of training, which included training to become an infantry rifleman, Woody was on his way to the Pacific.

The first island he stepped foot on was New Caledonia, a former French colony that served as a depot where replacement troops waited to be assigned to their units. Woody was a replacement, a gentle way of saying that he was stepping in for a dead or wounded Marine.

At New Caledonia the Marines waited and waited for their assignments. The green replacements were quickly growing bored, eager to see action. Woody and some other immature Marines observed the natives climbing trees for coconuts. They decided to try it, too. "They made it look easy," Woody told me, "so I said let's go get some coconuts."

Although Woody was able to make it to the top of the tree, his attempt to pull off a coconut was nothing short of a disaster. As he pried at the fruit, he lost his balance and slid down the tree, bear-hugging it with his body. Woody skinned himself from head to toe before hitting the ground.

"I was in tremendous pain, and as my buddies carried me to the aid station, we waded through salt water to get to the other side of the island," Woody remembered. As Woody's freshly-shaved skin hit the ocean, the saltwater stung his body, sending him into shock.

The Marines were afraid he would be kicked out of the replacement depot. Injuring yourself during wartime could get you court-martialed. Woody's buddies hid him in the back of the aid station and didn't tell anyone about the accident. During formation they would yell "Here!," making it sound like he was present during roll call.

Woody eventually healed up. Finally assigned to a unit, he and the other replacements boarded another ship to meet the Third Marine Division on the island of Guadalcanal, where the Marines had set up headquarters in the Pacific.

"We were finally given all the gear we needed—packs, sleeping systems, entrenching tools, and other items," Woody said of his last days on New Caledonia. While opening boxes of equipment, Woody encountered the flamethrower for the first time. "I saw an iron gas tank," he remembered. "The other boxes included mixing ingredients to create a flammable jelly."

"Are you seeing this?" Woody shouted out to his fellow Marines.

"What is it?" someone asked.

"The manual says flamethrower."

As the two stared in fascination at the weapon still in its box, Company Gunnery Sergeant Daniel Edward Hemphill yelled out, "Get only what you need and hurry up!" The young Marines closed their boxes and scurried off.

Gunny Hemphill had been a Marine in China in the 1930s. He had tattoos from his neck down to his belly button. "He was as hardcore as Marines got," Woody said fondly. "We respected him greatly. He was old Corps."

The next day, Gunny Hemphill returned to the company. While the men were in formation, he read off a list of six names who would be the company's new demolitionists. Woody was on the list. He was promptly reassigned to the company's headquarters to be utilized as needed by the platoons "to destroy stuff."

Woody had never received demolition training. Gunny Hemphill trained him right there on Guadalcanal. The training was hardly rigorous; it was all experimental. The flamethrowers did not come with a training manual, just a pamphlet that named the different parts. It was up to Gunny Hemphill, Woody, and the other five demolitionists to figure out how to use it.

The flamethrower was an odd weapon. "It was like spraying a water hose," Woody told me. "It wasn't that easy to aim. After seventy-two seconds of trying to place your stream-like flame into a makeshift bunker or foxhole, you would run out of fuel." Since the flamethrower could only carry four-and-a-half gallons of fuel, missing one's target would leave it combat ineffective. While they began the training by spraying the gun from longer distances, Gunny Hemphill began to have other ideas.

Hemphill was determined to change the tactics for operating the M1A1 flamethrower. He wasn't impressed by the spectacular plume of flame that shot out of the weapon's mouth and knew that they would have to find a new way to use it to be effective. If he only had seventy-two seconds to use the flamethrower, he wanted every second to count. He wanted it to be as powerful as possible.

The first thing Gunny Hemphill decided to tinker with was the flamethrower's fuel. Under his direction, the men began to experiment with several different types of liquids. They used motor oil, kerosene, phosphorous, and octane gasoline, but Hemphill was still determined to find something better.

One morning Hemphill showed up with a barrel. "We didn't ask how he got it, but the next day he came in rolling a big drum," Woody said. That drum held fifty-five gallons of 130-octane airplane gasoline, better known today as jet fuel. "Once we mixed this into the flamethrower, it was like a whole new weapon. It was more accurate and burned at 3,500 degrees Fahrenheit."

Finally satisfied with the deadly ingredient, Hemphill ordered the Marines to practice with the new and improved flamethrower. He taught the men to lie in the prone position when opening fire, rather than shoot from the hip and risk having flame blown back in their faces. Firing from the ground allowed a long heavy stream of flame to roll into its target. A great big orange ball formed at the end of the stream. The 1700-PSI air tank pushed the flaming ball directly into the openings of caves, pillboxes, or in whatever direction they wanted. Lying on the ground also prevented the wind from affecting the weapon.

The Third Marine Division's objective was to take the island of Guam. The six grunt Marine demolitionists prepared thirty to forty-five flamethrowers, mixing the gases and preparing the compressed air tanks. Despite their preparations, the men never used flamethrowers in action on Guam. Since the entire island was made of solid coral rock, the enemy couldn't dig or construct fortifications that required a flamethrower to destroy. The island terrain was also packed with dense jungle, which made the flamethrowers useless in the field.

Since there was no need for Woody as a flamethrower-wielding demolitionist, Woody went back to being a rifleman. The Guam campaign was his first combat experience. It was the first time he saw a Japanese soldier, the first time he shot rounds at an enemy, and the first time he stood over a dead Marine.

Before landing on the beach, Woody was given an M1 Garand rifle, even though he was initially trained to be a Browning automatic rifleman. He was assigned to Company C of the First Battalion, Twenty-First Marines, Third Marine Division. Upon taking the beach, the Marines advanced on the peak of a heavily defended ridge. "We lost a lot of Marines taking that ridge on Guam," Woody told me, "but one Marine in particular stands out to me. Clevenger."

Clevenger was given Woody's Browning automatic rifle when Woody was picked to be a demolitionist and temporarily reassigned to HQ Company. He was Company C's machine gunner. After five days of heavy fighting, Company C finally took the ridge the Japanese had occupied. But the Japanese did not go down without a fight, launching wave after wave of banzai charge counterattacks against the Marines. "The banzai attacks always came first thing in the morning, as the sun was coming up," Woody remembered. Though Company C warded off each banzai charge, Woody found out that Private First Class Clevenger had been overrun in a forward outpost and killed. "It would have been me if I hadn't been chosen to be a demolitionist," Woody reflected.

Clevenger was hardly the only Marine Woody remembers from Guam. In Guam, Woody became close with another Marine who had been chosen for demolitions, Vernon Waters. After clearing out the Japanese on the island, Woody and Vernon spent three months working side by side to turn the island into permanent living quarters for the division. As trained experts with TNT, they blew craters into the ground, clearing the rocks and trees for tents, chow halls, and other buildings. Daily training exercises continued for all the men. It was only a matter of time before they would be tasked with another mission.

After months of waiting, rumors began to swirl about the company's heading to another island. Sitting in a tent one day, Vernon got Woody's attention. "Hey, Hershel," Vernon said. "I want you to return this to my father if anything happens to me." Vernon took off a ring and showed it to Woody. Woody in turn removed his ring, given to him by his girlfriend at the time, Ruby. "I want you to return this to Ruby if something should happen to me, too," he told Vernon. The pair shook hands in agreement.

Soon after that, the men were told to pack their things. They knew they were heading out, but they didn't yet know where they were headed. The entire Third Marine Division loaded onto troop carrier ships again. While at sea, a Marine officer displayed a giant map on a wall. It showed the volcanic island known as Iwo Jima.

"We are only in reserve! The other divisions will be landing in the morning, and we will stand by in case they need us," an officer shouted to the men. As Woody's ship floated out, the men started to get worried. The other divisions had 80 percent casualties on the first day. While the officer may have thought they wouldn't see action, it became quite clear to the men that the military brass would soon tap the reserves. By nightfall of the first landing day, the Third Marine Division was notified that they would be joining the fight.

As Woody and the other men lay in their racks, a Marine officer on the intercom notified the Marines to be prepared to land on the beach. "At about 3:00 a.m., they woke us up, and we had steak and eggs," Woody remembered.

As the sun came up, the Marines of Company C climbed down the nets of their troop carrier and into small Higgins boats. They rendezvoused with other landing crafts and circled the beach for hours, waiting for the signal to begin their approach. They had to wait for a long time. The beaches on Iwo Jima were so crowded with destroyed vehicles, casualties, and bunched-up companies of Marines that there was nowhere to land another division. The Higgins boats brought the Marines back to the ships instead.

The next day, February 21, Woody's battalion finally headed for an open beachhead. As the landing crafts got closer to the black sand beach, Woody witnessed scenes he would never forget. "I have come to terms with the fact that I'll never be able to eradicate those memories from my mind," Woody wistfully told me. "There were destroyed tanks, flipped-over vehicles, and burning landing crafts. Yet the one image I still can't shake was the Marines. Piles of dead Marines, stacked like cords of wood. There was nowhere else to put them, nowhere to bring them. Some were wrapped in ponchos one on top of the other. Hundreds, it seemed."

The Marines who were killed on the beach and farther inland were all brought back to the foot of the beach. They were piled five feet high in some places. Woody hurried past the bodies to link up with the rest of the company; since the beach was still being shelled heavily, there was no time to waste.

It would be a slow two-day advance for C Company to their first objective. Their first mission was to capture an airfield, and the fighting between the beach and the landing strip was bloody. On February 23, Japanese mortars began to rain over the ground, halting C Company's advance in its tracks. Every platoon in the company was pinned down by enemy machine gun fire. As more firefights broke out with an invisible enemy, the battalion's casualties mounted.

While C Company lay on their bellies taking cover, waiting for a miracle to happen, Marines began to cheer and shoot their rifles in the air. Woody raised his head to see what had caused the sudden change of atmosphere. To his left, off into the distance, Marines were raising a flag on top of a mountain. It was the iconic event later known to the world as the flag raising on Mount Suribachi.

Although the flag raising boosted morale and was surely a victorious moment for some Marines on the island, it did absolutely nothing for Woody and his company. They were still in a fight for their lives. The flag raising might as well have been on the moon, but it motivated the Marines enough to find it in them to make it across the airfield.

"As we sprinted across the airfield under fire, you tried to find cover as much as possible," Woody told me. "You ran from hole to hole, but sometimes Marines would already be occupying them. It was mass confusion."

Just beyond the airfield, the Marines were stopped cold by enemy pillboxes pouring fire at them. "We couldn't see the enemy," Woody said, "but we were certain that the fire was coming from the eight-inch apertures of those fortifications. Shooting back was difficult. The openings of the pillboxes were only big enough for the enemy gun barrels."

As the Marines got bogged down again beyond the airfield, each attempt to destroy the pillboxes failed. They seemed impossible to take out. Woody remembered the most minute details: "All the concrete pillboxes were reinforced with metal rebar. Then several feet of sand were dumped on top of them. Bazookas could not penetrate them, and neither could our aircraft. Our tanks couldn't make it towards the positions either. They were stuck on the beach. Their tracks would spin and kick up sand."

In a desperate effort to save the remaining Marines in his company, a Marine captain called for an emergency meeting in a giant shell crater not far from Woody. "I wasn't even going to go to the meeting," Woody recalled, "but he demanded that all NCOs possible be there, as only two officers remained in the whole company." Woody jogged over and crawled down into the crater, where several men huddled around the captain. Woody noticed that he was the only demolitionist. The whereabouts of the others were unknown. They were probably dead or wounded.

The captain looked directly at Woody. "You think you can do anything with a flamethrower against these pillboxes?" he asked. It felt like the whole universe was being put on the twenty-two-year-old's shoulders.

"I'll try," Woody answered honestly.

The captain informed Woody he could choose any four men to accompany him. They would be assigned to protect him and give him covering fire during his dangerous task. Woody immediately picked two Marines he knew, PFC Tripp and PFC Schlager. He also chose two Marines he didn't know who were equipped with automatic weapons. It was important to have two riflemen and two automatic rifles for proper covering fire.

"You're with me," he said to Schlager. "You other guys spread out as best you can." Woody and his four guardians left the shell crater to begin to outflank the first pillbox. "We knew where this pillbox was. It had been shooting at us all day, and we decided to creep up on it."

As Woody's assault team inched closer, mortar rounds fell on the area between them and the pillbox. The pillbox was still engaging other Marines in the distance. Schlager carried the demolition charges while Woody wielded the flamethrower. The two headed towards the bunker. Suddenly the Japanese occupants inside spotted them. Rounds began to zip between Schlager and Woody. It wasn't long before Woody lost track of the other riflemen in his team, but he had to keep running forward.

As Woody lay on the ground taking cover, he saw a ditch in front of the pillbox. Under fire, he and Schlager sprinted for it. Woody was feet away when several bullets ricocheted off the tank of his flamethrower. Luckily, both terrified men made it.

The Japanese Nambu machine gun sticking out of the aperture of the pillbox was still firing, but it was unable to hit the two Marines due to their defiladed position. "That's when I realized we had advanced far enough that the gun couldn't hit us anymore," Woody said, "but if we backed up, we would be in its radius again."

It was Woody's chance to advance the several feet and strike the pillbox with flame. "Crawl with me!" he yelled to Schlager. Woody began to inch his way out of the ditch, with his pole charge man following.

Suddenly a round struck Schlager's helmet, sending him flying back into a shell crater. "I immediately crawled back to see if he was dead," Woody said. In the depression, Schlager lay dazed. The round had penetrated his helmet and wrapped around his head, only shaking him up. Once Woody confirmed his friend wasn't dead, he kept moving. He had made it this far with the help of his assault team, but now he was forced to advance by himself.

"I climbed back out of the shell crater and up to the side of the pillbox," Woody described. The scared Woody, with the flamethrower mounted on his back, boosted himself up onto the pillbox. With a quick glance, he saw smoke exiting the top of the pillbox. "I assumed it was the smoke from their machine guns exiting this pipe. I took a few steps over to it and saw that my flamethrower nozzle fit perfectly inside of it."

Woody inserted the flamethrower into the smokestack and held down the trigger. It poured a violent stream of fire down into the fortification. In a single act, he burned the occupants to death and silenced the machine guns that had killed dozens of U.S. Marines.

"There wasn't a pause or time to reflect after that," Woody said. "It was still an active battlefield. Enemy artillery was still coming in, and other pillboxes were still firing at my company."

Unable to see any of the original riflemen assigned to him, Woody followed a second ditch to another pillbox. "This fortification was smaller, and there was no smokestack on the roof I could see."

Woody had to eliminate this one the way Gunny Hemphill had taught him—from the prone position, rolling his flame into the apertures. Woody raced over within fifteen to twenty yards of the pillbox. He lay down on his stomach and raised the nozzle of his flamethrower. Without hesitation, he released his inferno into the pillbox.

After burning out the second pillbox, he ran off to take better cover. "I knew I probably needed a new tank after this, but I can't recall how I obtained it," Woody said. "It's something I have discussed with mental health professionals my whole life."

Woody probably went back to obtain another full flamethrower from headquarters. Once serviced with a new one, he must have set back to advance on another pillbox. Jogging his way past the destroyed fortifications, Woody was again yards away from another Japanese bunker. As he aimed to take out the position, Japanese soldiers screamed. "Roughly five or six Japanese soldiers came running out of the pillbox. I can only assume they were out of ammo, since they were charging right at me with bayonets," he recalled.

The enemy soldiers bunched up as they ran toward Woody. Remaining on the ground, he released a burst of flame. This time, the flaming stream of diesel and gasoline struck the Japanese soldiers head-on. The 3,500-degree heat collapsed their lungs, and they dropped dead where they stood. "Their hands went up in the air and they fell to the ground, dropping their weapons."

February 23 was a day like no other. Within four hours and with six flamethrowers, Woody eliminated four more enemy positions—a total of seven pillboxes. Woody's actions were credited with opening a new lane of advancement for friendly forces. They made their way farther into the island of Iwo Jima.

The battalion was debriefed several days after the airfield and pillbox ordeal. Woody found out later that the two other Marines, whose names he didn't know, were killed during their attempts to cover him while he took out the enemy positions. "They died trying to protect me," Woody remarked ruefully. "It's something I haven't ever forgotten."

Woody eventually entered the burned-out pillboxes with more Marines. They reported as many as seventeen dead Japanese soldiers in one bunker alone. Although Woody had gone above and beyond the call of duty, the island itself was far from being in friendly hands.

The war raged on. A couple weeks later, on March 6, C Company advanced farther north. Another fierce bombardment fell on the Marines. Woody slid into a shallow shell hole, but one of his legs stuck out in the open. Suddenly, an explosion rocked the ground around Woody.

"I felt a burning pain in my lower left leg," Woody recalled. "I had been hit with shrapnel. I called out for a corpsman. Sure enough, one came running over to me. He cut my dungarees half off and removed the shrapnel. He poured sulfur powder on my wound and wrapped a pressure bandage on it."

To Woody's dismay, the Navy corpsman tagged his dungarees, implying he would be medically evacuated. Woody broke protocol, removed the tag, and disobeyed the corpsman by telling him he wouldn't leave the front line. "He cursed me out. We were told once a corpsman gives you an order medically, he had the final say, but I couldn't bring myself to quit," he told me.

It was an ironic twist of fate. Later that day he discovered the dead body of his friend from Guam, Vernon Waters. Woody limped over to

Vernon's body. He was lying facedown, stretched out on the ground. Vernon had been killed by what the Americans referred to as a "knee mortar." It landed on his head, killing him by concussion. "When I looked down at his hands," Woody vividly told me, as if it were yesterday, "I could see his ring was still on his finger, the same ring I promised to take care of."

Kneeling over his body, Woody knew he had to return the ring to Vernon's father. "Taking anything off a fallen Marine's body could land you a court-martial, but I had made him a promise."

Woody nervously tried to pull the ring off his friend's finger, but it was extremely tight. He tugged and pulled but couldn't slide it off. "We hadn't showered in weeks. His hands were filthy, black from dirt and sweat." Woody spat on Vernon's finger and the ring finally came off. Woody placed it in his pocket, intent on keeping his promise.

Woody didn't pick up another flamethrower for the rest of his time on Iwo Jima. He was assigned as a regular rifleman to a company with only seventeen men left in it. Twenty days after Vernon was killed, Iwo Jima was declared secure on March 26, 1945.

In the 36 days on the island, some 7,000 Marines were killed in the intense fighting. Another 20,000 wounded Marines were packed into hospital ships sailing to bigger medical facilities elsewhere in the Pacific. Of the 22,000 Japanese who had held the island, only 323 were taken alive. Corpses littered the island.

The operation soon made its way into U.S. and Marine Corps history. In the days following the island's capture, Iwo Jima was made useful for B-29 bombers and fighters that needed to make emergency landings while bombing Tokyo.

Woody and what was left of the battered Marines of the Third Division were shipped back to Guam. Many assumed they were going to wait there until given the order to attack mainland Japan. They tried to make sense of all their fallen friends. "While I was there, word got passed down to me that I was going home," Woody remembered. "When I asked 'What for?' they told me I was getting the Medal of Honor. It didn't register because I had never heard of it."

As Woody waited on Hawaii for another aircraft, he pondered what this medal could be. He boarded and sat in the only seat available. The rest of the seats were occupied by men so skinny that they did not look human. They were American prisoners of war, rescued from camps across Japan. The only reason that a seat was available for Woody was because one of the POWs had died on his way to the aircraft. Woody was shocked by the emaciated appearance of the men. They looked like they weighed between seventy and ninety pounds.

On October 5, Woody was back in the United States. He was one of thirteen Marines and sailors to receive the Medal of Honor from President Harry Truman on the White House lawn. "One Marine who got the medal with me that day looked at me almost like a surrogate father. His name was Jack Lucas," Woody said.

Jack was the youngest Marine since the Civil War to receive the Medal of Honor. At seventeen years old, he had jumped on not only one but two hand grenades while on Iwo Jima. Jack and Woody remained friends throughout their lives until Jack's passing in 2008. "I'd say he was the most interesting of all Medal of Honor recipients I've ever known," Woody told me.

In October of 2018, after seventy-four years of wondering and through extensive research, he found the names of the other two Marines who had died while he attacked the pillboxes on February 23, 1945. "Corporal Warren Bornholz and Private First Class Charles Fischer died so I could wear this medal," Woody beamed with gratitude. "So when I do wear it, I'm wearing it for them and others who gave their lives, not me."

In January of 1946, Woody and his wife, Ruby, drove from West Virginia all the way to Froid, Montana. A local car dealership loaned them a car. They fixed flats themselves along the away. The purpose of the trip: return Vernon Waters's ring to his parents, as promised.

After several days of driving, Woody drove up the road leading to Vernon's home. Vernon's family was from a line of wheat farmers. Woody and Ruby drove for miles before they reached a home surrounded by wheat fields.

Vernon's parents greeted Woody with anticipation. "He also had some brothers and sisters there," Woody noted. "It was very emotional; we all cried." The promise was kept, and the ring was returned to its rightful owners. Woody and his wife spent some time with Vernon's family and then continued on to California to see other Marine friends who had survived the war.

Woody went from not knowing what the Medal of Honor was to having it alter his entire life. For seven and a half decades, Woody has worked with every generation of veterans—from World War I to Afghanistan. He spent thirty-three years working for the Department of Veterans Affairs and started a nonprofit organization to encourage communities throughout America to erect monuments for Gold Star Families, to remember their sacrifice. Their loved ones would not be forgotten.

I sat on Woody's couch and glanced at the clock. I had been there for five hours. Woody wasn't winded or exhausted from talking for so long, as many of the other veterans his age had been in their interviews. He might as well have been sixty years old. He handed me back the rifle after adding his signature. While other veterans steadily wrote their name, Woody was so used to signing autographs for people that he did it without second thought. He said, "How about some dinner? I know a nice country place."

Woody jumped into his car with Medal of Honor license plates and had me follow him to a local diner. As we walked into the restaurant, it went silent. Some of the patrons at their tables stared at us as we waited for a seat.

"Hi, Woody," a waitress greeted him. She brought us to an empty table. One by one, different residents made their way up to our table to say hi to the local hero. Even the sheriff approached and let out a, "Hell! They'll let anyone in here!"

Woody decided to ask me questions. We chatted about politics, world issues, and my personal life. He even shared stories you can't find on the internet about different men belonging to the Medal of Honor Society.

"Being a police officer must be tough these days," he said as he chewed his food.

I agreed with him.

"So many protests and lack of respect," he continued. "But you know, the first veterans to ever march in a peaceful protest were the World War I veterans. They were promised a bonus and never got it. But they were successful with their demonstration afterwards."

I wanted my meal to last forever. I could have talked to the man until the end of time. He was as gentle and calm at ninety-four as he most likely was when he was seventeen, a clear representation of someone raised by a loving mom who only wanted to protect her son.

I'll never forget the six hours I spent with Hershel "Woody" Williams. As I left town, I saw a giant billboard that read: "Ona, West Virginia. Proud to have CWO2 Hershel 'Woody' Williams Residing in Our Community."

Hershel "Woody" Williams with the rifle. *Photo courtesy of the author*

CHAPTER SEVEN

Raging Bull

Carl DiCicco
U.S. Army, Thirty-Fourth Infantry Division

Norristown, Pennsylvania

"Do not call back here!" Carl DiCicco yelled, slamming the phone down. I was the person on the other end of the line.

Carl, then ninety-three years old, assumed I was a scam artist when I tried explaining my project. Carl had been in the same division and regiment as my great-uncle Andrew. He was a piece to the puzzle I was trying to put together, so I wasn't going to give up that easy. Plus, the number of signatures on my rifle was growing, and I still had not met any veterans who had fought in Italy yet, which was the original purpose of the journey to begin with.

I discovered Carl after reading two hundred pages of after-action reports from the Thirty-Fourth Infantry Division's fight in Italy. I found his Silver Star Citation. The date on the citation read September 17, 1944, the same exact day Andrew was killed. They were in the same offensive.

Through a quick internet search on Carl, I found a white pages listing of his phone number and residential address. When I called, I was thrilled to hear a voice on the other end; his response was less encouraging. He was the only survivor I could find from that bloody day.

I decided to revert to old-fashioned ways and put pen to paper.

Then I had another idea. I started to dissemble the rifle by removing the upper handguard, which was made of five inches of wood. The piece could easily be replaced if lost. I wrote Carl a letter and included pictures of the other veterans signing the rifle. I took the letter and the section of the dissembled rifle and bundled them together, then shipped the package to Norristown, Pennsylvania, Carl's home. I might never see this part of the rifle again, but it was a chance I was willing to take.

Two weeks later, a small package arrived at my doorstep with a Norristown return address. I opened it to find the piece of the rifle inside, and, to my surprise, it was signed by Carl. Attached was a short note. "I'm sorry. I thought you were a scam. I turned ninety-four today. Good luck with your project."

I hopped back on the phone and called him right away to thank him. He invited me to come and talk with him anytime.

It was several months before I called Carl back to set up a meeting. To my disappointment, a "Temporarily out of Service" notification came up. I searched the internet for an obituary, but nothing appeared. Then I searched his name on social media and found a younger woman with the same last name living in Norristown. I couldn't believe my luck—it was his grandson's wife. His grandson, John, told me that Carl had had a bad fall and was now in assisted living, but arranged for me to meet his grandfather. Nearly a year after first calling him, I was off to meet the only survivor I could find from my great-uncle's regiment.

I drove out from Washington, D.C., to visit Carl on Memorial Day 2018. Carl's new home was two and a half hours away, a nursing facility in Pennsylvania. His grandson met me outside. He was hesitant. "Hey, man," he said nervously, "I don't think we should bring a rifle in here. Maybe I should ask or something?"

"If we ask, there is no way they will allow it," I said, speaking from experience. "He is not getting any younger. It's now or never."

John nodded, went inside, and came back with a towel. We wrapped the rifle in a half-assed disguise, but it worked. We walked past the nurses and receptionist to his grandfather's room. Carl was sitting in a wheelchair, facing the TV screen with the volume turned all the way up.

"Carl, how are you?"

He turned away from the TV and replied, "Wow. You really are persistent."

Knowing he was annoyed, I cautiously approached and sat in front of him. "You're a handsome bastard, though!" he cracked.

I got right to business. I wanted to preserve his energy for my questioning. He was undoubtedly in bad shape, with a bag draining his gallbladder attached to him. I felt guilty for bothering him.

But as I put the rifle into his hands, the sick, hunched-over Carl perked up. A smile lit up his face. "It was eight pounds the last I remembered it. It seems heavier now!" For a second he forgot about being sick and ignored the medical equipment attached to his body.

He started telling me his story.

Raging Bull

"There's no atheist in a foxhole," an old military saying goes. The phrase first originated in World War I, when digging holes and trenches was a widely used battle tactic. The saying's truth was reinforced by people like Carl during World War II, who struck his own deal with God when he was under four feet of rubble on the Anzio beachhead. He'd been buried alive and thought he was a dead man.

Carl began his service as a replacement for the Thirty-Fourth Infantry Division, also known as the "Red Bulls," a nickname based on their unit crest—a bull's skull. The crest was worn on their shoulders. The unit had finished the North African campaign and was ready for its next mission: Italy.

After completing basic training at Fort Riley, Kansas, Carl set sail for North Africa. He landed in Casablanca, then took a train to meet up with thousands of other young replacement troops in French Algeria.

They made up for the casualties suffered by the Red Bulls during the fighting in Tunisia and the Battle of Monte Cassino in Italy.

After several weeks in Africa, Carl was shipped to Italy and met his new division right outside the town Benevento. By a curious twist of fate, he had returned to his father's birthplace. Before Carl could get situated or familiarize himself with the Monte Cassino–hardened vets, he was placed in the 135th Regiment, Company G, and was shipped instead to Anzio, a coastal city in Italy. Anzio was strategic not only for its port but also because if the Allies held Anzio, they could obtain an easier route to take Rome from the occupying Germans.

At the Anzio beachhead, the first objective was to relieve the Third Infantry Division, which had been bogged down in fighting for two months. They had been in a stalemate since the Third Division's initial January landings. It was now March.

When they arrived on the front lines, the 135th found that the 3rd Division had built intricate tunnels, dugouts, and caves. The defenses were unusual—shallow trenches that wound about the battle lines. Digging any deeper would strike water, defeating the purpose of the defensive positions. The men often lay prone in trenches barely deep enough to cover their perpendicular bodies.

By day three, Carl's platoon had taken over responsibilities for a series of dugouts and partially destroyed homes that a squad from the Third Division had been using as observation posts. Carl took up a position in the second floor of a dilapidated building alongside his fellow infantryman, James Craig. Exhausted from being awake for several days, both men agreed to take turns getting some shut-eye while the other kept watch. Before they could agree on who would sleep first, enemy artillery shells started landing several yards away from the house. "The explosions were massive, bigger than ordinary artillery," Carl remembered. "These rounds were coming from a German railway gun known as Anzio Annie."

The rounds got closer and closer to the half-destroyed house. Keeping low to the ground for fear of enemy snipers, Carl began to inch his way to the exit. "We better get the hell outta here," he told James.

The next explosion was so close that debris and rock burst all around Carl, taking his helmet off his head. German artillery zeroed in on the home. Before Carl and James could make a run for it, the next shell was a direct hit. The defensive position collapsed, and Carl's vision went black. Completely deaf and unable to see, Carl tried to move, but he was pinned and could hardly breathe.

He had been buried alive.

Carl spit the dirt out of his mouth and began to yell out to James. "Jim! Jim! You there?" Carl was standing but was hunched over, pinned by dirt and concrete. James began to reply, but faintly. He was pinned in a much worse position than Carl. He had been lying down when the collapse happened.

After several hours, the situation looked grim for both men. Carl yelled out to James again. "Jim, this doesn't look good. We ought to pray!"

"I don't know how to pray," James replied.

Carl told James not to worry and to repeat what he said. "I tried to lead him in the Act of Contrition. 'Oh my God, I'm heartily sorry...' We made it halfway through the prayer when James began to scream and curse."

James was in tremendous pain and began to snap, "Fuck! Son of a bitch!" Then he went silent.

"I didn't hear much from him after that." Carl began to fall in and out of consciousness. His limbs began to lose circulation and cramp. "I told God that night that if I were able to make it out of there, I would go to church every year on that exact date." Carl begged God for his life and soon passed out.

The sound of an air raid woke him up. Planes were dropping bombs around the area, and the vibration rocked his body. Suddenly he could hear voices. They were from an approaching American squad.

"Hey! Hey! We are in here!" Carl yelled, coughing. The American squad responded. They could hear Carl but told him he needed to remain quiet to keep from alerting the Germans of their presence. Despite the commands, Carl continued yelling to his buried friend in excitement.

"James, they're here! James!" Carl belted out, but there was no reply from the other buried soldier.

Rock by rock and boulder by boulder, the rescuers cautiously dug out the trapped men. They did not want to be seen by the German artillery observers. Removing a large amount of dirt, they eventually saw the hair on Carl's head. They cleared more rocks, allowing Carl to breathe more easily. It was now nightfall, and the men postponed the rescue efforts until the next morning. One soldier named James Barkley was specifically assigned to Carl and ordered not to leave him. "He was giving me sips of coffee and water," Carl remembered.

Barkley began to dig with his bayonet. He did so until the sun came up, freeing Carl's upper body. After two days of trying to excavate Carl, the other American soldiers debated cutting off Carl's leg to free him. Carl prayed more. He was still drifting in and out of consciousness, having recurring dreams that he was trapped in a city with four walls.

But Barkley didn't stop digging, using his bayonet to carve out the dirt and rock from around Carl's trapped leg. Finally, after three days, all the men joined together to pull Carl out of the ground with one last yank. They slowly dragged his body out from the rubble.

Having had no circulation for three days, Carl's leg was swollen and unable to bear weight. The soldiers placed Carl on a stretcher to evacuate him towards the beach. German machine guns began to fire on his rescuers. The medics dropped Carl on the ground and jumped into a trench. When the coast was clear again, they ran out, picked him up, and brought him to the nearest hospital ship.

The ship brought him and hundreds of other severely wounded soldiers back to Naples, Italy, to a more elaborate field hospital. His leg was elevated with a sling. Doctors informed him that the stress wound was a simple fracture but that the lack of circulation had caused some severe nerve damage.

"For the next few months the nurses would visit me with a black box. The box had wires inside of it and they would put it around my leg," Carl said of his daily medical procedure. For several weeks, the field nurses shocked Carl's leg muscles to regain sensation in his nerves. "I would scream out every time. It was painful, but after two months of this therapy, I was able to walk again."

Carl was awarded his first Purple Heart, but being able to walk again only meant one thing: Carl had to return to his unit. Doctors made sure he was mentally stable enough to return to the battlefield. "They asked me all kinds of weird things, like had I ever screwed my mother," Carl said with a puzzled look on his face. "I could have gotten out of going back, but I didn't."

It had been two months since Carl last saw his own regiment. He rejoined them just in time to witness the fall of Rome. "We marched right by the Colosseum," Carl said of that spectacular day.

But Carl also received some bad news upon his return. "It wasn't long before I found out that James Craig, the other soldier buried with me, had died under the rubble that day."

Italian civilians treated the Red Bull division as liberators and celebrated in the streets. However, the massive victory of taking Rome was overshadowed by the Allied forces' invasion of France. The liberation of Rome took place the day before D-Day, and as a result the milestone in the Italian campaign did not receive the attention it deserved. The French invasion would have been nearly impossible if not for the U.S. forces in Italy. Without the invasion of the continent from the south, thirty more German divisions would have been free to reinforce Normandy instead of defending the Italian peninsula. The soldiers that fought the Axis powers in Italy would go down as the Second World War's relatively unsung heroes.

Eventually, Carl and the other soldiers were placed into trucks and moved north up the Italian coast to Livorno, known to the Americans as "Objective Leghorn." During the transport, they saw how essential the U.S. Army Air Corps had been to their previous efforts. German railway guns and artillery pieces lay destroyed along the route. Carl and his fellow soldiers could make out the same guns that had killed troops on the Anzio beachhead and, Carl speculated, the one possibly responsible for burying him in a mound of rubble.

As soon as the regiment moved into the towns of Cecina and Rosignano Marittimo, just outside of Leghorn, they hit stiff resistance. Men who had marched many miles with no activity were now blindly stepping on mines, dying instantly upon detonation. Sniper activity also picked up. The regiment was now engaging the first German forces since the Nazis' retreat from Rome.

U.S. forces were also greeted by Italian freedom fighters known as "partisans." They briefed the Americans the best they could about the ongoing situation in the area. They had harassed the Germans in the area for months, working as a guerilla militia in the Italian countryside and towns. With the enemy troop numbers in the hundreds, the American regiment began their house-to-house fight. Small arms fire turned into long-lasting firefights, and small skirmishes became raging battles.

With no time to evacuate before the fighting got serious, civilians were trapped in the towns. Many were killed when shells fell on their homes. Both armies fired on houses suspected to be enemy observation posts. In the confusion of war, the collateral damage began to increase.

The Germans always had the high ground in the towns, from which they pounded American positions with rocket and mortar fire. Through June and July 1944, the civilian death toll mounted. Bloated bodies littered streets and homes. Nervous that disease would spread, the Army ordered the burning of dead civilians whose corpses the partisans failed to remove.

Even with impressive tank support, the Americans were nearly surrounded. The only way out of their increasingly precarious position was to take out the German artillery in the hills. They advanced on elevated German positions. Allied artillery batteries made their way up the Italian coast. Once they arrived in the contested towns on the coast, they were able to launch counterstrikes on the camouflaged pillboxes that were peppering the battle lines with artillery fire and gunfire. The presence of friendly artillery allowed the 135th Regiment to break the deadlock. Freed up from the constant artillery threat that had been keeping them pinned, the 135th started to make significant progress pushing through the towns. The Germans began to retreat, using oxen to pull their artillery. Some of the recovered enemy equipment left behind was Russian, which the Allied forces surmised had been captured by the Germans and shipped in from the Eastern Front.

As Carl's company advanced farther towards Leghorn in the direction of Pisa, an enemy bullet tore into his shoulder, just missing the bone. Carl dropped his M1 rifle to place pressure over his wound as best he could. Medics ushered him to the rear for further treatment. Carl wouldn't see the progress up the coast from the front lines.

Upon finally reaching Leghorn, they found that much of the city was booby-trapped and rigged with mines. The Germans had decided to fight in a delayed style, using mines and scattered artillery fire to inflict casualties on the Allied troops. While Carl recovered from his wounds for a second time, more amputees than ever were transported to the medical tents. The lives of young kids, only eighteen and nineteen years old, would never be the same.

Before abandoning the city, the desperate Germans had also filled in the Leghorn harbor with concrete to blockade the port. When U.S. airpower bombed the Germans holding out in the area, they began to surrender in droves. Objective Leghorn and other eastern coastal cities were officially captured by late July. The Americans could now embark and debark from a new northern Italian port.

The battle-worn regiment was given the entire month of August for rest and relaxation. They had fought through May, June, and July and needed to recover. Engineers cleared the beaches in Leghorn, allowing men to go swimming. The American Red Cross set up movie theaters and ice cream parlors. Some of the men even got to witness a surprise visit from English prime minister Winston Churchill. As Carl's shoulder healed, he received his second Purple Heart. Toward the end of August, the men started training again, preparing for a new offensive in Italy's Apennine Mountains.

In early September, the division advanced into the mountains to assault the German defense positions known as the Gothic Line. Once again, the

American forces were tasked with taking on Germans in elevated, defensive positions. While the mountains worked as natural obstacles, the Americans also had to break an intricate defense system that spread from one side of the country to the other. The men knew the situation could quickly deteriorate into the harshest fighting they had yet faced. The Germans were slowly being pushed out of Italy, but Hitler wasn't going to let it happen that easily. Despite their brief vacation, morale plummeted as the men realized their work was not yet complete.

On September 12, the 135th Regiment was tasked with breaking the Gothic Line. The Red Bulls rushed through Florence virtually unopposed. Their objective was the city of Bologna, roughly 70 miles to the north and on the other side of the impressive defensive fortifications.

The Gothic Line was made up of camouflaged pillboxes, machine gun nests, snipers, foxholes, and barbed wire. The trees in the area had been shell-burst by both armies; splintered logs were littered across the field. Much of the ground had been muddied by rainfall and friction from troops and vehicles. The gorgeous landscape and vineyards of Italy were now a hellish scene.

By September 17, their momentum had slowed. Twenty-five miles into their northward march from Florence, the U.S. Army was stopped dead in its tracks in and around the hills of Barberino. The fighting was at close quarters, violent, and uphill. The Allied forces were using pack mules and donkeys to bring gear and equipment to summit the terrain. Enemy artillery fire increased. One shell landed between two donkeys and exploded, setting them on fire. The mules, along with the American equipment attached to them, fell off the cliffs.

As Carl's squad pushed farther up the hill, a distant enemy pillbox was seen. Two American soldiers, Platoon Staff Sergeant Davis and Lieutenant Polson, crept ahead on their own. They wanted to give the Germans occupying the position a chance to surrender. Earlier that day, Davis and his squad had killed two Germans and captured another eighteen. He had been told by the German POWs that others would be willing to surrender if given the opportunity.

As the two men approached the pillbox, their humane plan was cut short by a burst of machine gun fire. A bullet pierced Davis's forehead, and he dropped dead instantly. The lieutenant ran for his life, but he tripped and smashed his face on a rock. He scrambled back to his feet and ran towards the rest of the squad at the bottom of the hill.

"They just killed Davis!" Lieutenant Polson yelled as he neared their position. He was bleeding from the mouth. Carl told the lieutenant to stay put and take care of his injury; he would take over for the wounded lieutenant.

Carl took a few of his squad members to outflank the pillbox. With the sun setting, the Germans were having a hard time making out American movements. They shot flares into the sky to try to increase their line of sight.

Carl handed off his Browning automatic rifle (BAR) and grabbed an M1 Garand with a rifle grenade attached to it. The men hooked around the hill as quietly as they could and then advanced. Enemy mortars fell around them as they attempted to low-crawl under a series of barbed wire obstacles set up by the Germans. "I could see the concrete pillbox," Carl said. "It was shaped like a cone, and there was a German shooting flares. Once free from the barbed wire, I got in the prone position and fired the rifle grenade off the M1."

A German officer exited the pillbox entryway to shoot another flare, but the air-bound grenade hit a berm in front of him and detonated on impact. The shrapnel from the explosion took the German officer's head off his shoulders.

With the flares eliminated, Carl switched out his rifle for a BAR. The mortars were practically useless without the light provided by the flares, so Carl could take more risks. He was able to crawl several meters forward and under more barbed wire set up in front of the pillbox. A piece of shrapnel from a mortar firing blind managed to graze Carl's left shin, which he didn't even notice until the chaos was over.

Free from the barbed wire, Carl set up his BAR and began to pour fire into the German pillbox opening. "I started throwing grenades when I got closer. I always had five grenades with me," he recalled.

Carl threw three or four grenades at the defensive emplacement. One grenade bounced off the pillbox and rolled down the hill. It exploded and wounded an American soldier from another platoon—Captain Kibbler—who was also leading an attack on the pillbox. Neither Kibbler nor Carl knew that American men were attacking from opposite sides.

Carl's platoon had advanced within several feet of the pillbox when seven Germans came out with their hands up. "One of them was waving a white flag," Carl remembered. He instructed them to keep their hands up, taking a Walther P38 off one of the soldiers. The other Germans dropped their machine pistols on the ground.

It wasn't until the next morning that other American soldiers commented on the fate of the German officer near the pillbox. "Did you see what you did to that guy's head?" one of them asked Carl. Carl shrugged it off and continued to nurse the new cut on his leg. He was on to his third Purple Heart.

Captain Kibbler ordered Carl to take the German prisoners back to battalion HQ. Carl left his BAR, took up an M1, and marched the captured enemy a mile down the road. A U.S. Army colonel was walking in the opposite direction. "I informed the colonel what had happened and he handed me his swagger stick," Carl said.

"You wanna use this on them?" the colonel asked. Unwilling to beat the German captives, Carl declined and transported the prisoners to the rear.

Several months later, Carl was awarded the Silver Star for his actions on the hill that day. Staff Sergeant Davis was posthumously awarded the Distinguished Service Cross.

The regiment eventually penetrated the Gothic Line, but at a terrible cost. Throughout the months of September and October 1944, hundreds of Red Bulls were killed or wounded. Private First Class Andrew Biggio, my great-uncle, was among the casualties.

Up until that point, the enemy had surrendered their positions fairly easily. However, they began to become more fanatical. Rumors spread that Adolf Hitler had become more insistent about keeping Italy in Axis hands. The entire Fifth Army, including the Thirty-Fourth Division, used the rainy, slow months of November and December to regroup, count their losses, and rebuild.

As Carl once again healed up, the men celebrated Christmas and honored the war dead. Replacements filled the ranks, and Carl was promoted to staff sergeant. Nearly a year after he had been buried alive at Anzio, Carl was leading his own new squad, pushing farther into northern Italy's Po Valley. Carl's combat experience prepared them for a harsh reality. In the final stages of the war, a hidden German machine gunner ambushed the men in an open field.

"Bullets whizzed right between my legs," Carl told me. "The entire platoon ran and left me abandoned in a hole I found cover in." Carl had become so used to being under enemy fire that hitting the deck and taking cover was natural to him. As he tried to make a break for it to catch up with the rest of the platoon, fragments from a machine gun burst grazed his leg. Although wounded again, he ran back toward the town they had passed. The platoon was waiting there and cheered up when they saw him walking into the village. Carl wasn't so cheery.

"I was furious they left me," Carl barked. "But deep down inside, I couldn't blame them. We shouldn't have been taking any unnecessary chances that late in the war."

The division soon reached the outskirts of Milan. Carl's company marched by Benito Mussolini's dead body hanging upside down in the city square. The dictator had been killed hours before by partisans. Before he, his mistress, and his right-hand men were shot, they were strung up and their heads were caved in with rocks. "It was a barbaric sight," Carl reflected, "but this man destroyed their homes and country."

By the end of the war, the U.S. Army's point system took effect. Soldiers needed a certain number of points to be able to return home to the States. Points were determined by time in service, awards, and campaigns in which each soldier participated.

A paperwork mistake incorrectly calculated Carl's points at eighty-four, rather than the eighty-five needed to get home. Carl knew this was incorrect, but he had no one to turn to for recourse. With time on his hands, Carl was sent back to Leghorn, the city he had helped take months earlier. He attended typewriting school—and saw how the rear echelon lived with fresh meals, tents, and entertainment. "It felt like there were three hundred men for every one man on the front line," he remembered.

During his stay in Leghorn, Carl's paperwork was straightened out, bringing his points to ninety-four, more than enough to go home. The entire Thirty-Fourth Division made it home before he did. He was thrilled he did not have to go to the Pacific, a concern all the soldiers in Italy shared.

Carl returned home to Norristown, Pennsylvania, and never left again. During the 1980s, his wife and kids planned a trip to Italy, and Carl refused to go. He attended only one reunion for the Red Bull division, and only because it was hosted in Carlisle, Pennsylvania, not far from where he lived. For a moment, Carl sounded bitter: "Colin Powell turned down our offer to be guest speaker because it wasn't enough money."

The Red Bull division still holds the record for most days in combat, totaling over five hundred. Carl began his military career as a draftee; he finished it with three years of service, a Purple Heart with three Oak Leaf Clusters, and a Silver Star.

Despite his heroic deeds, Carl refused to talk about the war until 2006—first with a local historical society, and then with me on Memorial Day weekend of 2018. He hardly had any energy left after talking to me.

There was a knock on the door. A health aide made her way into the room. I tried to hide the rifle, but instead Carl began to raise it towards her. "Take a look at this!" he said, showing off the rifle.

I panicked that our cover was blown. The Haitian woman stared at us, curious but not alarmed. I knew that it was time to get going. I thanked Carl and packed up my things. He wasn't exactly sad to see me go, but I knew our time had brightened up his day. I drove seven hours home to Boston, thinking about what Andrew Biggio, my great-uncle, had gone through in Italy in the last hours of his life.

Carl DiCicco and the author with the rifle. *Photo courtesy of the author*

CHAPTER EIGHT

Man o' War

John Katsaros
8th Air Force, 401st Bomb Group

Haverhill, Massachusetts

As John Katsaros and I sat talking at his kitchen table, the rifle was laid out in front of us. Ever the airman, he wore a dark green flight suit.

"So, what's the difference between a waist gunner and a belly gunner?" I asked.

John had been in the Army Air Corps, which later became the U.S Air Force. It was a topic I really didn't know much about. There was a pause, and then he said, "Wait right there" and left me in the kitchen.

John, now ninety-five years old, returned hugging a large model plane of a B-17 "Flying Fortress" bomber. The model was nearly the size of his body. "This is the tail gunner, these are waist

John Katsaros. *Photo courtesy of John Katsaros*

gunners, ball turret, and nose gunners," he explained, pointing at all the different machine guns hanging out the windows of the model plane.

I appreciated the visual. He juggled the model a little before setting it down next to the rifle. "You know, they are making an HBO miniseries about the Army Air Corps. It comes out next year," I told him.

"Oh, yeah?"

I pulled out my iPhone and showed him the trailer. During the three-minute preview, a B-17 bomber attempted to fly through flak while being shot at by German fighter planes. The men in the plane were yelling at each other, giving commands during the chaos. The trailer ended and John handed me back the phone.

"God, what the hell was that?" he said. John explained to me that it is impossible to converse in a plane flying that high with that much noise going on. It could only be done with headphones and an intercom system. The noise of flak and gunfire and the roar of the engines would drown out the sound of voices. This is what I loved about meeting these men. I was about get the real-life story from the veteran himself, not from a movie.

Man o' War

The Katsaros family was happy to have their son, John, back from the war. Other families in the neighborhood were not so lucky.

Mr. Katsaros lay in bed one hot summer night, kicking around, trying to cool off. As he tried to get back to sleep, he heard noises emanating from John's room. Maybe John was having trouble sleeping too, he thought. But as he laid there, the sounds grew louder and louder. They sounded worse than a restless sleeper, more like feet stomping.

He rolled out of bed. "What's going on?" his wife asked. He walked down the hall to his son's room, slowly opened the door, and quietly asked, "Is everything okay?"

To his surprise, John was out of bed and opening his window. "John, what are you doing?" he shouted. John didn't react. He put both feet out the window, preparing to jump. John was sleepwalking again.

Mr. Katsaros ran over and pulled his son back from the window. They both tumbled to the floor. John snapped out of his night terror, covered in sweat. When he came to his senses, he realized that he was back home in his childhood bedroom. Just seconds prior, he had thought he was bailing out of his burning B-17 bomber again.

John Katsaros would go another sixty years without telling his parents, future wife, and kids what had happened during his time with the Eighth Air Force during World War II. Besides being sworn to secrecy, he wasn't comfortable talking about his experience. A phone call with legendary Air Force pilot Chuck Yeager in 2008 gave him the courage to share his story with his family—and the rest of the world.

John enlisted in the Air Corps well before his twentieth birthday. After attending basic training in Miami, Florida, John got word of what his actual job would be in the Air Corps—an aerial engineer. "The engineer is the eyes and ears of the plane," John told me. "When both pilots are too busy flying, they can't take their eyes away from the cockpit windows or they may crash into another plane. We flew with hundreds of planes in formation during a bombing mission. One false move and you can kill everyone. I was there to sit between the pilots and read the gauges. I could tell them fuel level, elevation, distance, and speed, so they could focus on flying."

In 1943, John headed to Salt Lake City and then to Texas as a fully trained aerial engineer. He met his new crew and laid eyes on a B-17 bomber for the first time. John practiced his new skill set as an engineer while the men learned how to work together as a team in flight. Most men had dual jobs. If the plane came under attack on missions, the navigator and bombardier would become nose gunners and the engineer would become a top turret gunner.

But some men had permanent jobs. There was a belly gunner who sat in a rotating glass ball encasement underneath the plane with dual .50 caliber machine guns. A tail gunner in the rear of the plane always covered their six o' clock. Two waist gunners sat in the center of the plane, picking up both the left and right side of the aircraft. The plane was guarded by a total of thirteen .50 caliber machine guns. Although that sounds like a lot of protection, it proved not to be enough.

During their training, John and the rest of the airmen were told about the ongoing raids against Nazi Germany. They hadn't realized how dangerous the bombing missions were until they heard the stories from Air Corps members. "About halfway through our training," John recollected, "the Eighth Air Force took off from England and did a major bombing run over Germany. Sixty-two bombers were shot out of the sky. Then a week later, another sixty planes went down due to enemy fire. That's over 1,200 men who didn't return from two trips."

The Eighth Air Force was devastated and needed reinforcements. Higher command ordered the green airmen to skip the third phase of training, promising that they could finish their preparations in England. When they got to England, John's men shared several bases with the Royal Air Force. Training with the British proved complicated because the Royal Air Force had different tactics than the Americans. The British didn't bomb in the daytime, only at night, and they never flew in big formations, only in straight lines. Before John could go on any real bombing missions, he trained for several weeks in Deenethorpe, England, with the 401st Bomb Group. He learned how to fly with some fifteen other bombers nearly wingtip to wingtip.

John was on the airfield when a group of B-17s returned from a bombing run. As one plane circled overhead, it dropped three red flares out its windows. "This meant they had wounded aboard and were given priority to land first," John explained.

Groups of medics and other airmen ran towards the airfield carrying stretchers and first aid kits. "As they began to land I saw they were missing wingtips, were full of holes, and had lost the use of some of their engines," John said. He had an uneasy feeling seeing the damaged planes. It was also depressing that none of the returning airmen wanted to talk to the new guys, but it was understandable. They had just lost crew members and been through hell on a ten-hour flight.

John's training concluded after nearly a month. His first bombing mission came on February 11, 1944. Sleeping in their huts, the men were awakened by a whistle at four o'clock in the morning. After a quick breakfast, some three hundred airmen and officers were packed into a room. A map of Europe hung on the wall. Target: Frankfurt, Germany. The raid's mission was to take out factories that were building parts for German fighter planes.

They were briefed on the route there, weather, enemy planes, enemy flak, and the route back. As the gathering concluded, a captain asked which of the men could operate a video camera. John had attended a combat camera class while in the States and volunteered. "You're going to take these," the captain said as he handed John three different cameras.

Over the course of the war effort, the United States Army realized that it needed footage to confirm the success of bombing missions. Human reports weren't good enough. They also wanted new film for intelligence purposes, as well as for teaching and training tools. Assigned to be the combat camera man for the first mission, John was moved from his position as an aerial engineer to right waist gunner and photographer. This move would end up saving his life on a later mission.

Leaving the briefing area, the new airmen speed-walked to the flight line. The veterans took their time, perhaps less eager to board their planes. John came face-to-face with his aircraft. The sun came up, reflecting off the dull metal of the plane—a well-worn B-17 bomber, F Model. She was already broken in and combat-tested, armed with four engines, thirteen .50 caliber machine guns, and three tons of bombs. Painted on her nose was her name: *Man o' War*.

One by one, the planes on the runway started their engines. They waited in line for the green light in the tower to indicate when it was their turn to take off. They took off in thirty-second intervals.

"Over the English Channel, everyone would warm up their guns and fire a few rounds to make sure they were working properly," John said. As the right waist gunner, John attempted to fire a burst from his .50 caliber machine gun. The weapon kicked back violently through the window. The gun and ammunition hit him square in the chest before falling inside the plane, with the barrel awkwardly pointing at the tail gunner.

"I was distracted with my new job as combat photographer and forgot to prep the gun properly using the clamp and adapter to hold it in the window," John explained. The left waist gunner saw what had happened. Luckily no rounds went off inside the plane, and the two men picked up the sixty-five-pound machine gun, placing it correctly in its window. John's first mission was off to a shaky start.

The planes rose high into the sky, ascending at three hundred feet per minute. At ten thousand feet, the pilots came over the intercom and ordered all the men to put on their oxygen masks. After several hours of standing at the open window of his machine gun, John grew cold. Temperatures at high altitude fell to forty degrees below zero. As a newbie, he hadn't adequately prepared for the cold. All he had for this first mission was his leather bomber jacket and gloves. John tried to focus. They eventually reached twenty-seven thousand feet. He was informed their formation could be engaged by the enemy as soon as they crossed the English Channel.

Two violent bangs came from the front of the plane, as if a sledgehammer were striking it. "It startled me and the crew," John said. Only able to communicate with headsets and microphones, the men began to yell. "Did you see him?" the top turret gunner yelled.

The pilots shot back, "Where did he go?"

A German fighter Focke-Wulf Fw 190 had taken a shot at the cockpit. John gripped the handle of his .50 caliber and scanned the sky. "I knew he was out there. I knew he would pass on our left or right side," he said.

Suddenly *Man o' War* opened fire. "One o'clock high!" the nose gunners declared over the intercom while shooting. More yelling ensued on the crew's headsets. The German plane was coming in from the front again. John gripped the handle of his .50 caliber, ready to engage the first plane he saw. Suddenly the large black Iron Cross decal, which was on all Luftwaffe planes, appeared in his sights. He squeezed the trigger.

As John's machine gun pumped rounds into the sky, his last volley of bullets damaged the rear of the German fighter plane. "I saw his tail break apart, and immediately began to yell in excitement to the tail gunner," he recalled.

The tail gunner watched as the German pilot parachuted out of his crashing plane. "He's bailing!" the tail gunner shouted out in glee.

With the first enemy attack repelled, the excitement died down and the bombers continued in formation to the target at Frankfurt. "As we got closer to the objective, I experienced anti-aircraft guns for the first time," John remembered. Exploding puffs of black smoke filled the sky. Known to American airmen as "ack ack," the German anti-aircraft guns fired 88 millimeter shells from ground positions. German fighter planes would radio in the Allied bombers' elevation and speed to the gunners below. This gave the Germans, some of whom were women and teenagers defending their homeland, the ability to set the distance of their guns with accuracy.

Black clouds of anti-aircraft shells exploded, seeming harmless at first. As clouds of shrapnel drew closer, the feeling of danger intensified. *Man o' War* barreled through, taking little damage but vibrating intensely. Exposed in a window with no real way to cover himself, John saw a smoking friendly bomber descending rapidly out of the sky. "I see a plane in a spin!" he yelled over the intercom.

One of the B-17s in formation took flak damage. It spiraled down to the earth. "Count any chutes?" the pilot asked.

John counted only six parachutes. The aircrew was made up of ten men. Some had not gotten out in time. Realizing he had not heard from the tail gunner in a while, John looked towards the rear of the plane and saw him slumped over. With a portable ten-minute oxygen tank, he crawled over to him. The man had not been wearing his own mask properly and had passed out. As John began to revive him, the gunner awoke in a total panic and started fighting John inside the plane.

The struggle was heard over the aircrew's headsets, and the navigator rushed down to help John subdue the tail gunner and give him oxygen.

While the men aided him, *Man o' War* flew over its target, the German city of Frankfurt. The B-17 dropped three tons of bombs, destroying several factories that were manufacturing Luftwaffe fighter planes.

As the rest of the formation emptied its payload over the area, the aircrafts completed a large turnaround maneuver. It was back to England for the bombers. *Man o' War* was in good shape, even though the plane had taken minor damage from flak. The tail gunner was back to normal, and John was now a combat airman.

Looking through his window on the six-hour return trip, John saw England emerge on the horizon. After landing, John and some other men sought medical attention for their frozen hands and feet. All aircrew members from the mission were offered a shot of Scotch so they could unwind before a debriefing took place.

Flying mission after mission, John became a hardened airman. The battered *Man o' War* earned its stripes as a legendary warplane. "Every time we came back from a mission, we usually had a couple days off," John told me. With this standard schedule, John figured it was all right to go out and have drinks with the other airmen at a pub not far from base. After one such night, John jumped into his rack only to be woken up a couple hours later. Someone yelled into his hut: "Katsaros! Hey, Katsaros! You're flying as a replacement gunner. Get up!"

"But I flew yesterday." He fell back to sleep.

The voice grew louder. "It's an order. You're going!"

John angrily got up and put on his flight clothes. At the morning briefing, the target was revealed to the airmen as Berlin, Germany, one of the most heavily defended parts of the country. The mission was to destroy a factory that made ball bearings, the key ingredient to German tanks, planes, and other vehicles.

Highly annoyed, John joined a random crew that he wasn't familiar with and a brand new rookie pilot. "Before takeoff, we were assigned to be the last plane in formation, also known as 'tail-end Charlie.' To some, it's known as the 'Purple Heart corner.' When birds fly in a V, the last one in the V formation is usually picked off by a predator. It's no different when fighter planes attack us. In other words, it was the worst place to be," he explained.

"Before we boarded the planes, another fellow came running up to me and asked if I was a cameraman," John continued. "When I told him yes, he asked me to film his plane dropping bombs, because they would be flying next to us in formation. I told him no problem."

As some five hundred planes took off for the seven-hour flight to Berlin, another three hundred planes took off from Italy to join the bombing raid. It wasn't long before John, who already had eight missions under his belt, realized how inexperienced the pilot was. As the bombers approached France, the B-17 was falling out of formation.

The hungover, irritated John informed the pilot over the intercom that they were falling behind. "We ought to keep up with the rest of the planes or we are sitting ducks out here!"

His transmissions were ignored. The pilot would close in, then fall back, over and over. The pilot continued to struggle, dragging considerably away from the other bombers over Germany. John's patience was at its end. He called over the intercom, asking the pilot to keep up. "If you don't stay off this intercom, I'll have you court-martialed!" the rookie pilot yelled.

John snapped. "If you don't keep this plane in formation, I'll come up and fly it for you!" he shouted back.

John thought back on that moment and said, "As soon as those words left my mouth, we heard a *BRRRRRRAAAAP!*"

A German fighter pilot had shot up their B-17. The rounds entered the bomber, going through the plane's radio and almost killing the radioman. "We kept taking direct hits. Our plane was starting to look like Swiss cheese," he told me.

Six German fighter planes were attacking the formation. Every one of the B-17's guns was firing back, each unloading over 250 rounds. Smoking bombers within the formation began to plummet out of the sky. "I saw three bombers alone go down from being shot up by the fighters," John remembered. "The fighters harassed us for a while before radioing our elevation and speed to the anti-aircraft on the ground. It was a wake-up call for our pilot. He made sure he stayed in formation perfectly after that."

Getting closer to Berlin, John experienced more flak than he had in any of his other missions. "When we were over the target," John recalled, "I made sure I began filming that kid's plane dropping its payload. He was the left waist gunner and was waving to me. I waved back, and fifteen seconds later the plane took a direct hit from ack ack."

The B-17 alongside John's exploded into a fireball, crashing down to earth like a meteor. There was no possibility of any airmen on board making it out alive.

"Was that real? Did that really just happen?" John asked himself. Fifty more planes were shot down, but his bomber managed to drop its payload and head back to base.

"I had never been so happy to land after a mission as I was that day. I kissed the ground when I got off," John said.

As he rose, the rookie pilot approached him. "I'm sorry for threatening to court-martial you," the pilot told him.

John placed his hand on the officer's shoulder. "Sir, it takes some guys six missions to learn how to fly like you did," John reassured him. "Today you became a combat pilot."

John returned to his crew waiting in their huts. They looked at him like they wanted to know how it had gone, but John, exhausted, kept to himself. The bombing raids proved to be successful against Berlin in the early part of March 1944. Although Allied warplanes took serious casualties in their missions to the heart of Germany, the Luftwaffe was never the same. From then on, German fighter planes only defended cities that were deemed absolutely necessary to Nazi survival, leaving some parts of Germany completely unprotected.

On March 20, 1944, *Man o' War* returned to the skies of Frankfurt. The city had been John's first mission—and it would be his last. Factories were the targets again, but these factories were not making bit parts like the industrial centers on which the previous bombing missions had focused. These factories manufactured the new jet engine for the German Ho-2 bomber, rumored to have the capability to reach New York.

Man o' War was locked and loaded, engines rolling and ready for takeoff soon after the morning briefing. The men were given electric heating suits to plug into the aircraft to help stay warm. John was again assigned to be right waist gunner. John was with his usual crew. William Mock was the navigator, Ted Kroll the bombardier, Jack Dunaway the pilot, Henry Kane the co-pilot, John Crowley the left waist gunner, Francis Mastronardi the navigator, Walter Rusch the ball turret gunner, and Marvin Benz the tail gunner. All the men had flown together since training in Texas. Their crew would never be the same again.

As the plane ascended over the English Channel, inauspicious weather brewed in the skies. It was the worst weather John had flown in since joining the Air Corps. "All the pilots had trouble controlling their planes," John remembered. "The dense cloud cover was very bad."

Soon after takeoff, two B-17s collided and crashed down on the English countryside. The bombers shook violently due to turbulence. Many pilots couldn't see other aircraft due to the weather, which made flying in formation dangerous.

Over France, the weather wasn't any better; the sky was still dense with cloud cover. The top turret gunner yelled over the intercom that the B-17 above them was about to crash into them. Pilot Jack Dunaway put the plane into a dive to escape the collision. As the plane fell rapidly from twenty-seven thousand feet, the centrifugal force caused John's body to slam against the wall of the plane. He was stuck, unable to move. The pilots used every muscle in their bodies to straighten out the plane.

Once below the clouds, they were out of formation. *Man o' War* began to make its way back up into the clouds to join the rest of the bombers. Rising to their previous elevation, they found that the rest of the Allied planes were nowhere in sight.

"Anyone see the formation?" the pilot asked over the intercom. All the crew members searched high and low, but they could not make out a single American plane. "I think they might have gone right," John said.

But with no way to be sure, *Man o' War* instead stayed its original course towards Frankfurt, alone.

"We were ordered to maintain radio silence during this mission," John explained. To be as stealthy as possible, the Eighth Air Force avoided all radio traffic so the Germans wouldn't know the Allied bombers' destination. Meanwhile, during *Man o' War*'s near disaster, the lead bomber in the formation had received orders from England to change targets due to the dangerous weather. Unbeknownst to John and his crew, their single B-17 bomber was now flying over enemy territory to its original destination of Frankfurt on its own.

The enemy flak started as the lone bomber flew over Frankfurt. Hundreds of anti-aircraft guns set on the single plane. "As soon as we dropped our bombs, we lost two engines on each side due to ack ack," John recalled. Smoke poured from *Man o' War*'s wings. More flak began to penetrate the plane's interior as it turned to head back to England.

But the trouble wasn't over. Six German Me-109 fighter planes began to strafe the bomber. One after another, the enemy planes' 20 mm shells exploded all over the B-17, killing the engineer manning the top turret. "A 20 mm round must have hit him in the neck, because his head was rattling around in the bomb bay doors," John said, wincing as he remembered the gruesome scene. "His body was between the pilots. He was the first of the crew to be killed in action."

Every gun on *Man o' War* was firing rapidly. The plane filled up with thousands of shell casings in a matter of minutes. "We knew it would be only a matter of time before we were going to have to bail, but we wanted to make it over France first," John told me. "We were afraid of being killed by German civilians for all the collateral damaged we caused. We heard stories of some men killed by farmers' pitchforks."

Man o' War's guns scored some successful hits on the German fighters, but the limping bomber made a tragic scene. William Mock, the navigator, was severely injured. The crew could not tend to him immediately, as fighting off the attacking planes was the priority. The bombardier would later throw Mock from the plane in the hopes that he would be rescued, but his parachute malfunctioned. He died on impact.

John had just gone through the last of his ammo when another set of enemy rounds tore through the center of the plane, sending shrapnel into his back and legs. John called over the intercom to notify the pilot that he was hit—and out of ammunition.

The pilots asked the status of the other crewmen. At the end of the plane, John saw the tail gunner, Marvin Benz, lying on his back. John crawled to reach him. "He was covered in frozen blood, with multiple wounds to his chest," John said, choking up as he remembered how he had tried to revive his tail gunner. "I performed chest compressions, and he came to for a short minute, but then died in my arms."

Hearing the emotion in John's voice snapped me out of his gripping story. The war had never really left him, even now at ninety-five years of age. The surreal events of that fateful day still stuck with him; the memory of a fallen comrade was still heart-wrenching today after a half century had passed. As he continued to tell me the details of *Man o' War*'s last mission, I quickly regained my focus on his story.

Unable to save Benz's life, John sat in the tail end of the plane for a moment. Another enemy aircraft closing in on *Man o' War* grabbed his attention. John saw the enemy aircraft coming up on the rear and, glancing at the .50 caliber, noticed it still had ammunition. He dove for the machine gun and began firing at the incoming German fighter. "I hit him directly with all my rounds and saw his cockpit explode and his aircraft drop fast out of the sky. There was no parachute, and I had no regrets killing that pilot," he said. "I'm sure he was the one who killed my buddy Benz."

John crawled back to the center of the plane and saw left waist gunner John Crowley slumped against the wall. "He was bleeding from the neck pretty bad," John recalled. "The freezing temperature was causing it to congeal. I tied a scarf around his neck to help stop the bleeding."

As John was administrating the limited first aid he could, the radioman—Frank—ran over to help. Both men knew that if Crowley didn't get help he would soon be dead. Both John and Frank strapped a parachute to Crowley's chest and threw him from the plane at twenty-eight thousand feet. "We did this in the hopes that whoever found him could give him better medical care than we could at that time," he told me.

John prepared to bail from the aircraft himself, but Walter Rusch, the belly gunner, was stuck in the ball turret. The crew of the battered bomber had fired so many rounds that shell casings had rolled into the gear box of the bull turret, causing it to jam and trapping the gunner inside. John and Frank ran over and picked spent shell casings out of the gear box one by one until the gears were able to move, freeing Rusch.

As the enemy planes made another strafe on *Man o' War*, John and Frank were hit badly in their arms by shrapnel. The surviving men, all wounded, helped buckle each other into their parachutes. "The pilot came over the intercom for the last time," John remembered. "He told us that one of our wings was fully engulfed in flames, and we were given permission to bail."

The pilots sounded a bell that blared throughout the plane, notifying the men to bail immediately from the doomed aircraft. The navigator, bombardier, and pilots all made it out of the plane. In the last-minute rush inside the plane, Rusch's parachute snagged on something and inflated. John and Francis helped him bunch it up again. He had to jump out of the burning plane hugging his bunched-up chute.

The wounded John limped his way over to the doors before rolling out into the sky. John free-fell some twenty thousand feet, passing out from his injuries while still in the air. Coming back to his senses, John pulled his chute with his one good hand just before it was too late. The late dispatch caused him to hit the ground hard, fracturing his ankles, cracking his head, and breaking six of his ribs. Severely injured from the fall and the wounds he had sustained in the aircraft, he watched the descending parachute of the radioman, hoping that he would land nearby. But the radioman's parachute dragged him farther and farther away from John, slamming him into a tree at the edge of the tree line.

John had landed on what was once a World War I airfield, now overgrown. As he struggled to free himself from the chute, a German fighter pilot slowly passed him. "I could see the pilot. I thought he was going to shoot me," John said, "but he saluted me instead."

The German pilot made several passes by John, ultimately giving his position away to ground forces. Completely immobile, he looked on as the radioman, Frank Mastronardi, was captured by a German patrol. John lay there helpless until he, too, was surrounded by the Nazi secret police, the Gestapo.

"They placed me into a wheelbarrow and brought me into a nearby farmhouse. The Gestapo spoke perfect English, asking me questions. I kept repeating my name, rank, and serial number," John told me.

As the temperatures were significantly warmer on the ground, John's arm began to thaw, which caused the bleeding to pick up. He sat in the barn, falling in and out of consciousness as blood spilled from his arm. The Gestapo offered minimal aid, leaving him there to die. "I must have been there for three or four days, when suddenly three armed men walked into the farmhouse," John said. "They were in civilian clothes. One of them walked over to me and put his finger over his lips, indicating for me to keep quiet." The three men were not just ordinary citizens. They were French resistance fighters.

They were later identified as Jean Joly, Pierre Demarchez, and Rene Felix. The trio crept into the back room where John's German guards were stationed. "That's when I heard a pop, pop. I found out later they had killed both the guards," he said.

Although happy that he was getting rescued, John still figured that he was doomed. The Germans had his dog tags, and it would be no secret that he was with the French resistance. John's new captors transferred him to the nearby home of Rene Felix. "That night at his home was the most horrible night I ever had," John told me. "My pain increased so much, I couldn't stop moaning and groaning." In fear that he would be heard by Germans occupying a nearby home, a woman in the house who spoke English informed John that if he couldn't keep quiet, they would be forced to hand him over to the Germans. She told John that he could get the medical attention he needed from the Germans. "Hell no!" John fired back. After John asked whether the resistance could offer medical treatment, the woman told him that a doctor would come help him in the morning if he could make it through the night. John agreed to tough it out, allowing the French woman to tie a cloth over his mouth for him to chew in order to muffle his groans.

The next morning a horse-and-buggy taxi arrived. John was put in the back. As the buggy passed German troops, they waved. The German soldiers were familiar with the local cabbie and didn't suspect that he had an American airman as his passenger.

The cab arrived at a medical clinic in Reims, France. John was brought upstairs and met with a doctor. His arm was in bad shape, especially after several days without proper medical attention. "They put a mask over my face and put me under. The doctor began surgery, but I woke up in the middle of it because they ran out of ether," he remembered.

The doctor decided he would have to halt the surgery until they could get more ether, which had to be smuggled from a different hospital. Once the sleeping agent arrived, they began a second surgery, only to run out again. John faced another sleepless night wracked with pain.

The next morning, the doctor got his hands on more ether, and John's third surgery was underway. The doctor diverted to stitching John's head and back instead, which also had lacerations, meaning that John woke up with an unfinished surgery for a third time. The poor treatment was beginning to cause severe complications in John's arm. On day three, the doctor examined the arm again and told the young American that it might have to be amputated. The arm was showing early stages of gangrene, the doctor told John.

John lashed out, refusing to consent to any amputation. Whether out of desperation or foresight, he disagreed with the doctor's diagnosis. His outburst prompted the French resistance to point their firearms at the doctor. They ordered the doctor to save John's arm.

When John came to for a fourth time, he woke up to see his arm wrapped in a cast. With a sigh of relief, he thanked God that his arm hadn't been amputated. However, his feeling of accomplishment soon faded. Extremely dehydrated, John began ringing the bell in his room for water. When the French nurses came, they had no water. Instead, they rushed the recuperating airman down the stairs and out the door of the clinic.

An unstable John fell into the gutter, still too weak to stand on his own. German soldiers walked by. They were drunk and had female dates. They laughed and ignored John, assuming he was the town drunk. He later discovered that the woman who worked the front desk of the clinic was a Nazi sympathizer. She had wanted nothing to do with harboring an American airman, and had alerted the Gestapo of his whereabouts.

As John sat in the gutter, a couple on the street helped him up and dragged him to another building, pushing him up a flight of stairs. They placed him in a jail cell. The building had belonged to the French cavalry during World War I but was being operated by another group of the French resistance. John didn't recognize any of the members from his original rescue, so he started to give them his name, rank, and serial number. He didn't know if the men were pro-Nazi or not.

By this point, several weeks had passed since his crash. John had lost considerable weight from lack of food, and his injuries had made him lose his appetite. He was able to down some food and water in his new holding area, but one morning a French cavalry colonel came in and ended the kindness. "If you don't give us some information, we are going to shoot you," the oddly dressed military officer threatened.

German soldiers often parachuted into France pretending to be Americans. Once the French rebels took them in to give them medical treatment, they would infiltrate and sabotage the resistance from within. John understood this concern, but he still refused to give information. He didn't know whether the people holding him were truly on his side, and he was adamantly opposed to providing information to enemy combatants. So John ignored the man's questions. The next day, the woman who had told John to hush when he was in agonizing pain at the first safe house entered his cell. "You need to give them more information," she told John. "They are not pro-Nazi. They are a rogue cell. But they don't believe you are an American. They really will shoot you."

When the French cavalry officer returned, John gave him more than just his name, rank, and serial number. He described who he was and the base from which he had flown, providing as many details of his background as he could. It satisfied the colonel, who ordered John to relocate again. The constant moving was hardly ideal for a man in John's physical condition, but it was needed to keep anyone looking for him off-track.

The third safe house John moved to was more than just a hideout. It was the home of Pierre Demarchez, one of the liberators who had killed John's German guards in the first farmhouse. Pierre's home contained an arsenal of weapons used by the French resistance. The weapons were hidden under a chicken coop. "There were machine guns, rifles, pistols, grenades, and time bombs," John noted. "He gave me civilian clothes to change into."

John was finally getting his strength back, and eating well at Pierre's home helped. After being shot down a month before, John was now a member of the French resistance. "I was equipped with a British Sten gun. We would go out and collect equipment that the Royal Air Force dropped for us," he said. "Pierre always told me that if a plane were ever to land to board it and get back to England. Sadly, the opportunity never arose, so I continued to carry out missions with them."

One day Pierre came back to his home and told John that he believed an American plane had landed in a nearby field. When John asked what kind of plane, Pierre could not answer. "Can you take me to this plane?' John asked.

Pierre agreed, taking John by foot. "Sure enough, when we got there, it was a P-51 Mustang. Our bombers were finally getting escorts, and one of them had made an emergency landing, but the plane was now guarded by German soldiers," John recalled. "I told

Pierre we had to find a way to destroy the plane or else it would be used by the Luftwaffe."

Pierre was way ahead of John. The men went back to the safe house, and Pierre took a time bomb with a couple of sticks of TNT out from the chicken coop. They returned to the plane.

Pierre had befriended the German soldier in his earlier visit to the aircraft. The fact that he was a bakery owner in town convinced the German guard that he and John were harmless, curious locals. The soldier allowed Pierre and John in for a closer look at the plane. Diverting the German's attention, Pierre removed the sticks of TNT from his waistline, placed them under the pilot's seat, and set the timer. He thanked the German soldier and they left. An hour later, the plane exploded, killing the German.

John's fun with the French resistance didn't last long. A $10,000 reward was offered for the location of American airman John Katsaros, and, sure enough, someone ratted him out.

"I was standing in Pierre's kitchen when I heard the door open," John said. Three armed Gestapo officers walked in, arresting him and Pierre's wife. They proceeded to transport the two to the regional Gestapo headquarters in Reims, France. Once they arrived, the secret police wasted no time separating the two prisoners. They began torturing John's former hostess, turning on a loud cement mixer to drown out her screams as they pulled out her fingernails.

Listening to the screams of Pierre's wife made John wonder what he would do under questioning. "I came to the conclusion that I would have to suffer the torture if it came to that," John told me in a somber tone. "I could never give up the people who saved my life."

But John wouldn't face torture. Before the screams from the next room subsided, John was taken out of the compound and placed in a car with two more Gestapo personnel. "They were more interested in her than they were with me," John speculated.

The car pulled up to a roadblock, where John was removed and placed into another automobile. Mysteriously—to this day he's not sure how it was arranged—he was transferred to the car of the Reims chief of police, a leader in the French resistance. The chief handed him a police uniform to wear and then brought him to another safe house that contained a British airman who had also been shot down.

Over the course of several weeks, the two Allied airmen were shuttled from resistance safe house to resistance safe house. At one point, they had to lower themselves down a well during an unexpected visit by Gestapo checking on the residence they called home. After moving them from place to place, the French resistance finally decided to put an end to stowing the two men away. They made fake identification cards for John and the British airman, took them to a train station, and sent them on a train headed to Paris.

Upon arrival, they were met by the chief of police of Paris. "They gave us information to pass on to our intelligence about different German bases to bomb if we ever made it back to England," John told me. "They also informed us that the only way out of France was to head south and climb over the mountains into neutral Spain."

John was ready to do whatever it took to return home. After a short stay in Paris, John boarded another train with six other Americans, a British airman, and seven Jews escaping the Holocaust. They headed to the Spanish border.

They arrived at the base of the Pyrenees mountain range. The men were wearing casual civilian clothes with dress shoes, hardly the appropriate attire for hiking the impressive mountains. The resistance members who had taken them south told the group to wait for their Spanish Basque guide, and then disappeared. "The guy didn't meet us until a day and a half later," John told me, still visibly annoyed. Worried about the possibility of being captured, the group considered attempting a pass over the mountains on their own. "We almost left without him," John continued. "Thank God we didn't. We most likely would have died."

With a guide to lead them, the party began the arduous trek across the Pyrenees. After two days of climbing, John's hunger and months of malnourishment began to get the best of him. He had no idea that climbing the mountains would take four days and four nights. Unable to keep pace with the group, he began to lag behind the escaping refugees. Worried that he might compromise their flight, John begged them to leave him with a compass and make for safety as fast as possible. The men refused, pulling John with a stick in the steep areas of the mountains. "There was nothing to eat," John said of the arduous journey. "We slept under the stars and drank melted snow."

Eventually descending into Spain, the men were spotted by government officials. They were rounded up and arrested by the police and brought to a Spanish prison. As the doctors evaluated John, they informed him he weighed only eighty-seven pounds. "When I asked the date, they told us it was the first week in June, and that the Allies had invaded Normandy, France. That's how I'll always know that I was climbing the Pyrenees on D-Day," John said.

The prison commander notified the men that he would contact the British Embassy in Madrid. The British Embassy asked that the men be delivered to them. They ate and enjoyed meals for the first time in a week. Now under British caretaking, the group was sent to Gibraltar and rescued.

After almost three months of running around behind enemy lines, John found himself on a British Royal Air Force transport plane. "When I returned to my original base in England, there were not many men I recognized," John said. "Everyone had been shot down, captured, killed, or wounded. They were also in the middle of moving the base to France now that the invasion had taken place." Without a job in the Air Corps anymore, and still battling poor health conditions, John was sent back to the States. He only separated from service at the end of the war.

Like many veterans of the Second World War, John didn't talk about his own war experiences when he came home. His story of perseverance, determination, and good fortune would go unknown until he started writing his own book, *Code Burgundy*, sixty years later. "When I decided to go through with writing the book, I had to go back to France several times to get the correct places and names of people who helped

me escape and personally thank them," John said, beaming with gratitude. "I had a few reunions with my French resistance friends. I'll always
be in debt to the French people for what they did for me."

Photos of John dressed in French police garb and French resistance
armbands hang on his walls. A painting of his B-17 going down in flames
hangs in his living room. He brought out a copy of his book, *Code Burgundy*, for me. I reached into my pocket to pay him, but he refused my
money. "I should be paying you," he said as he steadily signed my rifle.
His only request was that I drive him and his wife to lunch. I enjoyed my
beer and food with the last surviving crewman of *Man o' War*.

John Katsaros with the rifle. *Photo courtesy of the author*

CHAPTER NINE

Last-Minute Marauder

Stanley Sasine
U.S. Army, 5307th Composite Unit

Atlanta, Georgia

I met Stanley Sasine by accident. By the end of our chance encounter, he had drunk me under the table.

I had traveled to Atlanta, Georgia, to meet a veteran who fought in Bastogne, Belgium. Our interview did not go as planned. The veteran I had traveled all the way down to interview quickly described how badly the Germans had shelled his unit during the Battle of the Bulge, his first action in the war. In those opening moments, he admitted he had succumbed to "shell shock" and been taken off the front line, never to return.

I admired the man's honesty. I would have eaten up anything he told me, but he insisted on telling me his true story. He was ninety-six years old. Unfortunately, due to his short stint in the war, he was not able to answer the questions I had for him.

While I was certainly honored to have the man sign my rifle, I was now stranded in Georgia with plenty of time to kill before my flight home. Sitting in a coffee shop, my eyes fell an article in the local paper: "93-Year-Old WWII Vet Skydives." I read about Mr. Stanley Sasine, a combat veteran of Burma, who had wanted to skydive for his birthday.

I knew I had to find him. If jumping out of a plane at ninety-three wasn't cool enough, the rifle could use the signature of someone who had fought in Burma.

The white pages listed Stanley in an assisted living home a half hour from me. I decided to drive over there and try my luck with the adventure-loving veteran. When I arrived, I left the rifle in the car to make sure I didn't freak anyone out inside the home. I walked through the automatic doors and was greeted by a woman at the front desk. How was I going to smooth my way into this place, not being a friend or family member?

"Can I help you, sir?" the woman asked, in a tone that made it clear she ran the place.

The words flew out of my mouth. "Yes ma'am," I replied. "I'm traveling the country interviewing World War II veterans for a documentary, and I'm here to meet Mr. Stanley Sasine."

The woman cut me off before I could tell her my credentials. "Oh, Stanley is one of my favorites here!" she said, clearly quite enthusiastic that Stanley had a visitor. "You go right on upstairs, to the sixth floor. He is probably in the bar."

I thanked her. I had just finessed my way into a very impressive assisted living home in the South, and now I was riding an elevator to talk to a guy who had no idea I was coming. He didn't know one thing about me. The odds of his telling me to beat it were high.

When I got to the sixth floor, I looked through the dining facility windows. There he was, with an Army beret on his head featuring the Purple Heart, Bronze Star, and Combat Infantryman Badge. He had a goatee and was surrounded by five women, all listening to him attentively. I pulled up a chair and began to listen, too.

I caught the tail end of the conversation, when Stanley declared to the women, "You should have seen me when I was forty-four!" The table erupted in laughter, but I was too late to catch the joke. As soon as the laughter died down, I introduced myself.

Stanley immediately treated me as if we had served together. He slapped my shoulder and thanked me for my own service. But the five women surrounding the table looked at me with distrust, perhaps assuming that I was a con artist. As I began to tell Stanley about the rifle, he said, "Go get it! We'll slam it down right here!" pointing to the table in the middle of the dining room, now packed with some fifty other elderly residents.

"I don't think that's a good idea. I really don't want to scare everyone." I laughed nervously as the faces of the women around the table continued to look on, unamused.

We agreed to meet in his room. The women began to whisper to each other.

Coming from the rental car, I had to walk past the lovely woman at the front desk again. "He's allowing me to interview him!" I said excitedly, holding the rifle case in the air, pretending it held a video camera. I made my way to Room 225. When I knocked on the door Stanley shouted, "Come right in."

As I entered his apartment, he stood there brandishing a rifle of his own. "This belonged to the bastard who shot me!" he cried out, holding up a Japanese sniper rifle. The rifle was in rough shape, and the buttstock, which was splintering, was duct-taped together. The tape was aged. Could it have been applied more than seventy years before?

The rifle still had a chrysanthemum engraved into it, which was the mark of the Japanese emperor. The rifle was truly a "bring back" and not an aftermarket, or else the emperor's marking would have been scrubbed off. The U.S. government allowed Japan to scrub its emperor's markings off before surrendering a large cache of arms to Allied forces.

"I wasn't even supposed to be in Burma," Stanley started. "I was slated to go to Europe with everyone else, but I signed some volunteer form that was put in front of me. I thought it was for clothing issue." He paused. "Have another glass; we got nowhere to be!"

Stanley poured me another glass of straight Ciroc vodka and started his story from the beginning.

The Last-Minute Marauder

In the summer of 1995, Stanley Sasine won one million dollars in a *Reader's Digest* sweepstakes. He and his wife, Renee, celebrated in complete joy as a giant check was presented to them in front of their home in Atlanta, Georgia. Neighbors, family, and friends joined for the photo op, and a few weeks later he and his wife discussed what they would do with the money.

"We can travel the world now," Renee said excitedly.

Stanley agreed. The couple went down a list of countries they could visit.

"What about going back to India?" Renee asked.

Stanley was shaving, looking in the bathroom mirror. He cleaned off his razor and said, "Absolutely not."

He took a towel off his right shoulder to dry his face, exposing a deep hole. In fact, whenever his shirt was off he draped a folded towel over his shoulder to hide the scar that had developed where he had been shot by a Japanese sniper.

Stanley rejected his wife's suggestion so offhandedly because he knew that part of the world would only bring him back to the jungles of Burma in June 1944. He didn't have pleasant memories of those days. In Burma, U.S. soldiers of the 5307th Composite Unit suffered from such bad dysentery that they had to remove the seams from their pants. Rather than continuously pulling their pants down to defecate, removing the seams allowed them to roll over and let the feces fall out of them as they fought. "It was better than shitting ourselves like we had been doing during combat," Stanley grimaced.

When the Long Islander's troop transport ship had pulled into England in April of 1944, most of the men were let off, but not Stanley. "A few days before we got docked in Great Britain, I got duped into signing some paperwork that I was told was for new uniforms," Stanley explained. "Instead, it was a volunteer list to go to India."

A few days later, the Jewish kid who had never left New York was in Calcutta, India. He was supposed to have a cushy job driving a jeep around England; now he was in the jungles halfway across the world. In less than a year, Stanley went from being a freshman at Cornell University to being in a land he had only read about. "There were elephants, snake charmers, people in crazy outfits," Stanley told me.

Only a few thousand U.S. troops served in Burma during the Second World War. They had the least amount of resources of any front during World War II, and yet they had two enemies: the Japanese and disease.

They were resupplied mostly by airdrop. Their original purpose was to support Chinese and British forces from India. However, their mission evolved into being a hit-and-run unit, used to disrupt Japanese supply lines in Burma, actions that would later result in the birth of the Seventy-Fifth Army Ranger Regiment.

In the meantime, the nickname given to this small group of men was "Merrill's Marauders," after their commanding officer, General Merrill. I sat across from one of the last living Marauders, ninety-four-year-old Stanley.

He went on: "We received no training in India. Me and some others were handed weapons and grenades and were told we had to catch up with the rest of the battalions who were already marching through the jungles of India and into Burma. We were made up of truck drivers, mechanics, supply men, and other soldiers. We were being sent to help Merrill's Marauders in their final mission Their ultimate objective was to march hundreds of miles and capture an airfield in Myitkyina, Burma. It was being used to resupply Japanese forces occupying China."

Stanley continued: "After several days and a short plane ride, we caught up with the other men. As our plane was getting ready to land in an open area, the pilot told us to jump out and run into the woods on our left side."

Stanley and the other reinforcements jumped out of the moving plane and sprinted into the jungle. Japanese artillery fire struck the landing strip. Upon entering the jungle, they met what remained of the original Merrill's Marauders. "They had donkeys and pack mules carrying their equipment. The battalion was gearing up to ambush a Japanese camp nearby," Stanley recalled.

Stanley, a fresh soldier with a clean uniform, introduced himself to what was left of the special unit. The men were filthy, skinny, and sick. They had marched hundreds of miles through the mountains and jungles of Burma. They took hundreds of casualties from both the enemy and illness.

"They were not a division. They were not a battalion. Only a thousand men remained of what was once three thousand. They asked me how I got stuck with the unit. I told them I didn't know. I'll never forget the day I went from being just a truck driver to being accepted by Merrill's Marauders," Stanley told me.

In just under a week, Stanley was part of Merrill's Marauders, preparing to meet the Japanese enemy for the first time. The enemy camp the men were getting ready to raid was spotted by reconnaissance scouts. It was blocking the route that would ultimately bring them to their final objective, the Myitkyina airfield.

The camp was occupied by garrisoned troops, not frontline infantry fighters. The enemy soldiers were mostly tasked with organizing supplies, and the base was home to wounded soldiers in recovery. "These were the easy kills," Stanley said of his first real military action. "There were less than fifty of them, but I have lived with this first engagement for almost forty years. My wife for a long time would wake me up out of nightmares and clean the sweat off my forehead."

Stanley and his squad crawled close to the camp, coming within eyesight of the opposition forces. The Japanese soldiers were sitting by a fire. As the Marauders rushed the camp, Stanley raised his Tommy gun and began to run. One Japanese soldier who saw the invading Americans started running towards the onrushing men without seeing Stanley coming from the brush. "We passed each other," Stanley recalled. "It took a second to realize it. My finger was already on the trigger, and when I turned, I was quicker than him. I watched my bullets hit his body from two o' clock to eight o'clock. That's just how the Thompson fired."

Stanley nearly cut the Japanese soldier in half with six .45 caliber rounds from his Thompson submachine gun. As the rest of Merrill's Marauders stormed the camp, he went through the dead soldier's bloody clothing. Reaching into his uniform top, he found a photo of two Caucasian children, a boy and a girl. Written on the back was "Merry Christmas, Dad."

"I never could find out who those children were. I only assume the picture was originally taken off a dead Australian or English solider," Stanley said with some regret. He reached into a folder and took out the picture, which he had kept all those years.

The U.S. soldiers ran riot in the camp, taking no prisoners. As the din of battle subsided, Stanley and his fellow Americans noticed that the Japanese stationed at the outpost were living in filth and squalor. After taking the garrison without casualties, the men had to fight an invisible enemy. They started getting sick.

The same men who had bravely taken the enemy base were soon keeled over with high fevers, dysentery, and typhus. Merrill's Marauders caught their sickness from the Japanese soldiers. Though they had taken a key position on their march to Burma, the disease that now spread among them would haunt them for the rest of their campaign. The men marched on, but the monsoon rain and mud only made their diseases worse. Some of the 149 soldiers would die from their illnesses.

After one hundred miles of travel, the sick, tired, and hungry Merrill's Marauders reached the outskirts of the Myitkyina airfield. Their numbers had dwindled over the arduous journey, but because of how fast they moved through terrain, they were able to take the airfield by complete surprise.

"On May 17, 1944, we descended onto the airstrip with two Chinese regiments," Stanley noted. The Marauders swooped in and seized the enemy position with minimal resistance. The initial mission was such a success that news of the Marauders' accomplishment was soon on the front pages of the English papers. Even Winston Churchill praised the Americans, acknowledging that his own British troops hadn't gained that much ground that quickly in Burma.

However, the success was celebrated too soon. The Marauders were promised no more heavy lifting after taking the airfield, and they were told that Chinese forces would take over the nearby city. "We were told that planes would be arriving any day to replenish us with food, ammo, and medicine, and that our job was done, so we waited," Stanley told me.

Instead, the Marauders were dismayed to discover when the planes arrived that they weren't carrying anything except tools to repair the airfield. Feeling completely let down by the military, the Marauders' morale cratered when they needed it most. The city outside the airfield, which could have been taken right after the airstrip was seized, had been reinforced with another 3,500 Japanese troops during the days of delay.

"If we hadn't been told we were getting resupplies and food, we would have gone with the Chinese to take over the town," Stanley scowled, still upset over the lack of support from central command.

The Chinese regiments attacked the city without the Marauders' help, but it was an epic failure. Two Chinese regiments fired upon each other in the confusion of the assault, causing great casualties. Allied forces were in jeopardy of losing the airfield they had spent months trying to capture, and the entire Burma campaign was in jeopardy as the Japanese advanced to take back the airport.

In desperation, General Merrill was forced to put his men back into the fight. "Even though 80 percent of us were infected with dysentery," Stanley told me, "we were ordered to dig defensive positions at the Myitkyina airfield and prepare for a counterattack."

Truck drivers, engineers, and rear echelon troops were flown in on small planes from India to provide whatever reinforcement they could. Even the severely sick soldiers, barely able to stand, were ordered out of the aid stations and into the fighting.

Despite the fact that all hands were on deck, the grossly outnumbered Americans had a hard time holding the airfield. "The Japanese were infiltrating us," Stanley recounted. "They threw grenades into our makeshift field hospital along the airstrip. As they ran off, I fired on one, striking him in the back. A really pissed-off medic and I began to crawl through the jungle to hunt down the rest of them. We ran right into a sniper, and a bullet struck the medic in the head, taking part of it off!"

Lying on the ground taking cover, Stanley saw the sniper who had just killed the medic. He was hiding in a tree. "I knew if I exposed myself, I could get hit too, but I said maybe if I can rise to my knees, I'll be OK," Stanley recalled. Coming up on his knees, Stanley aimed at the camouflaged sniper with an M1 Garand and fired into the tree.

He hit his mark. But as the Japanese soldier fell out of the tree, Stanley felt a heavy blow to his back. "It felt like someone had hit me with a bat," he said. An enemy bullet, possibly fired by the same sniper, had skimmed Stanley's beard and entered his right shoulder. The round exited his back by blowing apart his shoulder blade. "I began to crawl back towards the aid station when some other soldiers found me. They bandaged me up as best they could and placed me on an oxcart to be evacuated."

Before the animal-drawn ambulance left the area, a soldier stopped it. "Sasine, this fell out of that tree," the unknown soldier said, placing a Japanese Arisaka sniper rifle across Stanley's chest. "The locals then guided my oxcart several miles outside the fighting to an area where a small plane could land on a sandbar," Stanley said. "I was loaded onto the plane and sent back to Calcutta."

Stanley underwent surgery on his shoulder in an Army field hospital back in India. "It took me ten years to be able to swing a golf club after the war," Stanley said of his injury, "and it's still not the same."

By July of 1944, the Allied forces in Burma had succeeded in pushing the Japanese out of Myitkyina. Stanley rode out the rest of the war recovering in India, making some pocket money by trading Japanese swords. "I would sell them for fifty dollars apiece to the pilots," he beamed, "then me and my buddies would live like kings in a Calcutta whorehouse!"

Living like kings was short-lived, as Stanley soon had to return home burdened with injury, bad memories, and nightmares. Yet through threat and disease, his acts of courage and heroism made him stand out among Merrill's Marauders.

I looked over at Stanley's dining room wall. The highlights of his life hung there: photos of his family, his Army Ranger tab, medals, and the framed newspaper article from when he had won the one million dollars. My rifle and his Japanese rifle lay side by side on the kitchen table.

"Now you, my friend, are going to take me to get some more vodka," Stanley said when the interview concluded. I happily drove Stanley to the

Stanley Sasine with the rifle. *Photo courtesy of the author*

store to purchase a handle. "You're gonna help me with this when we get back, right?" he asked.

I wanted nothing more than to raise another glass with one of the first ever Army Rangers. "I wish I could, but I have a flight to catch," I told him. "I promise to send you what I write for your approval."

I dropped him off at his senior citizen facility. "I'm sure gonna love whatever you write," he replied as he slammed the car door shut.

My journey to Georgia had come to its end. I was left with a nice vodka buzz for the plane ride home, thanks to a last-minute Marauder.

CHAPTER TEN

An Italian American's War in Italy

Santo DiSalvo
U.S. Army, Thirty-Sixth Infantry Division

Leominster, Massachusetts

When Santo DiSalvo got up to take his medication, I looked at the pictures on the wall. He was ninety-six. His wife had passed away, and he was now living under his daughter's roof in Leominster, not far from where he had grown up.

He walked by a bird's cage and into the kitchen. A green parakeet, his only company while his daughter was at work, squawked as Santo took his pill. The rifle lay on the floor with its case half-open. When he signed the rifle, I realized it was almost as big as he was. Santo was now just over five feet tall.

After the war, Santo spent thirty-one years as a firefighter, had a family, and led a successful life. But the odds had been stacked against him. Serving in one of World War II's hardest-hit units, the Thirty-Sixth Infantry Division, he hadn't experienced anything in his three decades as a first responder that could ever compare to what he had witnessed fighting in Italy, France, and Germany.

As an Italian American myself, I had to ask, "What was it like to be Italian fighting in Italy?"

He wasted no time responding. "The Italian people were so grateful for us," he beamed. "Most of them had cousins and family living in the United States." Santo's mood turned melancholic. "Their homes were pulverized in some places," he said, choking up. "The Germans stole everything from them, yet they still gave us what little they had."

I could feel that Santo was still tormented by what he had seen in Italy, and he was four years away from being one hundred years old. Although I knew it, and so did history, Santo was too loyal to admit that most of the destruction in Italy had come at the hands of an American, General Mark Clark.

General Clark was described by his men as a headline hunter and a medal chaser. Those who served under him believed he did not care for their lives, only for his legacy.

But don't take that from me, a kid born more than forty-five years after World War II. Take it from the survivors of his own command who called for a congressional investigation into the general's actions after the war, in 1946. General Clark was ultimately cleared of any malicious wrongdoing during his control of the Fifth Army in Italy, but the men who served in those divisions never forgot his actions.

"He nearly wiped out our entire unit," Santo whispered, as if there were others in the room. "All because he wanted to capture Rome and make the history books."

Santo was as honorable when I interviewed him in 2018 as he had been when he was a twenty-three-year-old soldier. He didn't like bad-mouthing his higher-ups.

An Italian American's War in Italy

By early May 1945, Santo DiSalvo and what was left of the Thirty-Sixth Infantry Division were at the base of a mountain in Austria. Hitler was dead. What was left of some of his most loyal SS troops still held out in the elevated terrain. After trying to negotiate with some enemy troops holding out up the hillside, a squad of U.S. soldiers descended the hill with one soldier who could speak German. They had a message for the rest of Santo's company.

"They said they would only surrender if they are allowed to keep their weapons," one soldier yelled out.

"No way! Surrender now or get killed," Santo shot back. The games were over. After nearly two years of frontline combat in Italy, France, and Germany, the men had had enough.

Although Santo meant what he said, the last thing he wanted was more fighting. He had already escaped death a few times, and he had lost personal friends. Suddenly the group of Germans began to march down the mountain road. They had their hands up and, miraculously, were unarmed. Santo took a deep breath as he watched them walk with their white flag towards the U.S. soldiers.

Santo and another man in the company began to pat down and search the Germans. An SS soldier pointed at the Thompson submachine gun Santo had slung on his shoulder, speaking in broken English. "Da bullets, .45? Go in make a small hole, come out, make big hole!" the German combatant exclaimed. The enemy held American weapons in high esteem.

After the Allied landing at Salerno, Santo had joined a unit composed mostly of men from the American South. The Thirty-Sixth Division was a National Guard unit out of Texas and Oklahoma, and Santo was one of the few "Yankees." The division had already seen combat during the initial landings in Italy. Santo was a replacement, helping take Naples and many other towns. "We had to go up and down so many hills," Santo complained. "I had no idea how hilly Italy was, my God!"

The fiercest fighting occurred when Santo's regiment, the 143rd, reached a town called San Pietro, a small village on the way to Rome. Santo and his brothers-in-arms were charged with taking the town and clearing the roads so that the trucks and convoys could continue their movement north. As they approached the town, Santo made his way through a few hundred meters of vineyards. "That's when we started to get shelled terribly," he remembered.

The men broke out into a sprint, running from different defiladed positions through the vineyards as German artillery landed around them. One shell landed not far from Santo. "I took cover, and when dust cleared, I saw human body parts still soaring through the air," Santo said of the aftermath. "There was a leg. It must have been a direct hit on the soldier in front of me."

Getting up again to run for his life, Santo sprinted toward the outskirts of the town and took cover by a stone wall. Suddenly another shell landed behind him. Rock and dirt landed on top of his helmet, but this time shrapnel pierced his right shoulder. Bleeding heavily, Santo turned to another soldier for help. "There is an aid station not far back!" the soldier yelled.

Santo ran back through the gauntlet of artillery fire to the rear, where a field hospital was set up. He held his rifle with one arm. "I spent almost seven days in the hospital, then another five months in a replacement depot," Santo said. "I couldn't rejoin my unit because they had advanced so far up into Italy, they couldn't get me up there."

Getting wounded in San Pietro probably saved Santo's life. His regiment advanced toward the Rapido River, a move many saw as unnecessary. As part of the Germans' defensive Winter Line, the Rapido River was an obstacle preventing the Thirty-Sixth Division from capturing Rome. The impressive defenses around the river meant that Santo's division would see tremendous casualties, despite the fact that two other divisions had the German position surrounded. Allied beach landings at Anzio were only two days away, meaning that the American forces had a much easier way to reach the Italian capital. Santo's division was needlessly sent into a buzz saw.

On a cold January night, two regiments of the Thirty-Sixth Division carried rubber rafts to cross the Rapido River under the cover of darkness. The Germans had flooded the river banks, turning them into swamps, so the rafts had to be hand-carried to where the water was deep enough to put them in. On each side of the river were rows of barbed wire, mines, and cut trees. The Americans had nowhere to take cover.

As the regiments pushed towards the river, a wall of artillery emerged in front of the men. The German guns zeroed in on the area perfectly. Mortar and machine gun fire caused American infantrymen to fall left and right. Most who made it to the water held useless rafts that had been penetrated by shrapnel. Screams for medics sounded across the banks, but the medics, killed and wounded by the abundant mines, were nowhere to be found. The few boats that made it into the water were blown up and cut down by machine guns.

Soldiers fell out of the boats, weighed down by their heavy equipment. Some drowned on the spot; the ones who ditched their gear were pulled downstream. The few who miraculously made it across the river had to dig foxholes with their bare hands and helmets since their weapons had sunk to the bottom of the river. "One officer who survived said he made it to the river," Santo told me, "and turned around to signal his men to advance when an artillery shell took out his whole platoon."

Of the four thousand men who attempted to cross, only a couple hundred made it to the other side. Stranded, they protected themselves with the little ammo they had.

Santo's regiment fell back. The first attempt to cross the Rapido River had been a devastating failure, but the men were forced to brave the waters again, this time during the day. The men of the Thirty-Sixth Division saw what was going on: they were being massacred for no reason. If the plan didn't work at night, why would the daytime be any better? This was clearly a desperate rush to take Rome, motivated more by their general's desire for glory than strategic considerations.

With replacement rubber rafts in their hands, the regiments made their way to the banks. They lowered their heads, closed their eyes, and ran toward the river at 4:00 p.m. The mud and rock under their feet became soft as they got closer to the water, and men began to trip. They walked over the bodies of American soldiers killed the night before. The corpses were stacked four and five bodies high.

The crossing was only twelve feet deep and fifty feet wide. It wasn't supposed to be this hard. The enemy bombardment let loose again. The survivors stranded on the other side from the first crossing could do nothing but watch as their fellow soldiers were vaporized by enemy artillery.

A small footbridge was eventually established but was cut apart by enemy machine gun fire in a matter of minutes. No heavy bridge could be constructed for tank support by the end of day two—or ever. The remaining men on the other side of the river surrendered to the Germans.

"Seventeen hundred men were killed and wounded, while another seven hundred were captured," Santo lamented. "We lost so many guys trying to cross the goddamn river, I don't even want to begin to remember any more of it." Santo held his hand up in a pausing motion with his head down, as if he would have considered dementia a blessing. He clenched his fists as he described one of World War II's biggest tragedies, still irate over the senseless loss of life incurred on that day.

After the Battle of Monte Cassino, Santo eventually rejoined the battered Thirty-Sixth Division. It wasn't much of a reunion, since hundreds of replacements now made up the regiment.

The division regrouped in Naples, where they had entered Italy almost a year before. However, they found out that their next objective had nothing to do with Italy. They were being shipped to France to relieve the pressure on the units fighting in northern France.

After a few practice beach landings in Salerno, the division set sail for Marseille, France. "We landed with no opposition," Santo said. "We rode on tops of tanks through the city and people were cheering us on. I was so distracted by the hero's welcome that when the tank hit a bump, I nearly fell off. Some woman in the crowd thought she was going to have to catch me!" For the first time while telling his story, Santo was able to laugh.

As Santo and his company advanced into the Alsace-Lorraine region of France, an area heavily occupied by Germans, they reached the outskirts of a town called Mittelwihr. The signs of heavy fighting became more apparent with each step they took.

"Our division was getting held up by opposition," Santo said. A painful memory came to him. "I was advancing along a wet, muddy road when I saw a dead American soldier. It was a good friend of mine since Italy, PFC Donderro. He had just gotten back from a few days off the front lines."

Private First Class Donderro was one of many Thirty-Sixth Division soldiers killed in the heavily occupied German area. Santo paused again as his memory caught up with him. "I hated seeing him in the road like that," Santo sighed. "He'd just come back from a nine-day furlough. He was happy." Santo paused in telling his story. In the ensuing silence, a bell sounded from his parakeet flying around in its cage in the kitchen. Santo was trying not to cry. He started again.

The company marched off the road and into the woods, going around Mittelwihr. Taking the road into the town would only be asking to be ambushed or to hit mines. While creeping though the woods, Santo and his men received intel reports suggesting there were enemy troops in the area. It was time to dig in. Upon setting up their defensive positions, Santo's squad began to patrol from their new foxholes. Suddenly a machine gun and some small arms opened fire on the men. Santo rushed forward, drawing enemy fire upon himself, giving his men time to fall back and take cover in their foxholes. Santo returned to his own foxhole as the sun was going down.

With his friend Donderro on his mind, along with all the other lost lives he had witnessed in Italy and France, Santo decided to take matters into his own hands. "I said to myself, 'I'm not staying stuck here in a foxhole forever!'" he recalled. Santo took his rifle, along with three rifle grenades, and crawled back up the hill towards the enemy machine gun nest that was harassing them. "I began launching the grenades in the direction of the machine gun, one after another." As he got closer, Santo saw that the MG 42 machine gun was abandoned. "I crawled back down the hill and let my company know. The next morning we headed back up, and we didn't get shot at this time."

As Santo's squad advanced on the enemy machine gun emplacement, they could see the havoc Santo's rifle grenades had caused. Three German soldiers, feet from the position, lay dead, blown apart as they had tried to flee Santo's wrath. "I didn't go look at them," Santo confessed. The other men told him what they had seen.

Santo had single-handedly captured the enemy emplacement and opened up an avenue of approach for his company to advance into Mittelwihr, France. As the 143rd Regiment reached the town, they soon realized that they wouldn't be sweeping through the town from house to house looking for enemy combatants. When the Americans made it to the town, German artillery, miles away, began shelling the town heavily. The destruction reached epic proportions. Houses crumbled and burning fires raged. Farm animals ran frantically about the area. As Santo moved through the town, an enemy mortar landed behind him, sending more shrapnel into his back, where his previous injury was. Thankfully his rucksack stopped the metal from penetrating his body.

The artillery finally ceased as the Americans captured the town, causing German forward observers to retreat. As the month of March came rolling around, the division called for a giant formation in an open field. Now that the Germans had retreated from France, it was time for a ceremony. "They brought the band in and told a bunch of us we were getting medals," Santo recalled.

Santo was awarded the nation's second-highest military decoration—the Army's Distinguished Service Cross—for his actions taking out the German machine gun team. It was unexpected. "Many men got medals that day—Crosses, Silver Stars, and Bronze Stars," he remembered. With the honors distributed, the men began their push into Germany.

The 143rd Regiment passed by destroyed German towns and prison camps. "I didn't see any prisoners," Santo said of the camps. "They had already been freed, but I saw the ovens." He was referring to the cremation ovens the Nazis used to dispose of the bodies of their Jewish victims.

By April of 1945, the Thirty-Sixth Division had reached Austria. The war was at its end. Soon enough, Santo would be back home, working to put out fires rather than start them. In civilian life, Santo had a new enemy. He fought fires at factories, restaurants, and residential homes in central Massachusetts just as valiantly as he had fought the Nazis. The action brought him reprieve from the thoughts of his previous battles. "I never thought about the war when battling fires and saving lives," he told me. "It was a form of therapy."

Santo's parakeet was still squawking in the background. "I just want to say one thing, and you can write this down," Santo said as he looked at me with a tear in his eye. "Whenever General Eisenhower needed the job done, he told us he could always depend on the Thirty-Sixth!" These words had carried Santo for seventy-four years.

Santo DiSalvo with the rifle. *Photo courtesy of the author*

Santo was one of the most loyal men to sign the rifle. He was as honorable at ninety-six as he was when he got pinned with his Distinguished Service Cross. He regretted nothing, and he refused to play into the "should have, could have, what if" questions I baited him with. He was a good man, a living testament to the qualities that patriotic service inculcates.

CHAPTER ELEVEN

Two Paratroopers, One Island

Nelson Bryant and Ted Morgan
U.S. Army, Eighty-Second Airborne Division

Martha's Vineyard, Massachusetts

The Eighty-Second Airborne is one of the most well-known Army units of all time. They played a pivotal role in World War II, and I wanted them represented on my rifle. Through research, I found an article on the internet about a Mr. Nelson Bryant from Martha's Vineyard. The article told the story of how, in 2017, a Dutch man found a bayonet in the attic of a house in Holland. That bayonet happened to have Nelson's full name on it. It had been seventy-three years since it was initially discarded in the countryside. It had been recovered and moved several times over the years. The Dutch man took it upon himself to fly to America to return it to Nelson.

I reached out to a few people I knew in Cape Cod and, sure enough, they were able to connect me to Nelson. His caretaker and partner, Ruth, set up a meeting for us. I strapped the rifle to the back of my Harley Davidson and rode from Boston to Cape Cod with a couple of friends. From there, we took a ferry and sailed over to Martha's Vineyard.

Riding along island roads, we eventually reached Nelson's home, a converted goat barn. He couldn't miss the rumbling of our Harleys as we parked. Dressed in overalls, Nelson came to the door with a walking stick.

Nelson was amazed by the motorcycles. "Does that thing play music?" He pointed at my speakers.

"Sure does. Want to go for a ride?"

"Ha, ha. No way!" As Nelson spoke, I noticed something in his mouth. He had a lip full of Skoal Long Cut tobacco! I couldn't believe he was still packing lips at ninety-five years old.

His home was the typical Cape Cod house. Pots and pans hung from the kitchen ceiling, and his yard was full of homesteading material and plants.

When we sat, I showed him the rifle. He grabbed it immediately and began to aim it, left-handed. "They only taught us how to shoot righty, ya know. I had to teach myself how to aim with my left because I had a lazy eye!" he exclaimed.

Nelson was a true grunt and wouldn't let go of the rifle. "You won't believe this shit!" Nelson howled. (He also swore like a truck driver— and I loved it.) "Some guy called me last year and returned my bayonet and sheath to me. He came all the way from fuckin' Holland!"

Although I had already heard the story, I knew that hearing it from his mouth would be priceless.

Two Paratroopers, One Island

Before he started his story, Nelson walked over to a chest in his living room and opened it. He reached in and grabbed what was easily recognizable as a bayonet, along with a green piece of silk. He slammed the bayonet down on the dining room table next to the rifle. The green cloth, it turned out, was a piece of camo parachute. "This was the chute I used in Operation Market Garden," he told me. That was the last time he had seen his bayonet before the Dutchman returned it to him seven decades later.

But Nelson's story didn't start in Holland. It began in Normandy, when Nelson successfully jumped from his C-47 on June 6, 1944—D-Day.

Nelson was a member of D Company, 508th Parachute Infantry Regiment, of the 82nd Airborne. Although most of the division was scattered, he landed and regrouped with hundreds of other paratroopers. "We were able to occupy a hill known as Hill 30 three days after our jump," Nelson said. "From there, we dispatched squads to patrol the local villages for German activity."

Nelson Bryant. *Photo courtesy of Nelson Bryant*

During one patrol, as Nelson approached a farmhouse, German machine gun fire tore through him and the point man at the head of the patrol. "The point man was screaming out for help, but I had a bullet through my chest and was knocked back myself. He died quick," Nelson told me. He lay there in disbelief, not far from his dead fellow paratrooper. The bullet had entered the right side of his chest, gone through his lung, and exited below his shoulder blade. "A medic ran up to me and hit me with morphine. The squad had to continue the attack, leaving me behind," he remembered.

Nelson lay alone, dying. "I could hear cows mooing in the pasture, and figured it was over," he said. Out of nowhere, a second medic knelt next to Nelson, hitting him with more morphine. "I tried to tell him I had already been given morphine, but I couldn't speak, and obviously the first medic never marked me properly."

Gunfire began to erupt closer to Nelson again. After eliminating the enemy machine gun, the squad hit more resistance and was forced to fall back. "Bryant, unless you want to be a POW, I suggest you get your ass up now!'" an officer yelled at Nelson.

With the assistance of other paratroopers, Nelson found the strength to get up, but he soon toppled over. "I knocked over the paratrooper assisting me and sent the bayonet on his rifle into the ankle of the officer in front of us," Nelson said of the scene. He had been made clumsy by his wound and double dose of morphine. Despite being weighed down by a discombobulated Nelson, the paratrooper managed to get them back to Allied lines. Nelson received medical treatment and was soon shipped off to England. He needed several months to recuperate, as the bullet had left a hole the size of a fist in his back as it exited his body.

After three months in an English hospital in Wales, Nelson learned that the Eighty-Second would soon be gearing up for another combat jump. By that point, Normandy was well secured. This time, they'd be going to Holland. It was September of 1944, and Nelson didn't want to miss out.

"I asked the doctor for permission to return to my unit," Nelson said. "He said no, and asked me if I was nuts." Determined to rejoin the Eighty-Second Airborne, Nelson left the hospital without permission and hitchhiked back to the airfield.

"I got there a few days before the jump," Nelson said. "I was weak, but my superiors pretended not to notice." Later, as the men were filling up the airplanes, Nelson scrambled to gather gear. "I obtained a light M1 carbine. I wasn't strong enough to hold up the M1 Garand yet."

Nelson was thrown a parachute that was too small for him. "I ran from plane to plane asking everyone if they didn't like the way their harness fit, so I could trade with them," he told me. By luck, Nelson found a paratrooper who was willing to trade. The only issue was that the new harness was still too small. Running out of time, Nelson had no choice. Still weak from recovering in the hospital, he was helped by two other soldiers who squeezed together his parachute harness until it buckled together. They then used combined muscle strength to push him into the aircraft.

In the early morning of September 17, after a successful jump, Nelson and thousands of other paratroopers found themselves floating down into the Dutch countryside. Once Nelson landed, he couldn't unbuckle his chute on his own. "It was too tight, and I was too weak," he said. "So in a hurry I pulled out my bayonet and cut off my harness. I took off running after that because we came under fire. I guess I didn't realize I left the bayonet behind."

That was the last time he held his bayonet before accidentally leaving it in a field in the village of Groesbeek—until, of course, in his home in Martha's Vineyard, when a European stranger found him.

In the chaos after leaving his bayonet, Nelson watched his friend Wally Berstorm get shot in the head by a sniper as he was temporarily taking off his helmet, an event that still haunts him. The Americans later reached the outskirts of the city Nijmegen, where the civilians were thrilled to meet them. Nelson watched as a little girl on a bicycle, no older than twelve, was shot by a German sniper while attempting to visit the Americans. The incident put the Americans in a rage. Nelson called up the 88 mm mortar team and asked them to drop some rounds on the sniper's position. "I was hesitant because I knew we were all-around low on ammo, but when I told them why, they launched their first round immediately," Nelson said. "Two mortar shells exploded around the sniper's foxhole. However, it wasn't until the third shell that we saw the sniper's helmet get blown into the air. I always hoped we hit him, or at least wounded him."

Nelson went on to fight in the Belgian Ardennes after Holland. "Although I was shot in Normandy, the Battle of the Bulge was the worst part of the whole war. Something about combat in the winter was a whole 'nother level of depressing," he said.

By December of 1944, Nelson was acting platoon sergeant during the advance through the Ardennes Forest. Filled with rolling valleys, caves, pine trees, and rivers, the Ardennes extended into Germany, France, and Luxembourg. Nelson's men set up defensive positions on a hill, keeping their wounded in a cave to keep them out of the snow. As Nelson went to visit a wounded comrade in the cave, he told the rest of the men in his charge on the front line that under no circumstance should they start a fire to keep warm. "Creating fires only notified the enemy of our exact locations," he explained to me.

After his visit to the cave, Nelson headed back with his frozen Thompson submachine gun slung on his back. "As I got closer, I was horrified to see the men had started a fire," Nelson recalled. Nelson broke out in a full sprint towards the men in an attempt to rapidy put the fire out. "Just as I began to reach them, German artillery began screeching overhead. A shell landed close by, then another one burst in the trees above us."

The tree-burst shrapnel knocked the men down. By luck, a piece of shrapnel had hit Nelson in the back but lodged into his Tommy gun, which prevented the shrapnel from entering his body. "I was lucky, but another soldier wasn't. He had been hit in the chest, and I could see his lung rising in and out of his wound," Nelson said.

Nelson shot the soldier with morphine and patched up his chest. "This is like the wound I got in Normandy!" he yelled into the soldier's ear, in an attempt to comfort him and show that he could also survive his injury. Nelson dragged his wounded comrade back to the cave where the other wounded soldiers awaited medical attention. "I can only assume it was this man who called me over fifty years later. His name was Charlie, and he was a Native American," he said.

Nelson had already told me the story of a mysterious phone call he had received in 1999. He was sitting at his computer, writing an article about duck hunting, when his phone rang. As an outdoors columnist for the *New York Times*, it wasn't uncommon for someone to interrupt him while he worked from his home office. Nelson picked up the phone

Nelson and the author with the rifle.
Photo courtesy of the author

before the second ring. It sounded as if
the caller on the other end was in a bar
or at a party.

"Hello?" Nelson said.

The caller waited a moment, then
finally spoke. "I just wanted to thank you
for saving my life," the stranger said.
Laughter and the clanging of bottles or
dishes continued in the background.

"Who the hell is this?" Nelson asked.
Confused, his mind began to race.

"You know," the man said. "It
doesn't matter anyway. Thanks again."
He hung up.

Ted Morgan. *Photo courtesy of
Ted Morgan*

Nelson figured it could only have been Charlie, a person Nelson
hadn't seen since the wintery days of the Battle of the Bulge. Staring at
the rifle for a second, Nelson seemed curious whether his assumption
was correct. Was it the man he had saved in the winter of 1944?

He picked up the white marker and proceeded to sign the rifle, making him the first Eighty-Second Airborne member to do so. I thought he
would be the only one until Nelson insisted that I go visit his buddy.
"Before you leave, you have to visit the only other paratrooper on the
island!" Nelson said.

On the island? How about probably the only one in Massachusetts. I couldn't believe I had worked so hard to track down Nelson
only to find another member of the storied division without even
looking. "We played high school football together," Nelson said.
"In England, he visited me before our Normandy jump and told me
what to expect. After all, he had already jumped into Sicily and
Salerno. Call him from my phone so he will answer. He is my
ex-brother-in-law."

Ruth, Nelson's caretaker, gave me the number for Mr. Ted Morgan,
who also lived on the Vineyard. I called from Nelson's home phone and

was excited to hear him answer. I informed Ted what I was doing at Nelson's house.

"Come on by," he responded.

I couldn't believe it. I rushed out of Nelson's house and fired up my Harley, bungee-cording the rifle to the back of my motorcycle. In his driveway, Nelson waved goodbye to us with his walking stick. We rode fifteen minutes to Ted's home.

To my surprise, he was out in front of his house, walking an English bulldog in the summer heat. He was dressed really well for a man his age, with a nice button-down collared shirt, khakis, shoes, and a matching belt—an outfit which would require a lot of energy for a man his age to put on.

I got off my motorcycle and shook Ted's hand. Looking the way he did, I thought Ted had to be in his early nineties. I was wrong. He was ninety-seven! Ninety-seven meant only one thing to me: Ted must have been in the war early and at a young age.

My hunch was right. Ted was one of only a dozen living men left in the country who had made all four combat jumps in World War II: Sicily, Italy, Normandy, and Holland. I had hit a jackpot of epic proportions for my rifle. Ted was a retired town selectman. In the Army, he had been a combat medic. This distinction also made him the only medic on the rifle.

His wife joined us on the back porch as he signed the rifle. I couldn't help but think of what this man had seen. Not only had he made all four jumps during World War II, but he had been a medic from the beginning of the war all the way to the end. The number of young kids he had seen die was probably countless. He had finished his wartime service in Germany, taking care of both the enemy and civilians.

"I was wounded once, in Sicily," he recounted. "Years later my wife and I took out some leftover shrapnel lodged in my back. We did it right in the bathroom of our home."

Ted Morgan had come home, grabbed life by the horns, and represented his community as a local politician. Whatever horrible memories he possessed, he turned them into positive energy and moved forward with his life.

My friends and I rode back to the ferry and loaded our bikes. How lucky was I? I had met two paratroopers on one island. Symbols of courage and strength. Members of the Eighty-Second Airborne who had made their mark on D-Day—and beyond.

CHAPTER TWELVE

Learning to Drive

Steve Domitrovich
U.S. Army, 575th Ambulance Company

Beaver, Pennsylvania

In his living room in Beaver, Pennsylvania, Steve Domitrovich smiled while touching the barrel of my M1 Garand with one hand. The gun was leaned up against his recliner. The buttstock touched the floor. Too weak to hold it, Steve was unable to stand and was hard of hearing to boot, but he knew the date—December 17, 2018.

It was the seventy-fourth anniversary of the day on which Steve had had a German Mauser pointed to his head, in an incident later known as the Malmedy massacre.

I came across Steve thanks to my wife. I was about halfway done with my rifle project when she surprised me with a trip to Bastogne, Belgium, for my thirtieth birthday. We flew into Brussels, rented a car, and began the drive towards Bastogne. Along the route were signs for a town named Malmedy.

Why did that sound so familiar? It didn't take long before I remembered what had happened there.

We took the exit towards the rural Belgian village and reached a stone wall. Eighty-four American names stretched out along the wall. The men had not been killed in action. They had been executed.

The deceased American soldiers had been members of the 285th Field Artillery Observation Battalion. They were not infantrymen, but forward observers, cooks, signalmen, and medics. Their small convoy was heading down a road when they were intercepted by Hitler's most aggressive forces, the Schutzstaffel, better known as the SS.

After the Americans surrendered, they were herded into a field and gunned down by machine guns at close range. It had happened on the very ground I was standing on. Peering over to my right, I could see a small museum. We changed course.

In the museum, I came face to face with a wax model of a man wearing striped pajamas with the number 42 hanging around his neck. It was Lieutenant Colonel Joachim Peiper, who had been the commander of the SS forces that day. The outfit was what he had worn to his 1946 court appearance for war crimes and other atrocities.

His men were known as the "Blow Torch Battalion." They had come from the Eastern Front, where killing Russian prisoners and civilians was a common occurrence. The havoc they wreaked earned them their terrifying name. On December 17, 1944, they lived up to their reputation.

Peiper served only eleven years in prison for the war crimes he had committed. In 1976, however, unknown assailants sought revenge and burned him alive in his home. *The man couldn't outrun his past*, I thought. As we continued through the exhibit, I found a list of names of those who had survived that day. Steve Domitrovich was one of them. Now here I was, sitting in his home, on the very anniversary of the massacre he had survived.

"I just played dead," he said, shaking his head.

I placed the rifle carefully into his arms. Steve was fragile, his touch light. I helped guide his hand along the rifle to where I thought his name belonged, to where he should sign.

He did the best he could. His position in the recliner made his already feeble hand unsteady, but we accomplished it. "He usually puts 575th Ambulance Company under his name," his son suggested.

It seemed that Steve was already out of energy, so I carefully wrote that under his name for him. After all, his ambulance was what had gotten him to Malmedy in the first place.

Learning to Drive

In the summer of 1992, Steve Domitrovich and his son were locking up the front door to their convenience store. Making sure all the doors were locked and the register was empty had become a systematic ritual. Aliquippa was not the same town it used to be. "It wasn't the same place I grew up in before the war. It got worse. I saw it change through the '60s and '70s," Steve said.

Just a year before, a man had jumped over the counter and attempted to rob the store, which was their family business. Steve and Stevie Jr. wrestled the would-be robber to the ground. As he squirmed to break free, he bit Stevie Jr. on the hands. The father and son were able to restrain the man until police arrived.

This time, after going through the usual motions of locking up the store, Steve and his son were walking toward their car when a masked man appeared. He was holding a gun in his hand and quickly stuck it in the face of Steve Sr. "Give me the . . ."

The masked man didn't get a chance to get more words out of his mouth. Steve slapped the pistol out of his hands. The silver handgun fell to the ground, making a clanking noise. The masked man ran away.

"It was the first time I had a gun pointed in my face since Malmedy, and I was not going stand in front of a barrel again," Steve said. Now bound to a recliner in his living room at the age of ninety-four, he went on to reminisce about the series of failed robberies he and his son had experienced. The two Stevens were not fighters, he told me. They were genuinely trusting people. But what happened at Malmedy shaped Steve Sr.'s intensity.

Slapping a handgun out of a would-be robber's grasp was an automatic reflex by someone who had already stared down death. Forty-five years before he had a gun pointed in his face in a Pennsylvania parking lot, Steve was on the side of a Belgian road with a German Mauser pointed at him in the same way. Then a helpless twenty-year-old, Steve had raised his hands and said, "Comrade, I give up." Steve had vowed he would never be that helpless again, which made the decision to fight an armed thug an easy one on that night in 1992.

"I had never driven a car before until I drove an ambulance for the Army!" Steve said excitedly. After the eleventh grade, he was drafted and sent to California for training. It was the first time the young Steven was behind the steering wheel of any kind of vehicle, let alone an expensive U.S. Army ambulance.

While trying to teach himself to drive, he would accelerate and then nervously slam the brakes. "Well, if your patients weren't already dead, they are now," the medic cracked to Steven once after the vehicle slammed to a halt.

Soon after learning how to operate the vehicle, Steven shipped out and went right to work throughout the Normandy campaign. He landed on Utah Beach on D-Day and was soon transporting wounded soldiers for medical attention. "I could transport up to seven patients at a time, but mostly I was transporting injured Germans," Steven recounted. He never spoke to them. "I was too scared. I just wanted them out of my ambulance."

As the months dragged by, Allied forces advanced through Europe. Steve's job stayed the same, and his ambulance was, again, loaded with wounded Germans. "We were leaving France and advancing into Belgium. My captain told me to find a way to get rid of these injured Germans. We had nowhere to put them," he remembered.

Steve took off in the middle of the night, driving his ambulance in black-out mode. He and a medic reached a heavily wooded area and began to unload the German patients. "They were patched up and medicated. Hopefully their own guys would recover them. I hopped right back in the ambulance. Like I said, I was scared," he said.

He nervously climbed back into the ambulance and sped off toward headquarters. Moonlight lit the way clearly. Suddenly a man waving his arms jumped in front of the ambulance. "I was so scared and couldn't stop in time. I ran him right over," Steve told me. Fearing it could be Germans, Steve continued back to the front lines. "I told my captain, 'I think I hit someone on the way back.' We drove back out there, but couldn't find anybody. I can only assume it was a German."

Steve's anxiety subsided. In the morning, four ambulances from the 575th Ambulance Company departed friendly lines to link up with a convoy of the 285th Field Artillery Observation Battalion. "We had orders in Belgium to make our way towards St. Vith. That's what I remember about the convoy that day," Steve said. He had never driven in the United States. Now here he was, behind the wheel of his ambulance for several hours, being mesmerized by the Belgian countryside.

However, Steve's captivation with the new environment ended when gunfire erupted from behind the convoy. Steve halted his ambulance. He saw a burning vehicle in the rear of the column. "More bullets and shells began to strike around us. The vehicles in the front of the column were disabled too. We got out of the vehicle and rolled into a ditch," Steve recalled.

"I think it's an air raid!" the assistant driver yelled.

"Whatever you do, do not stick your head up!" Steve yelled back. Most of the men were not combat troops and did not know how to identify where the fire was coming from. They exited their vehicles and hid along the road. "As I began to lift my head up, a German pointed his rifle right at me. I could only say, 'Comrade, I give up,'" Steve told me. The enemy soldiers shoved Steve aside.

The Germans began to strip the vehicles, rounding up their new American prisoners. Although the five-minute battle was over, some gunshots still rang out. Germans walked around kicking American GIs in the groin to see if they were playing dead. If they were alive, they were shot. "I just kept my hands up, and they marched us off," he said.

Steve and the remainder of the Americans captured from the convoy were forced into a pasture, where other prisoners already waited. "A German pulled me out of the group and pointed at my wrist. I had a red bracelet on, identifying me as an ambulance driver. They spoke in German to each other, then returned me to the group."

As Steve and the other men waited anxiously, more German armored vehicles approached. One German ran over and stopped an enemy half-track that was driving down the road. A heavy machine gun was mounted on the half-track. After a short discussion, the German soldier manning the weapon on the vehicle attempted to aim the machine gun at the group of American POWs huddled off the road. Due to the landscape and position of the gun, it couldn't be pointed low enough to hit the group.

The Americans saw their captors' clear intentions and became more than fidgety. "They are going to bring us to Germany, right?" a soldier next to Steve asked.

"No, they are going to shoot us," Steve replied with certainty. As the vehicle was dismissed, another German column appeared. The order looked as if it was given a second time, and this time the German rose from his vehicle and, without hesitation, began to fire his pistol into the crowded group of Americans. "We just stood there in confusion at first and let it happen. Then men began to run. That's when they opened up the machine guns on all of us," Steve remembered.

Steve immediately dropped to the ground. "I could hear the bullets hitting all around me, and hitting the bodies next to me," he said. Multiple machine guns, burp guns, and rifles sprayed the group of unarmed prisoners for several minutes. When the enemy vehicles finally drove away, helpless men lay there dying. Some groaned. Others yelled out. Another set of enemy vehicles drove by, dumping more rounds into the bodies that now littered the Belgian field. Several American soldiers unscratched from the first volley of fire got up and ran into a coffee shop across the field.

"I heard the German soldiers dismount from the vehicles and walk amongst us still lying on the ground," Steve told me. "Some of the guys who were dying were crying for their mom or God. The Germans mocked them, saying 'Mom' and 'God' back to them. Then they shot them in the head."

Steve continued to lie completely still on the ground. He heard a German soldier's footsteps come closer, until a boot landed next to his face. "I could see his boot. I thought, 'This is it. I'm dead.'"

To Steve's shock, the SS trooper fired a round into the man lying next to him, then continued to fish through the pile for more survivors to execute. They continued to shoot survivors, setting the coffee shop on fire. All of a sudden, it was quiet. The Germans were gone. "That's when someone yelled, 'All right! Let's go!'"

Several Americans got up and made a run for it. "A wounded man asked me to help him," Steve said. "I told him I couldn't because we needed to get out of there."

Steve and five others ran over the crest of a hill. "We saw a Belgian man," he said. "He wanted nothing to do with us but pointed us in the direction of the closest Americans."

As Steve and the other survivors trekked down the hill, they saw a U.S. Army jeep. "While we ran towards it, an enemy 88 shell came out of nowhere and blew the jeep apart," Steve recalled. The escaped soldiers almost fell back into German hands. Luckily, they made it back to friendly lines.

Steve could hardly explain the situation to the other troops. The men were delirious after what they had experienced. "The doctors gave me a shot, and I was out like a light," he said. He recovered in a hospital for thirty days. "In the hospital they told me I screamed at night, but after a month they sent me back to the front."

Steve shook his head in dismay. After all this time, he was still disappointed that the Army had thought he was fit to return to duty after his traumatic experience. "My captain was good to me. He hid me from those who tried to interview me or ask me questions about the massacre. He knew it bothered me terribly. As I left the hospital, a V-1 buzz bomb struck it and blew it up. It was the second time I escaped death," he told me.

Steve continued his service as an ambulance driver throughout the rest of the war. After returning home, he opened a store, calling it G.I. Dairy. After marrying his wife in 1956, he changed the name to H&S Dairy. "To this day, I can still see that German's boot in front of my face," he said.

A lot can be said about a man like Steve. If he had

Steve Domitrovich with the rifle. *Photo courtesy of the author*

wanted to, he could have never worked again a day in his life. After what he experienced, some men would have taken a mental discharge. Yet he never did, and to this day he doesn't collect disability from the VA. He is living proof that life goes on after war.

CHAPTER THIRTEEN

The Running Man

Bob White
U.S. Army, Seventeenth Airborne Division

The Seventeenth Airborne Division wasn't a unit I was familiar with, but once I learned about its members, I quickly realized that they were heroes. I needed one to sign the rifle.

I discovered the Seventeenth Airborne on the surprise birthday trip to Belgium that my wife had arranged. At the urging of a veteran, we visited a bar in Bastogne called the Café au Carré, a living memorial to the American soldiers who had liberated Bastogne from Nazi occupation. Photos of American soldiers hung across the bar's walls, each with names and divisions inscribed underneath. Photo after photo had the same unit tagged: the Seventeenth Airborne.

Who were they? What did they do? I knew nothing about them, but I had met enough Normandy and Holland veterans by now to know that

Bob White. *Photo courtesy of Bob White*

the Seventeenth Airborne had not jumped on D-Day or during Operation Market Garden. How could they be a World War II airborne unit?

I started my research right there in the bar room, reading up on the division. Its first combat was the Battle of the Bulge. The unit had not made any combat jumps until that point and was basically serving as a traditional infantry unit during the fighting in the Ardennes. Its logo consisted of talon-like claw with the word "airborne" above it.

I immediately thought about how deflating it must have been to train so hard to be a paratrooper only to end up serving as a basic infantry unit. However, I soon discovered that I was wrong again: the unit did make a combat jump, but only after fighting in one of the largest land battles of World War II at the Battle of the Bulge. They may not have jumped into France like their fellow airborne units, but they did jump into Germany.

It didn't take long for me to find the 17th Airborne fascinating. After briefly surveying the division's history, I knew that their experience was unique. Most airborne units are only introduced to combat after jumping into a war zone. The 101st and the 82nd jumped from planes without knowing what lay ahead in Normandy and Holland. They didn't know what fighting was like, for better or for worse.

The Seventeenth, by contrast, was introduced to combat *before* making an airborne jump, adding a new layer to their experience as paratroopers. They jumped from a plane knowing that once they landed they would be confronted by chaos. They had no illusions about what challenges they would face. The young men who made up the Seventeenth Airborne had already experienced war at the Battle of the Bulge; when they jumped from their planes into Germany, they would have had to steel themselves to face Nazi bullets again.

After my wife and I came home from our trip to Europe, I found a news article announcing that a veteran was being awarded his Bronze Star seventy-five years after his service. His name was Bob White of Hampton, Virginia, and he had served in the Seventeenth Airborne Division.

I reached out to Mr. White, and several weeks later a few cop friends and I took the eleven-hour road trip to Virginia from Boston. Hampton felt like the town that declared you had officially crossed from North to South, and Bob White's polite southern manners only confirmed my view. My friends and I wasted no time, meeting Bob, his girlfriend, and son for dinner at a Texas Roadhouse as soon as we arrived. We kept the conversation informal and resolved to save the war stories for the following morning. I didn't want Bob to hold back and knew it would be better to interview him one-on-one.

The next morning, I drove to Bob's house. It was the most patriotic in the neighborhood, complete with yellow ribbons on the trees and Old Glory hanging from the flagpole. When Bob let me in the front door, I saw his wall of fame to my immediate right, decked with dozens of medals, ribbons, awards, and plaques. But unlike many of the veterans whom I had interviewed, Bob's accolades weren't from the military: they were trophies from the marathons and road races that Bob had run over the years.

"Do you miss running?" I asked the ninety-six-year-old Bob.

"Miss it?" he scoffed. "I ran a 5k last week."

I stared at him, stunned.

"I only started running when I turned sixty," he explained.

Many people acquire new hobbies later in life, but I never imagined running marathons could be one of them. Bob's son appeared from the living room and guided me to the kitchen. I took the rifle out of its case and placed it across the kitchen table. Both of Bob's kids took photos of it with digital cameras. They were really proud of this moment and understood it to be historic, which made me feel accomplished.

"Dad never talked about this stuff until about three years ago," Bob's son, Charlie, said. Something had happened in World War II that Bob didn't want to talk about. Experiences in war vary, but Bob must have had it rough.

Both of Bob's kids left their dad and I alone in the kitchen to talk. After Bob added his name to the rifle, we began. He had grown up in Leland, North Carolina, and was a farmer until he got drafted in 1943. He did his basic training at Camp Blanding, Florida, where the military conducted routine physical examinations. Bob must have done pretty well on the hearing test, because he was soon named a communications private. After basic training and communications school, Bob was a certified radio operator and wireman. Before he knew it, he was on his way to England as a replacement, without a unit to belong to.

"They asked for volunteers," Bob said. "They told us because they had taken so many casualties in Normandy that they wanted new paratroopers. So dummy me, I raised my hand." Upon arriving in England Bob was rushed off to jump school. He had to make five jumps to earn his wings. "They were in such a rush with us that we made two jumps in one day," he said. "At the drop zone there were trucks, and they loaded us back up and drove us right back to the airstrip."

Bob and his fellow paratrooper trainees didn't know it at the time, but the Army was preparing this new airborne division for a jump into the Ardennes Forest in order to relieve units besieged in the beginning stages of the Battle of the Bulge. That plan would never come to fruition, as the landscape and sheer number of enemy forces rendered the proposed jump impossible. Instead, the Seventeenth Airborne Division was rushed by secret night flights into Reims, France. There they assembled and were soon trucked to the front lines in Belgium.

Bob was now part of the 507th Parachute Infantry Regiment. The regiment had once belonged to the 82nd Airborne and had been transferred, a rare circumstance. The men going into Belgium were now a fifty-fifty mix of combat vets who had already jumped into Normandy and green replacements such as Bob.

As nighttime turned into day, the Army trucks loaded with non–jump status paratroopers began their four-hour drive towards Belgium, arriving on New Year's Day 1945. The snow grew thicker as the trucks drove on. The men rocked back and forth in the trucks to keep warm as the wind made its way through the loose canopy.

Bob heard artillery fire in the distance. Soon after, he heard the sound of other trucks coming to a halt and their tailgates dropping as his own truck idled. "Get out now, and get in formation!" someone yelled from the ground. Bob dismounted with his radio and linked up with the rest of Headquarters Company.

The Twenty-Eighth Division had been badly battered, and it wasn't long before the Seventeenth Airborne began to advance in its place, clearing the western side of Bastogne of all German units. "We began to march through the snow, really just in the direction of the noise of small arms fire and explosions. We just walked towards it," Bob recalled.

Bob's company waded through the knee-deep snow towards a series of destroyed farmhouses and trees. Gunfire erupted. "Two men from my company were killed instantly by the incoming bullets," Bob said. Blood colored the snow where they had fallen and darkened their uniforms. Bob watched on as their bodies were put on the front of a jeep and hauled off to the rear.

It was Bob's first introduction to war. He hadn't even met the enemy, yet here he stood over two dead young Americans from his company who had hardly been in Belgium for two days.

"How did that make you feel?" I asked.

"I felt like I could have taken that gun right there and killed every last one of them," he answered, staring at the rifle lying across his kitchen table.

Watching those two men fall transformed Bob from an innocent farmer into a soldier who had to fulfill his duty in war. Our interview became harder from this point in the conversation. "Do you remember firing your weapon?" I asked curiously.

"I try to forget it," he responded, squinting his eyes.

I changed the topic, asking about the weather during their advance. The men of the Seventeenth Airborne Division dug in at the rear slope of what later came to be known as Dead Man's Ridge. The slope had a narrow strip of road that climbed from the village of Monty to Flamierge, about a half mile in length along the ridge. The men's feet were freezing and wet. "It got to the point where I didn't know if I had feet or not," Bob said.

Bob was half-frozen, and his second round with the Germans hadn't even happened yet. The men used blankets to cover their foxholes so their breath and body heat stayed inside. "That's when the Screaming Mimi's started," Bob told me as he made a screeching noise with his mouth, imitating the sound of incoming artillery fire. The regiment got hit with a lot of heavy gunfire on the ridge, taking more casualties.

After tenderizing the Allies with their heavy guns, the Germans began a counterattack on the fresh troops of the 17th Airborne. Luckily, the men of the 507th had Normandy combat veterans in their midst who modeled for the green replacements how a soldier was to respond to adversity. Although Bob was a communications man, he found himself firing his M1 carbine into the fog at several Germans attempting to break their lines.

"We stayed in this position for days," Bob said. The men urinated and defecated both in and around their foxholes. Artillery was extremely accurate. Men were being evacuated off the lines constantly, suffering from frostbite and trench foot. "At nighttime I would walk back and forth with my hands in my armpits to stay warm and carry my rifle over my back. I would sleep like that," Bob said. He told me that he slept while walking so he could stay warm. "If not, I would have died."

The men of the 507th Parachute Infantry Regiment, 17th Airborne, repulsed numerous attacks. Luckily, the Germans faced the same tortuous weather conditions and also struggled. After rebuffing the onslaught, it was finally time to move out from the ridge.

"We advanced, liberating a few Belgian towns, but the 88s were killing men. They were as accurate as that M1 rifle," Bob said, nodding at the rifle on the kitchen table. "They could pick a single man off with an 88 mm artillery shell."

Bob had been on patrol when incoming fire struck his platoon. When he went to check on one of his soldiers, he could see the man was covered in blood. "This one fellow had blood splats on him, but it wasn't his blood; it belonged to another soldier that got hit next to him. The soldier took a direct hit and exploded all over his buddy," Bob remembered. Throughout the months of combat, Bob grew battle-hardened. He discarded his shovel and pick for digging cover and steeled himself against the possibility of death. "At that point, I had seen so many casualties that I said, 'If it's going to happen, it's going to happen,'" he explained. "You just accept that you could be the next one." From then on, he only took cover in small ditches or behind trees.

The Seventeenth Airborne eventually pushed into Luxembourg, relieving other U.S. units that had been holding the line since early December. "The Germans began marching towards our lines with their hands over their heads, and we let them pass us and head to the rear where someone collected them up. Then they wanted volunteers to shoot the SS prisoners. I didn't have the heart to do it, but some guys did. They walked off with the prisoners into the woods and came back without them," Bob told me.

The Seventeenth Airborne had been on the front lines for over a month. It was now mid-February 1945, and they were being trucked back to France for rest. The division needed to replace some seven hundred casualties. Bob had his feet treated for frostbite and was awarded a Purple Heart, along with all the other men who had suffered frozen feet at the Battle of the Bulge.

Bob's regiment withdrew to a tent camp at Châlons-sur-Marne, France, in February of 1945. The men were able to clean themselves, exchange damaged gear out for new equipment, and receive mail. Rumors began to circulate that they would soon reenter combat. The men were not happy to hear it. "We knew we wouldn't just be delivered to the front lines again. We performed our sixth practice jump while in France. We knew we would be making a combat jump," Bob told me.

They soon learned that they wouldn't be making just any combat jump: the men of the Seventeenth Airborne would be jumping into Germany, the country that had started it all. "The night before the jump they pulled us into a great big tent. In the middle of the tent was a model terrain of the drop zones. I knew if there was any place the Germans would defend fanatically, it would be their homeland," Bob said.

"Did that scare you?" I asked. Typically when I asked a World War II veteran if he had been scared, he would give me a delayed response. Bob didn't hesitate: he had been scared, all right.

The jump would take place across the Rhine River. The Americans knew it would be heavily fortified with anti-aircraft guns and infantry. The job would be carried out by the British paratroopers in the North and the Americans to the South. They would not be liberators this time. This time they would be invaders.

The name of the operation was "Varsity." The U.S. Army tried to mimic Operation Market Garden as closely as possible, making it a daytime drop. That being said, the brass also decided to use a lot of new tactics and equipment in Varsity, such as towing two gliders in the air at the same time with bigger transport planes. The Army Air Corps would test out the new C-46s, which could hold almost twice as many paratroopers as the C-47s they were accompanying. Bob was given a British parachute, which had a knob for a quick release of the chute upon hitting the ground.

After four weeks of preparation, on March 24, 1945, Bob's regiment took off from an airport in Reims, France, to invade German skies. He remembers everything he carried. "I had a small radio, telephone, two bandoliers, two grenades, and a Gammon grenade I had made," he told me. The Gammon grenade was a sticky bomb made by soldiers in order to take out the tracks of Panzer tanks.

With all his gear loaded, Bob's C-47 was air-bound. "We kept making circles until all the planes got in the air, then we finally headed to our objective," he recalled. At approximately 10:30 a.m. on March 24, Bob knew they must be close to the drop zone, as anti-aircraft fire began to hit his plane. Bob's C-47 vibrated violently and the sounds of metal snapping could be heard throughout the plane. Fifteen minutes later, Bob and the rest of the Seventeenth Airborne Division jumped and became real paratroopers. They exited their planes and descended from the sky as flak burst around them. The gliders did their job, crashing violently onto German soil.

"I jumped from approximately four hundred feet. I could hear bullets penetrating my chute, but none ever hit me. A minute later I struck some trees, and my feet were just touching the ground," he recalled. The sounds of gunfire echoed across the area. Gliders slammed to the ground, rolling over German foxholes. Glider pilots fired Thompson machine guns out of their cockpits in order to give the glider infantry time to get out of their makeshift planes.

Bob twisted the knob to his British parachute harness, activating the quick release. "After I released myself, I saw a set of railroad tracks several feet in front of me. As a communications man, I recognized something," he said. Bob had spotted a ball of German communications wire. He took out his pliers and began cutting the enemy cables, interrupting their radio chatter. As he performed his best sabotage work, Bob came under fire from an enemy position in the distance. He cut as many wires as possible as enemy bullets snapped overhead.

After the job was done, Bob ran back into the tree line away from the enemy sharpshooters. "Hey, up here!" a man yelled. Bob looked up to see an American soldier hanging high up in a tree. "Some damn German shot me while I was hanging up here, I need help!" he yelled to Bob.

"As soon as I find someone, I'll tell them where you are!" Bob yelled back.

Bob crouched over the kitchen table. "Things were so unorganized; I didn't see a single person from my plane," he insisted. Bob was trying to justify to me that he forgot about the soldier dying in the tree. He never sent anyone back. This guilt had stuck with Bob for seventy-five years. It wasn't his fault. At the time, the twenty-two-year-old paratrooper's first responsibility was to save himself and reach his objective. In the chaos, his top priority was to survive; rescue missions had to wait. "I have been too scared to ask what ever happened to the man," Bob said, shaking his head.

"It's normal to have survivor's guilt," I suggested. Although I hadn't fought in World War II, it was still something I could relate to.

Bob's first distraction after seeing the dangling paratrooper was a bridge off in the distance being shelled. "To my left I saw the Germans shelling a bridge on our side of the river; I knew I wanted to stay away from there so I went right." Bob removed his compass from his jacket and began to follow it to his company's original objective. Firefights began to break out in the area and Bob ducked back into the woods. He halted. "I came up on a German sitting on some ammo crates with his rifle between his legs. I kept watching him. I was getting closer and closer, and he wasn't moving. I got right up on him and I . . . I . . ." Bob couldn't finish his sentence. He had shot the German, firing several rounds to make sure he was dead. "Back then I didn't mind shooting them, I shot as many as I could—now it's so hard to talk about," he said.

Moving out after his close encounter with the German, Bob had to witness another gruesome sight. It was a glider full of American infantry-men, dead. They had been crushed and mangled from a bad landing. "I looked right inside of it and none had survived," Bob told me. At this point, it was understandable that Bob had forgotten about that para-trooper in the tree hours before.

Bob scurried on, finally meeting up with others from his regiment to secure a dam. Beyond the dam, the 507th Parachute Infantry Regiment continued to advance around the area of Fluren, Germany, eliminating machine gun emplacements and dug-in infantry. The Germans began to dispatch small counterattacks, launching multiple tanks in the direction of Bob's regiment. "I took off my Gammon grenade and handed it off to another soldier. He ran up to the tank, placing the sticky bomb on the axle. When it exploded, the track fell off and the wheels just kept spinning."

The men of the 507th Regiment repulsed several attacks. German soldiers surrendered and retreated. A pontoon bridge was constructed by engineers as Bob's company guarded the area, and more supplies made it over the Rhine. The mission was a success. "One thousand Germans surrendered to us in one hour. I think it was a record," Bob concluded. Operation Varsity proved to be a success. The Seventeenth Airborne suffered two thousand casualties with the loss of some seventy aircraft that were shot down or crashed. However, the United States and its allies had a foothold in Germany. Thousands of men, trucks, and equipment could now start crossing the Rhine River unharmed. And with the exception of a couple more months of light fighting, Bob White's war service was just about over.

But Bob had one last harrowing experience in Germany when the Seventeenth Airborne discovered a forced labor camp. "We found people starved. Their eyes were sunken in the backs of their heads. I saw other people stuffed into trays that slid in and out of walls. I think they may have been put in there as punishment. You could see bullet holes along concrete walls where they executed others. I couldn't believe what I was seeing, and then my buddy said to me, 'You should see out back. There are mounds of dead bodies that were bulldozed!' I didn't have the stomach to go look," Bob remembered,

Bob White with the rifle. *Photo courtesy of the author*

After fulfilling his occupation duty in Germany, Bob returned to North Carolina. He worked in the shipyards in Wilmington, Delaware, and then in Newport News, Virginia, as a sheet metalworker for thirty-eight years. Working and raising five children kept his mind off the war. He never spoke a word of it, but then he retired. As thoughts of combat began to trickle into Bob's mind, fifty years later he needed a new hobby. He began to run.

He started off with a couple miles, then five miles, then ten miles. After he got up to fourteen miles, he was well on his way to completing marathons. All of his running started after he was already sixty years of age. Bob competed his first marathon in 1987, the Marine Corps Marathon in Washington, D.C. He went on to finish another eight marathons, including the New York City and Boston Marathons.

After I departed Hampton, Virginia, I stayed in touch with Bob. I saw photos appear on his Facebook page from his most recent 5k road race on the morning of Thanksgiving 2019, at the age of ninety-six. The marathon man was a symbol. He was a message for young veterans not to stop or slow down. He overcame the horrors of war by keeping busy. Even when your career path is completed and your family members are on their own, you still have to keep running. The memories, whether good or bad, will never go away, so you have to keep producing new ones. That's what the running man taught me.

CHAPTER FOURTEEN

The Most Interesting Man in the World

Roy Roush
U.S. Marine Corps, Second Marine Division

Woodland Hills, California

Growing up, I went to the beach as a kid. The majority of beachgoers wore flip-flops, bathing suits, and tank tops. Occasionally there was the one guy wearing jeans, a T-shirt, boots, and big silly headphones, waving a metal detector around. Families lying on their beach towels would stare at him as he wandered by and often remark, "What a goofball."

It never occurred to me that maybe that man might have been picking up another hobby to avoid thinking about what had happened to him fifty years before. It never occurred to me that maybe that man in the goofy headphones was just keeping himself busy to prevent dwelling on the war. It never occurred to me that maybe he was staying active in any way possible to avoid the memory of all the dead Japanese bodies that he had seen—so many that it had taken a

Roy Roush. *Photo courtesy of Roy Roush*

179

bulldozer to move them. It never occurred to me that maybe that man was just trying to cope with what he had dealt with on Guadalcanal, Tarawa, Saipan, and Tinian.

As I stared up at a mansion in the heights of Woodland Hills, California, I double-checked to make sure I had the correct address. After all, many of the men I had been visiting were in assisted living–type situations. Getting closer to the home, it was evident someone elderly was living there and that I was most likely in the right place. The beautiful home, in need of renovation, had overgrown vegetation. A 1970s Thunderbird sat in the driveway, covered in dust.

I walked up the stairs with the rifle in its case. There was a great view of Hollywood at the top. When I turned back around, I faced a large glass door surrounded by glass windows. I didn't need to knock. Whoever was inside had already seen me.

"Come in!" a voice called from a couch. Walking into the home, I saw the man I had come for: Mr. Roy Roush. Dr. Roy Roush. Corporal Roy Roush. Lieutenant Roy Roush. Author Roy Roush. Pilot Roy Roush. And last but not least, treasure hunter Roy Roush.

I had first been introduced to the man with a dozen titles when I graduated Marine Corps boot camp. Someone gifted me a large green book titled *Open Fire!* I skimmed through it a little. It was about one Marine's experience on Guadalcanal, Tarawa, Saipan, and Tinian. I placed it in a bag with some other gifts a new Marine receives and forgot about it for years. It wasn't until I started my rifle journey that I came across the book buried in one of my closets. Opening it again, a business card fell out. I gave the number a shot. Maybe the man who had given me the book was still alive. Sure enough, he answered the phone.

So now here I was, in his home. Roy began to stand up to shake my hand but struggled a little bit. But he still grabbed my hand with a vise-like grip, like no other ninety-four-year-old I had met. He was in a tank top and had good muscle mass. He sat back down and chugged the rest of his cough syrup from the bottle. He tossed the empty bottle, striking an orange cat sitting on the couch to his left.

"You're in amazing shape for your age," I started to say, but I was cut off when his wife, Lydia, walked over from the kitchen. "Now my husband can't just go signing things," she started. "I have to be present to know what's going on."

She was certainly protective of her husband, as she should be at their age. Instead of explaining, I opened the case and pulled out the rifle. Hardly any of the wood stock could be seen with all the signatures on it. Suddenly her concerns turned to silence. "That is magnificent," she said after a brief pause.

I wasn't surprised by Lydia's skepticism towards me. There was no way to tell if I was another person trying to scam the elderly or not. Luckily, the rifle spoke its own language and answered any questions she might have had about me.

"I got something you might want to see. You're going to have to help me with this," Roy said.

Roy told me to meet him upstairs. I walked up the spiral staircase and waited for him. He mounted an electric chairlift. It was exceptionally slow. When he reached the top, he dismounted and waddled over to a leather duffle bag. As he unzipped it, I knew what it was: a Browning automatic rifle (BAR).

He handed it to me. It was the first time I had ever held such a weapon. I didn't ask how he had gotten it or where. It was clearly still special to him.

The first time Roy Roush carried the BAR was in the Battle of Tarawa, although his first combat experience was on Guadalcanal. He referred to the Battle of Tarawa as "one of the Marine Corps's biggest blunders." "We simply were not prepared for what happened on that island," Roy said of the battle. "It ended up being the most heavily fortified enemy position of World War II. We watched for two weeks as the Navy shelled it. There should have been no way anything survived. When we came ashore, a big surprise was in store for us. The bombing did nothing."

The men encountered endless machine gun nests. "We walked right into a trap. Whenever we ran into a machine gun, it was never just one.

They always had more on the right and left sides," he recalled. "The only way to take out a Jap machine gun was to bust through and take the position from behind."

Roy dashed along the island, tossing satchel charges and grenades inside bunkers. "I'm not sure how many I killed," he said. "You really couldn't see the enemy until you walked right up on them, dead or dying." The charges exploded, burying Japanese soldiers alive. Their corpses probably remain there to this day.

For two months, the 2nd Marine Division fought through Tarawa, losing some 1,700 men. The Japanese casualties were nearly 5,000, with only 17 captured alive—1 officer and 16 enlisted. By late November of 1943, Tarawa Atoll was declared secured. "After we left that island, nearly 100 percent of us came down with malaria. A few of the men actually died," Roy said. Fighting severe sickness, the Second Marine Division continued to train for their next invasion.

In June 1944, Roy stormed another beach with the Second Battalion, Sixth Marines, E Company, this time on Saipan. "When I landed, I jumped into a shell crater," he remembered. "I was shaking and didn't know why. I said to myself 'Wait a second. I shouldn't be this nervous. I have already been in combat.'" When Roy looked down, he saw that his legs were crossed over another Marine sharing the same hole. The Marine was shaking uncontrollably, causing Roy's body to shake too.

"We were the first wave of the invasion, of the left flank. The extreme left flank. The only other people to our left were the Japs," Roy said. The first wave took fire as they headed into the beachhead. One amphibious tractor took a direct hit, sinking into the harbor. "It remained there for months," Roy added.

He began to dig in near the beach and glanced at the destroyed AMTRAC sitting in the harbor. He watched as more men, equipment, and two tanks came ashore. "The first night was quiet, but on the second night, they tried to infiltrate us," he told me.

That second night, a group of approximately one hundred Japanese tried to break through the Marines' fighting holes. "Navy ships illuminated the sky with flares so we could see. That's how the rest of the night went. No sleep!" Roy remembered.

After killing the infiltrators with accurate rifle fire, the Marines heard activity in the distance. "We could hear trucks dropping off more Japanese. I heard the tailgates slam and soldiers dismounting from vehicles. You could hear their mess kits jingling. We knew they were out there, but out of sight at night."

As the sun came up, Roy grew nervous. He knew the Marines expected an attack at any moment, possibly by hundreds of enemy fighters. He turned to the Marine sharing his foxhole. "We need some tanks up here."

"There aren't any," his sergeant replied from another foxhole.

"Bullshit!" Roy shot back. "I saw some come in on the beach before nightfall." Having experienced the carnage on Tarawa, Roy was restless.

"Well, if you know where they are, then go get them!" the sergeant yelled.

Roy handed off his BAR to the other Marine in the foxhole. After he climbed out, he made it roughly one hundred feet away and then stopped dead in his tracks. "All of a sudden, I could hear someone playing a bugle," he said. Roy slowly turned around. One by one, Marines began to raise their heads out of their foxholes to see where the noise was coming from. "I recognized the melody. The bugle was playing 'Charge!'" He spotted a Japanese soldier in the distance with the instrument raised to his mouth, playing the tune. "Right then and there I knew this wasn't good. Everyone was frozen with disbelief. As soon as he began to play it a second time, a Marine stood up and plugged him with one shot from his rifle."

As the Japanese soldier fell to the ground, squirting blood from his neck, rows of other Japanese began to run toward the Marines, firing from the hip, shooting wildly. Roy sprinted the rest of the way to the beach where the tanks were parked. He was aggravated to see the tank drivers sitting down drinking coffee. "The Japs are coming!" he screamed, waving his arms.

"I wasn't getting any fast reaction out of them," he told me. "So I began to climb on a tank and entered the hatch." The tank crewman then rushed over and took control. Roy rode in the tank back towards the front lines. "I was down by the tank commander's feet as he was hanging out of the hatch. As we got closer, he yelled down to me that he didn't see any Japs. I said, 'Keep looking, you'll see them any minute!'"

As the two tanks got closer to the front lines, the commander finally spotted the onrushing Japanese soldiers. After firing off an I-told-you-so to the commander, Roy insisted on getting out of the tank to fight from the ground. "I saw Sherman tanks burst into flames on Tarawa," he told me. "I didn't want to be stuck in one." Roy jumped out of the tank, taking cover in a shell hole. He watched as the two tanks repelled the attack for thirty minutes while firefights raged on.

"If it wasn't for me grabbing those tanks, the Japs would have broken through the lines," Roy reported proudly. Like many other enlisted Marines, Roy was never properly recognized for his efforts to alert the tanks of the attack. At the end of the day, some 1,600 Japanese lay dead in front of the Marines' position.

With the position held, the Marines were soon ordered to advance to the center of the island. On the way, Roy's company cleared the caves and mountains of Japanese civilians who were hiding there. They managed to lure them out with gifts of candy and water. "The civilians' fear of us was so heavy, they were trembling," Roy remembered. "They didn't trust us. The Japanese Army told them that the Americans would rape and kill them. I gave one guy some water, and he wouldn't leave my side. He wanted to be my friend and even offered to dig my foxhole for me that night."

The march continued for the men of E Company. Once they reached the other side of Saipan, they were taken off the front lines. The U.S. Army had formed a defensive perimeter, relieving the Marines for the time being. "We set up camp about half a mile away. That night we saw tracer rounds flying all over the place. We usually ignored firefights in the distance at night, but this one seemed like it was coming our way. A few stray bullets landed near our sleeping area," Roy said.

The next morning, Roy and the other Marines were ordered to gear up. They were informed that the Japanese had penetrated the American lines. Instead of getting much-needed rest, they would have to patrol the area in case the Japanese made their way over towards them.

On patrol, Roy saw utter carnage. "There was about a quarter of a mile of images a movie couldn't even produce," Roy said with a grimace. The U.S. Army had faced one of the largest banzai charge attacks of the whole war. Near one foxhole, Roy saw five bodies piled practically on top of one another. One American, one Japanese, another American, another Japanese, and again another American, all on top of one another.

When Roy reached the Marine Corps's artillery batteries, he saw a knocked-out Japanese tank sitting in front of the guns. The tank had a big opening in the front. When he asked what had happened, survivors told him that two .50 caliber machine guns had concentrated their fire on it, cutting the tank open like a can of soda. The scene only got stranger when Roy saw the artillery's position. While the Marines usually faced their artillery guns straight forward in the hopes that they could blast the waves of enemy soldiers at point-blank range, four of the howitzers were facing each other. "They had a duel!" Roy told me, still excited by the rare event. The Japanese had tried to commandeer two howitzers, and so two Marine cannons were forced to fire on their own equipment.

The Marines were now put in charge of the advance. They pushed on past the Japanese bodies littering the ground. "Some were playing dead," Roy remembered, "and we, well, we finished them off."

Coming upon a farm, the Marines saw a chicken coop in the distance. Roy and his men crossed over a ditch and into the farmland. Roy and another BAR man were leading the formation when a shot rang out. The BAR man in front of Roy dropped to the ground, bleeding out from a gunshot wound. "I hit the deck immediately," Roy said, "and a Japanese grenade rolled from behind and stopped in front of me." Roy grabbed his helmet and tucked his head, anticipating the blast. "Some shrapnel bounced off my helmet. I turned around to see where it had come from."

As Roy turned, he saw a hand reach out of a hole in the ground that he had just walked over. The hand pulled back a piece of wood to cover the hole's opening. "I had walked past a bundle of wooden railroad ties, thinking they were lying on the ground," he told me. "I was unaware they were concealing a spider hole."

Roy jumped up, spraying his BAR at the railroad ties, blowing the wooden planks away like twigs. "I reloaded a full clip and ran up to the hole. There must have been seven Japanese in there. I emptied another twenty-round clip into all of them," he recalled. "They had no chance. They were trapped."

Roy reloaded, making his way to the chicken coop from which the patrol had first taken fire. He passed the now-dead Marine who had been leading the patrol. "I poured fire into that bamboo chicken house a few times before entering," he said. In the coop, another seven Japanese were dead, cut down by all the returning fire from Roy and his squad. One was a dead officer.

"I got a Nambu pistol, a sword, and a flag off that dead officer," he boasted, right before he disappeared from the room. He returned with a samurai sword and a Japanese pistol. He loved showing off the beautiful weapons, unfazed by the memory of how he had acquired them. Roy seemed to look back on his days in the Pacific with the same sense of pride and curiosity with which he now looked at these souvenirs. He told his stories with enthusiasm, not remorse, and treated his war stories as neat collector's items he could share. I found it admirable, and thought it was evidence that Roy's life hadn't peaked in the Marines.

Roy went on to become an Air Force pilot and served in the Korean and Cold Wars. After surviving a bad crash, he became a private civilian pilot. When the opportunity arose, he became a technical journalist, writing flight manuals for Lockheed Martin. When that wasn't enough, he became a certified treasure diver and explorer. His willingness to try his hand at new things make him an example for every person exiting military service.

As I finished up with Roy, I buckled the rifle back into its case. I didn't want to leave. He was the first World War II veteran I had ever read about, and I had found him here fifteen years later, waiting for me. It was tough seeing a legend like him get old.

I shook hands with the most interesting man in the world, and then I was off to my next journey.

Roy Roush with the rifle. *Photo courtesy of the author*

CHAPTER FIFTEEN

"I Don't Want to Go Home"

Al Bucharelli
U.S. Army, Third Infantry Division

Port Charlotte, Florida

Meeting Al Bucharelli, a veteran who had been walking on a prosthetic leg for the last seventy-five years, was personal for me. Before I started my journey tracking down World War II veterans, I had started a nonprofit in Boston—New England's Wounded Veterans, Inc.—which helped amputees from the wars I'd served in, Iraq and Afghanistan.

Watching twenty-year-olds get fitted with state-of-the-art prostheses was a remarkable sight. It gave them hope after being wounded at such a young age. But there was always that nagging thought in the back of my head: What happens as they grow older?

Technology may advance, but the body only declines. Knowing that my fellow veterans could eventually be bound to a wheelchair because of their injuries always bothered me. But then I met Al.

Al was an amputee who had been fitted with a prosthetic leg for seventy-five years. Over the course of three quarters of a century, Al wore a variety of prostheses. He had witnessed more than seven decades of medical advancements for amputees firsthand. When I met Al and heard about how the VA had kept him out of a wheelchair for all these years,

I saw that there was hope for the wounded veterans I worked with through my nonprofit.

The first time we met, I brought along my friend, Brian. Although I usually did my rifle adventures on my own, I thought Brian might benefit from the meeting. He had lost his right leg and right arm in the Battle of Fallujah, Iraq, in 2004. Though sixty years separated him from Al, both men had the same injuries. As I watched them pass the rifle back and forth to one another, I developed a clear goal for the meeting: instill some motivation into Brian's long journey ahead as an amputee veteran.

Al could motivate and inspire him. When I asked Al if he was drafted or volunteered, he answered, "I didn't plan on joining." But he did serve, and as a result he was maimed for life. Al began his story.

■ ■ ■

Al Bucharelli lay under an automobile in his crowded garage, making the usual repairs. It was springtime in Charlton, Massachusetts, and his shop was piled up with cars in need of oil changes and other maintenance after a long winter.

When the shop phone rang while he was working under a vehicle, he never rushed to answer it. Getting in and out from under a car isn't easy when you have one leg. His prosthetic leg didn't allow him to go fast anyway, but on this day in 1963, the phone would not stop ringing.

Al cleaned off his greasy hands and limped over to the phone. He picked up the receiver, but he didn't have time to get a word out. It was his wife, crying and screaming on the other end, telling him to get to the hospital.

Grabbing a random set of car keys off the counter, Al took a customer's car straight to the hospital. In the lobby, he was stopped by police. "It's okay," another officer said. "He's the father, he's the father." They allowed him into the emergency room. Al barged through the door to hug his crying wife.

While squeezing her tightly, he looked over her shoulder. On an aluminum table lay a figure, covered by a sheet, that looked too small to be a body. That was because the body underneath wasn't that of an adult.

It was that of a seven-year-old boy.

His son.

Al limped over to the table and removed the sheet to have one last look at his youngest child.

A teenage driver had been speeding through town and struck his son as he was getting off the school bus. His child was dead and, even worse, no one had any answers. The bus driver appeared to have been drunk, and the chief of police was often his drinking partner. In typical small-town-politics fashion, it seemed that no real effort would ever be put into solving the matter.

The days turned into months, and no charges were ever filed. The teenager drove around in his new car like it had never happened. When Al got a copy of the police report, he grew irate. The report read that no one was at fault, that his son simply "ran into the moving car."

When he read the report, Al stormed down to the police station to give the delinquent officers a piece of his mind. He crumpled up the report and threw it at the enclosed windows of the police booth. "I want to talk the chief now!" he yelled.

The chief of police wasn't there, so Al stormed off, limping towards the door. Another officer came to the front desk from a back room and watched Al limp off. "What? Did he get hit by the car too?" he cracked to the other officer.

Al hadn't been hit by a car. His limp had developed almost twenty years before near Monte Cassino, Italy, when his leg was blown off at the knee. Yet losing his leg and being maimed for life didn't match the pain of losing his youngest son. He returned home that night and said two words to his wife: "We're moving."

In his Florida home in 2019, the ninety-four-year-old revisited the story of losing his youngest child—and it still crushed him. He got emotional about the son he had never forgotten. It still hurt after all this time. "Let's change the topic," his wife chimed in from across the room.

Perhaps some people might think that too much interview time was spent on the loss, but in my time interviewing vets I had come to learn that understanding the veteran was about more than understanding just the war he had served in. Telling a veteran's story required knowing details about the rest of his life, about the milestones and heartaches that had built his character.

■ ■ ■

Al never intended to join the military and head to war. In fact, he had tried to avoid it. "I became a welder and secured a job at a shipyard, which would have kept me ineligible from the draft," Al explained. "Two days before I was supposed to start the job, I got drafted. I never made it. Uncle Sam got me first."

After completing basic training in Starke, Florida, Al was shipped to Little Rock, Arkansas, where he completed his infantry training. From there it was off to Newport News, Virginia, from which Al was shipped out to North Africa.

Secured from Axis powers, North Africa became the staging area for convoys heading to Italy. When Al's convoy embarked for Italy, it was raided by German bombers on its way across the Mediterranean. As Al waited below deck, packed away with other fresh replacements from the United States, the German Luftwaffe dive-bombed the other ships in the convoy.

"Our escorts shot eight German planes out of the sky," he remembered. "As soon as the battle was over, we went topside." A few hours later, a submarine emerged from the ocean directly in front of Al's transport ship. "Everyone tensed up. We thought we were about to be sunk by an enemy sub."

Luckily, it was an American submarine—but the commander didn't have good news. A pack of German U-boats was nearby and would surely sink the convoy if it continued towards the Italian coastline. The Americans had no choice but to sail back to Africa. Taking their position in the war was delayed. A few weeks later, the convoy embarked again, landing safely in Naples, Italy.

"They removed all replacement troops from the ships and assembled us in a giant soccer stadium," Al recalled. There, he was told he would be part of Headquarters Company, Fifteenth Regiment, of the Third Infantry Division. Al was thrilled. "Being assigned to HQ Company, I figured I wouldn't be on the front lines as much."

However, his excitement subsided as the weeks passed. It turned out Headquarters Company would be in the middle of all the action. Once they pushed farther north, Al and the other soldiers were again dive-bombed repeatedly by German planes. Throughout the campaign, they were hit by Stukas. All they could do was duck, run, or dive under the trees when they were attacked.

Allied forces began to advance farther into Italy in November of 1943. They approached the vicinity of Monte Cassino, a Nazi stronghold. The German-held territory had been impenetrable. The bombardments only got worse for the men of Headquarters Company.

"We had a big switchboard set up to establish radio communications with all the different companies in the regiment," Al said. That responsibility put the men of Headquarters Company in added danger. They had to lay communication wire all over the terrain, including in open areas, a dangerous but necessary task.

The Germans took advantage of the Americans' vulnerability, especially when they were exposed in the wide-open areas. "They had a giant rail gun on tracks," Al said. "It would come out of a tunnel in the mountains. It would be wheeled out, fire, then reverse back into the mountain. Our airpower could never take it out."

The gun could lob an explosive round from nearly thirty miles away. As Al and a corporal he knew only as "Ray" laid wire in an olive field one morning, the Germans wheeled out their massive rail gun. Unbeknownst to Al and Ray, the Germans fired their state-of-the-art weapon at the men in the field. The massive artillery shell landed a half mile short from its intended target, landing—and detonating—in front of Al. He was violently blown back into the ground. He sat up and looked around. The corporal was gone. "He was killed instantly. He never knew what hit him," Al said.

Al didn't realize he was injured. He couldn't feel anything. A group of engineers ran over to him, put him on a stretcher, and laid him across a jeep. "My left leg was shattered. It was hanging off me," he said, remembering the gruesome scene that changed his life forever. "The only thing connecting it to my body was the main artery. So I carried my leg to the hospital with me."

Al's injury was clearly below his knee, but he was covered in heavy amounts of blood. "The doctors rolled me over and asked if I was with anyone. I told them I was, and they asked who, specifically. Apparently I had Corporal Ray's brains on my back and up in my crotch area," he said. It was important for the medical detachment to know who Al had been with so they could document the man as killed or missing, especially if they didn't have the body.

As the doctors cleaned the human remains off his body, Al blacked out. "When I woke up, my leg was completely gone. They amputated the rest of it. I knew right then that I didn't want to go home," he told me. In World War II, getting wounded was typically a blessing if it wasn't severe. A wound was your ticket home, or at least time off the front lines. Al wasn't so lucky. His wound handicapped him for life. He was embarrassed to face his family. He was scared of what their reaction would be when they saw he was missing a leg.

"You will be getting shipped back to North Africa for rehab," a nurse said as he looked down at his missing limb.

"No, I don't want to go home," Al replied in a frenzy.

"The doctor came over and said the same thing," he told me. "I still refused to get shipped back home. It wasn't until the priests, rabbis, and nuns all made their rounds to visit me that they talked me into agreeing to be moved. They motivated me to want to go home."

After being in combat only a month, the eighteen-year-old was back in North Africa. "They didn't waste any time trying to get me to walk. They threw me a pair of crutches and said, 'Get to it,'" he remembered. In North Africa, the Army didn't give Al any time to feel sorry for himself. As he began to hop around on crutches, he fell abruptly to the ground, splitting his nub and reopening the wound. Al didn't feel a thing, but the accident set his return to the United States back several months. The open wound on his nub was so bad that it required a second surgery.

The doctors ended up performing only a patch job on Al. He would need more extensive surgery. The military decided to ship the teenager back to Newport News. From there, they transferred him to Walter Reed Hospital for proper medical attention.

Upon arriving at Walter Reed, Al was fitted with his first prosthetic leg. Al vividly remembers the day. "It was two weeks before Memorial Day 1944," he told me. "The captain in charge of the wounded at the hospital made a bet with us. He challenged us to walk on our own, unassisted. Anyone who did would get a thirty day furlough. Well, sure enough, I walked on that prosthetic leg without crutches," Al said with pride. "I wanted to get home."

As Al thought about what he would say to his parents, a nurse entered the room. "You have a visitor," she informed him.

Al raised his head. It was his father, the man who had taught him everything. "It was the first time I had seen my father since I lost my leg," he explained. "I just went to hell bawling my eyes out." Al broke down, crying in the room with his father. That moment they shared still makes him tremble to this day. "He came down to visit me with one of the fellows who worked for him. The two spent the weekend with me."

His dad's two-day visit didn't last long, but Al would see him again soon. He was owed his thirty days' leave for his medical strides at Walter Reed. After taking the train back to Boston, he was just one bus ride away from Charlton, Massachusetts.

The bus was completely full. "I boarded the bus in my uniform and the driver told a man to get up for me to sit down," Al said of his first foray into civilian life as an amputee. "Who's going to make me?" the man responded.

Al got nervous. He didn't want to make a scene, but he needed the seat to make it through the ride home. He froze, unsure how to respond, but the bus driver quickly came to his rescue. "I will throw you off this bus if you don't give your seat to this soldier," the driver said to the intransigent passenger. The man got up and allowed the limping Al to sit.

"It was a rule to give up your seat for a service member in full uniform," Al explained. "The bus driver had the authority to enforce that."

At just after midnight, the bus finally pulled into the small town of Charlton. Al woke up his parents. He had not seen his mom since the start of the war. It was another emotional reunion for the Bucharelli family. "Seeing my parents gave me the confidence to carry my disability," he said with visible gratitude. "No one was going to say anything to me about having one leg, or else they would get an earful."

Al went straight to work just a week after getting home. He trained on the job in an automotive repair, towing, and machine shop—work that he would spend the next thirty-six years of his life doing before retiring in 1991. He only collected $115 dollars a month from the VA for his missing leg. While he was proud of his service and respected the men he had served with, he never got involved in veterans' activities. "I was too busy and had six kids to feed," he said.

The fear of being permanently confined to a wheelchair one day never concerned him. "I made up my mind I was going to walk forever," he said. Al looked over at my friend sitting across from us. Brian's prosthetic leg protruded from the love seat he was sitting on. "How about you, Brian? You want to be in a wheelchair one day?" Al asked.

Brian shook his head no.

Their injuries happened sixty years apart, in two very different wars. But the way they looked at one another told me they knew that they faced the same obstacles in life. For the first time since I started my project, I wasn't the only veteran in the room forging a deep bond with a soldier from another generation.

Al began to roll his pant leg back down, covering his fake leg. I knew this meant we were done for the time being. I unsnapped the rifle case and placed the rifle back inside it. There was hardly any space left on it. *Just a few names left*, I thought.

I thanked Al, but he was more interested in saying his goodbye to Brian. I was the odd man out in the room, but I didn't care. Al was hope for Brian, hope for the wounded, even seventy years after he served. They locked eyes, shook hands, and we each made our way home.

■ ■ ■

While this chapter was supposed to end right here, my meeting with Al nagged at me for weeks. In our interview, he told me that he had refused to go back to Italy when his family took a vacation there in the '80s. I kept thinking about him sitting at home while his family toured the country that shaped his life. Ordinarily, the veterans I interviewed who had served in Europe eventually returned to the location of their battlegrounds. They appreciated the chance to see with fresh eyes, in peacetime, the places that had turned them from boys to men. But Al was obstinate: he wouldn't go back. I wanted to know why.

Back in Massachusetts, I looked for a reason to call Al back and decided on some questions about specific dates and people for his chapter. When I got him on the phone, I snuck in another question. "I know you haven't been back to Italy, but would you ever consider going back these days?"

Expecting a definite "No," I was shocked to hear Al say, "I suppose I would these days."

I couldn't get off the phone fast enough to try to formulate a plan to pull this off. My charity for wounded veterans, which had been going on for ten years, was a perfect solution. We were already preparing aid for severely wounded veterans of Iraq and Afghanistan. Why not start

offering assistance to other veterans? After consulting with my commit-
tee, I had the green light: Al and his wife would go back to Italy for the
first time in seventy-five years.

I waited to surprise Al with the news at Boston's Wounded Vet Motorcycle Run. He was virtually speechless. His wife had tricked him into
getting a passport, saying that one of his grandkids was graduating from
college in Canada. It was a slick trick and, more importantly, it worked.

There was another veteran whom I wanted to bring along for the
trip. I had begun meeting every week with ninety-four-year-old Rocco
Telese of East Boston after he had signed the rifle nearly two years before.
Rocco had served with the 85th Infantry Division, 339th Regiment, on
the Italian front. We lived so close to one another that we couldn't help
but become friends.

After surprising Al with the news about taking him to Italy, I ran
right back to Rocco and invited him to come with us. Facing some health
issues, Rocco hesitated. I told him I would give him some time to think
about it, and he could even bring a nurse if he had to.

A week later I put the pressure on him. "Have you made a decision
yet?" I yelled, climbing up the stairs to his top-floor apartment. Rocco
looked like he wanted to tell me no, but he reached for his checkbook.
He wrote out a check for $2,500 and handed it to me.

"What's this for?" I asked.

"Buy the plane tickets," he said sharply. He was witty for his age,
still all there.

"This is too much money," I replied. "The tickets are not this much."

"That's because I want to buy your ticket as well!"

I argued back and forth with Rocco. He became visibly shaken that
I was denying his check, and so I finally accepted the old man's wish.

"You buy those tickets so we are there June 4," Rocco commanded.
"It will be the seventy-fifth anniversary of the liberation of Rome."
Rocco reached for his wallet and pulled out photos of him at the thirtieth
and fiftieth anniversaries of the liberation. He was even in a picture with
President Clinton at the American cemetery in Nettuno in 1994.

Not long after Rocco's stern request, his and Al's tickets were purchased and we were wheels up to Rome for the first week of June 2019. I needed help on the trip and had convinced four of my friends to travel with me. After all, I had two wheelchairs to push around Italy.

The trip started off bitter and disappointing, I am sad to say. Not a flag, banner, band, honor guard, or anything else acknowledged that it was, in fact, the seventy-fifth anniversary of the Allied forces reaching the Italian capital of Rome and freeing it from Nazi and Fascist rule.

It was Al's first time back, and he didn't seem to care, but for Rocco, who had been back multiple times, it was a disgrace. "I can't believe the president doesn't even plan to come!" he raged. "We took over 200,000 casualties over here!"

The more Rocco went on, the angrier I got. All over the news there was nothing but hype for the seventy-fifth anniversary of D-Day in France, which was a couple of days away, on June 6. Here we were in Italy on June 4, with not even a "Welcome back" from anyone.

I drove Rocco and Al down to the Colosseum, took some photos, and compared them to those from 1944. We enjoyed ourselves, even though we were quite possibly the only ones there who knew what June 4 meant. "This is the way it has always been," Rocco added. The liberation of Rome was completely overlooked because Allied forces landed on the beach in France a day and a half later.

As Rocco discussed this issue with me at dinner, I stared into my glass of wine. Italy truly was the forgotten front. Here I was, sitting with two men who were most likely the only American World War II veterans in the whole country. There should have been some recognition, some fanfare.

Al had no expression on his face. He had been quiet since we landed. This trip meant more than just sightseeing and a history lesson for him. He was returning to a place where his life had changed forever. He knew I had plans up my sleeve to bring him back to the vicinity where he had been wounded, but then it hit me. Where did they bury the other soldier who was with him and was killed on that day?

"Al!" I yelled across the dinner table to wake him from his deep thought. Then I lowered my voice. "What was the name again of that soldier who got killed in your incident?"

"Ray," Al answered. "I never did know his last name. He had just come back from a furlough." Al began shaking his head. It really bothered him that the young man was killed after returning from R&R.

I pulled out my iPhone and began searching the Sicily–Rome American Cemetery's roster of the fallen. Not having a last name made it difficult, but I got to sleuthing. Searching for "Ray" brought up a lot of results. There were nearly two hundred "Rays" buried in the cemetery. I scrolled through the names all night until I narrowed it down to four "Rays" who served with the Third Infantry Division. From there, I sorted them by regiment. Two were from Al's regiment. From there, I looked at the dates to see if one's death matched the day Al had lost his leg. I found him. At that moment, I learned Ray's full name. Ray James of Kentucky, killed in action November 12, 1943.

I kept this information to myself and memorized Ray's grave and plot number during our drive to the cemetery the next morning. The Sicily–Rome American Cemetery was a visually striking place, lined with 7,800 white crosses. Entering the cemetery with Al and Rocco made me think about how they carried themselves after the war, knowing that thousands of men never made it home. The Italian tour guides assigned to us rushed into the manager's office to inform them they were in the presence of two "real live World War II Vets!" It was a rare occurrence for them, the guide explained.

Al and Rocco were loaded onto a golf cart headed for the incline of the cemetery. My friends and I rushed to follow. We didn't want to miss these men's reactions to seeing the graves of the men whom they had served alongside. At Plot D, Row 19, the golf cart came to a halt. I knew the manager had stopped at Ray James's gravesite, but Al did not. When I caught up to the golf cart, I grabbed Al's hand and walked him in the direction of the grave. He was still unaware which white cross we were heading for. I turned around and raised my hands to stop the rest of the group. I wanted to give Al privacy for this moment.

I placed a hand on his shoulder and said, "Al, I'm just going to give you a second to visit Ray, Ray James, your corporal."

"Where?" he replied.

I pointed to the grave and Al made his way over. I stayed back, between the group and Al. As he walked over with his prosthetic leg, his cane began to shake. He was trembling. Al shed a few tears and started talking to himself—words I will never know or ask about. He made the sign of the cross. He wanted to be done at that moment, but his emotions still affected him.

After a few moments, I walked over and began to hug him, but I could not get any words out. Overcome, the breath was taken from me. I just turned around and waved for everyone else to join us. We all hugged Al.

"Oh Andy, I don't know how to ever thank you," were the first words he uttered.

I responded, but I don't know what I said. The emotion exchanged between veterans, young and old, tore into me. I felt gratitude, sorrow, and respect for the man I stood alongside in the cemetery. I felt a bond between two veterans that transcended the generations that separated our times of service.

Al continued to stare at the white granite cross. I took a photo. In it his chrome prosthetic leg gleams as it reflects the light of the sun. I'll never take a more powerful photo.

Just when I thought things couldn't get any more emotional, we headed for Tremensuoli, a suburb of Minturno, Italy. It was important for Rocco to visit this village. He had fought there with his regiment and helped erect a memorial there in 1992. The village was not even big enough for its own gas station. We ran into a few locals who were in their early sixties, sitting outside the town's only restaurant.

With a stack of photos in his hands, Rocco went up to them and began speaking in broken Italian. The men took the photos from him and began to point out people they knew in his pictures. Rocco had pictures ranging from the 1940s to the 1970s, and some from his short return in 1992 when he helped erect the monument. Our Italian tour guides and interpreters gestured for us to follow the villagers. They wanted to show us something.

We followed the locals down an alley. They began to knock on a few doors, and a few women exited their homes in confusion. A lot of Italian words were exchanged, and suddenly they began celebrating with joy. They were so ecstatic to point themselves out in Rocco's photos.

I couldn't believe it. Rocco's pile of documents became a celebration. The women were laughing and smiling ear to ear as they showed one another the photos of themselves. They began to bang on another door, waking up a ninety-six-year-old woman. Her house was still covered with bullet holes and shrapnel marks from the war. She, too, began to laugh and reminisce with Rocco's pictures.

The women began to hug him, and I had to walk away. Seeing the human emotion and what this ninety-four-year-old man meant to these Italian people touched me on another level. Rocco was no longer the elderly man I teased on Sundays over a cup of coffee. He was a savior. Everything I had held in from the cemetery until now came running down my face. I was crying, and crying hard for the first time since I was a child.

We often refer to World War II veterans as liberators and heroes, but actually seeing the residents of a once war-torn village greet a man who seventy-five years earlier walked through their town with a rifle, helmet, and boots was life-changing. Our tour guides were just as blown away as we were.

As we wheeled Rocco down the rest of the alley to the monument his division had erected, he got out of his chair, walked up to the statue, and beamed. "This will be the last time I see this bad boy," he exclaimed.

It was a kick in my gut, but he found humor in his own statement. This man was so satisfied with what he had done with his life that he didn't care that he was heading toward the end of it.

Not long after, it was time to get Al and Rocco back on the road and head for Rome. It had been a long day for both men, and they were physically and mentally exhausted. Worried that I might have pushed the envelope with their health, I was relieved that the long car ride allowed them the chance to sleep.

Al Bucharelli with Brian. *Photo courtesy of the author*

Suddenly my bitterness about the anniversary of Normandy stealing all the attention disappeared. This reunion of war fighters here in Italy was personal. We didn't need the news cameras, flyovers, and politicians. We didn't need Hollywood breathing down our necks. These two men had needed their privacy, and they had gotten it.

They educated me on an entirely new level, beyond my rifle. Our trip to Italy strengthened my passion for veterans tenfold, while sparking new ideas for working with them. However, it was one mission at a time for now. I needed to fill the rifle up with more names and hear more stories from men like Al and Rocco, men who connected to generations of veterans seventy-five years after their service.

CHAPTER SIXTEEN

Eighteen Hours

Masmeno "Smuz" DelRossi
U.S. Army, Tenth Armored Division

Masmeno DelRossi stared into the mirror, ready to put his uniform on for the last time. Taking a deep breath, he slipped on his U.S. Army jacket. The year was 1947. The war had been over for two years, and his brother John was finally being brought home.

John had first been listed as missing, but then was confirmed killed in action in the Philippines in December of 1944. All five of the DelRossi brothers, all Italian immigrants, were drafted into the military in 1942. Two of his brothers served in the U.S Navy; the other three, the U.S. Army. Masmeno, whose friends knew him as "Smuz," ended up in the European theater, while his brother John shipped off to the Pacific.

"I knew if something was going to happen to any of my brothers, it was going

Masmeno "Smuz" DelRossi.
Photo courtesy of Masmeno DelRossi

to be John," Smuz told me. "He liked to fight and would go headfirst right into things."

After he finished dressing, Smuz walked out of the house and got into the passenger's side of a Wakefield, Massachusetts, police cruiser. The chief had been kind enough to offer to give him a ride to the funeral home to greet his brother's flag-draped casket.

At the funeral home, a uniformed soldier waited by the door. "On behalf of the Thirty-Eighth Division, I'm sorry for your loss," he said dryly. "These are your brother's personal effects."

The U.S. Army death certificate read: "Bullet wound to the back. Location: Leyte, Philippines." As he watched Smuz read the paperwork, the soldier told him that his brother had been shot by a sniper.

Smuz crumpled the certificate and placed it back in the personal effects bag. John's casket was loaded into the hearse. Smuz and the soldier, whose name he didn't care to learn, loaded into the police car. Both vehicles headed to the cemetery. Residents of Wakefield stood along sidewalks holding American flags to pay their respects, having learned of John's return in the local newspaper the previous day.

The cemetery was full of family, friends, and townspeople expressing their gratitude. As Smuz exited the police car to serve as a pallbearer, a child no older than ten broke away from the crowd and ran up to him.

"Where did you fight in the war, Sarge?" the child asked innocently.

"Bastogne," Smuz replied, smiling.

"Are you a Screaming Eagle?" the boy asked excitedly.

Smuz shook his head no. He pointed to the triangle-shaped patch on his shoulder.

The confused boy stared and then ran back to his parents.

Smuz looked on as his brother's coffin was lowered into the earth. The funeral-goers were encouraged to join friends and family back at the American Legion for food and drink. At the Legion post, Smuz needed a shot of whiskey more than ever, ordering one for himself and one for his deceased brother.

A man approaching the bar yelled out, "I got those!" Smuz didn't recognize him, but the stranger paid the bartender and began to make small talk.

"It must be good to have him home," the man started. "Sorry for your loss. I grew up right down the street from him."

"It feels OK, I guess," Smuz conceded as he extended his hand. "Masmeno. Everyone calls me Smuz."

"So where did you serve over there?"

"France, Belgium, and Germany," Smuz muttered.

"Wow, I bet you saw a lot of action."

The trivial back-and-forth started to bother Smuz. It should have been obvious to the stranger that Smuz had seen heavy action. After all, the Combat Infantryman Badge and Purple Heart with an Oak Leaf Cluster didn't sit on his chest for nothing.

"What was the worst?" the man continued to pry.

Smuz grabbed his shot of whiskey off the bar and said, "Bastogne, the Bulge."

The man thought about the answer. "Well, thank God for those paratroopers, huh?" he prattled on after the brief pause.

Smuz had had all he could stand at that point. He rolled his eyes, shook his head, and knocked back the shot. He pointed to his brother's shot on the bar and told the man, "No one touches that one." Smuz walked away, leaving the shot of whiskey by itself on the bar top, and tried to be kind to the rest of the guests. If burying his brother wasn't hurtful enough, seeing his own military service trivialized added insult to injury.

The patch he wore on his shoulder that had drawn the inquisitive child's attention that morning was a yellow triangle with the number 10, which stood for the 10th Armored Division. But because of where he had fought in the war, Smuz was often presumed to be a member of the prestigious 101st Airborne Division, or the "Screaming Eagles."

Later, the HBO television miniseries *Band of Brothers* would explode the fame and popularity of the 101st; however, they were famous long before that. Popular media decreed that the 101st Airborne basically won the whole war. The standard World War II highlights always featured the paratroopers jumping into Normandy and capturing Hitler's Eagle's Nest.

The men from the 101st who fought and died in World War II deserve all the credit they can get, without a doubt. They jumped into active combat and fought their way to the Battle of the Bulge to save Bastogne. However, what's often overlooked is that they were not the first to reach the Belgian town of Bastogne. The 10th Armored Division was.

After seventy-five years, that topic was still a bitter one among surviving Tenth Armored Division veterans. "All the newspapers and films back then gave all the credit to the paratroopers. The Tenth Armored Division wasn't acknowledged at all in holding that strategic town. Our actions helped changed the tide of war," explained Smuz.

The closest the Tenth Armored Division came to Hollywood fame was when future late-night talk show host Jimmy Fallon played one of them, riding in a jeep during a five-second scene in *Band of Brothers*. Monuments in Belgium to honor the Tenth Armored were only erected as late as 2011 and 2015. By that time, most of the men who had served in the Tenth weren't alive to see them.

Some say this kind of mentality is needless jealousy among rival Army units. But for Smuz and other members of the 10th Armored, the fact that their heroic actions went unsung was a stinging rebuke to their friends who had sacrificed life and limb to take Bastogne. Even the commanding general of the 101st Airborne, General Anthony McAuliffe, once admitted to the 10th Armored's heroism. "If it weren't for the elements of the 10th Armored holding the Germans off for the twenty-four hours before we got there," McAuliffe said, "we would have never won the Battle of Bastogne."

Smuz told me how he took off his uniform that day after the funeral and hung it up forever. Although bitter, he found it amusing that no one knew the accomplishments of his well-disciplined unit. "It didn't matter whatever everyone else thought they knew," Smuz smarted, "I know what we accomplished."

Smuz was a member of Team O'Hara in Baker Company, 54th Armored Infantry. He was one of the first men in the U.S. Army to set foot in the Bastogne area. He and members of the 101st Airborne defended the town in the village outskirts until they were surrounded.

"I remember the day they moved us to Belgium," he began. "We were in France. It was on December 17, 1944."

Smuz was sleeping on the hood of his half-track to keep warm. "We took turns doing this. The heat from the engine kept us warm, even when it wasn't running," he explained. The men's sleep was cut short when the lieutenant began to wake them. "He ordered us to gear up because we were moving out."

Smuz got along with the lieutenant. Although Smuz was enlisted and the lieutenant was an officer, Smuz's age—thirty-two—forged a close bond between the two men compared to the relatively young members of the platoon.

The Tenth Armored Division had already breached the border between France and Germany and was ready to keep going. "When we were ordered to move out in such a hurry, I noticed we were moving in the opposite direction of Germany," Smuz noted. "Many of us thought we were getting a break in Paris."

The columns of tanks and half-tracks moved all day, stopping only to allow the men to relieve themselves. Even though the men were overwhelmed with constant travel, there was also excitement. Could they finally be getting some rest? They had been in combat since Halloween night.

"We had stopped quickly along the road so guys could piss when some French civilians asked about the Germans troops headed their way. We didn't know how to respond and dismissed it at as rumors. We figured we had the German Army on the run," Smuz remembered. The Americans remounted their vehicles and did not stop again until nightfall. They had traveled seventy-five miles.

"I don't remember seeing any signs for towns, but I was told when we stopped that we were in Luxembourg. It was officially clear we were not going to Paris. More townspeople were asking about how many Germans were coming. They knew more about the situation than we did, I guess," Smuz recalled.

The division's senior officers knew what was happening, but the men were often kept in the dark about the details. On December 16, a significant breakthrough occurred. Hundreds of thousands of Germans were reported to be conducting a major offensive. The enlisted men were told that the entire division would be rushed to the Ardennes Forest and half of them would be sent to a Belgian crossroads town. At this point, the town's name wasn't being shared, at least not to the common foot soldier.

This was the beginning stages of the Battle of the Bulge.

Before the sun rose, the division was split in two. Smuz and the rest of Team O'Hara were loaded into half-tracks, while the rest of the Tenth Armored Division stayed put. They marched another forty miles, stopping once. The terrain was tough, and the mud caused issues. They were finally ordered to stop sometime around nine o'clock that night.

The next morning, December 18, the men of the Tenth Armored Division were ordered to do something they didn't usually do much of: "Dig in."

"As an armored unit, we never dug a foxhole. We were always mobile and needed to move in a hurry. We knew something was up now," Smuz explained. The men were told to construct a roadblock, cut down trees, and lay mines, and under no circumstances were they to allow Germans to come through.

Instead of digging his foxhole, Smuz volunteered to take a group of engineers to lay mines alongside the nearest road. The engineers piled in the half-track, and they drove a mile or two down the road. They didn't leave the sight of the rest of the company. As the engineers planted anti-tank mines, a figure suddenly appeared in the distance.

"Contact!" an engineer yelled before dashing into a ditch alongside the road.

Smuz hit the ground and raised his M1 Garand as another soldier swung the .50 caliber machine gun around on the half-track and pointed it at the figure.

"Wait! He's one of ours!" someone else shouted.

The American soldier made no effort to clarify his identity. "He wasn't the least bit concerned. We almost killed him, and he just kept walking past us with a blank look on his face, as if we weren't even there," Smuz recalled.

The engineers let out a "Whoa" and stepped in front of the man, preventing him from walking over the mines they had just planted. "Where the fuck are you going?" the Tenth Armored soldier on the .50 caliber asked.

Smuz caught up with the soldier and grabbed his arm. He wore a patch from the Twenty-Eighth Infantry Division, a red keystone. "They were a unit out of Pennsylvania," Smuz said. "We were told they might be in the area but couldn't be positive." Smuz tried to question the soldier, but the erratic infantryman tore away from him.

"Fuck it!" the soldier yelled, clearly bothered by Smuz's generic questions.

The soldier operating the .50 caliber jumped off the half-track. "What did he say to you?" he asked, prepared to confront the wanderer.

"Let him go," Smuz responded.

The straggler from the Twenty-Eighth Division continued to walk off. He would be one of many that crept through the Tenth Armored Division's lines that day, some by themselves, others in groups of three or four. "They were completely overwhelmed by whatever German force was out there," Smuz remembered. "It was a creepy feeling. When they stopped coming, we had an idea of what was coming next."

None of the men of Team O'Hara slept comfortably that night. The thought of Americans hightailing it out of the area was disconcerting. The next morning, no one needed to be woken up. The men could hear explosions in the distance and were told the Germans were shelling another location to the north.

The fog on December 19 was so dense that the men couldn't see fifty feet in front of them. "Your ears were what kept you alive those first few days. You couldn't see very far. You could hear vehicles but couldn't see them," Smuz remembered.

Suddenly one of the men from the company began to shout. "Hey! Hey!" the soldier yelled in a frenzy. "He couldn't get the words out, but he was thrusting his arm as if he were trying to point at something," Smuz said.

Peering out into the fog, Smuz could see several Germans attempting to remove the mines the engineers had placed the day before. The American squad fired on the Germans. The enemy made a getaway in a small Volkswagen military vehicle.

"We had no idea how much of our roadblock was cleared because of the fog, so we stayed focused on that area waiting for more enemy," Smuz remembered. The men heard more enemy troops rumbling in the distance. As the fog momentarily shifted, the men could make out German tanks backing down the road to avoid the mines. Team O'Hara called for an artillery strike on the area. The Americans were hoping for good results.

Suddenly an enemy tank shell flew into their position, splitting the trees above their heads. Men began to shoot blindly into the fog, and their lieutenant screamed at them to cease fire. Unable to see the enemy, they were wasting ammo.

Anxiety ran high through the ranks on December 19. The enemy was steps away but couldn't be seen. The Germans had already been trying to penetrate heavily from the north when everyone began to scream and yell again. This time men were approaching from behind.

As the men turned in their foxholes and changed the directions of their machine guns, they could see a formation of soldiers approaching. Luckily, the Americans held their fire until the last minute. It was friendly forces.

"This was the first I saw of the 101st Airborne," Smuz said. "They were members of the 501st. It was also the first time I learned the name of the town behind us—Bastogne."

Ten hours after their arrival and eight hours after engaging the first German patrols, the 101st's Airborne's 501st Parachute Infantry Regiment was digging in on the left flank of the 10th Armored Division. The next morning, the 327th Glider Infantry showed up on their right side. There was now a 360-degree circle around Bastogne. "That's when it hit us that we could be surrounded," Smuz remembered.

The fog finally lifted, but the weather conditions didn't improve. Much to the men's dismay, snow began to fall. The Germans bypassed the Tenth Armored roadblock, entering the villages of Wardin and Marvie, to the left and right of Team O'Hara. "We started to get shelled heavily," Smuz said of the early action, "and we couldn't help the other units to our flanks because they were still sending enemy patrols in our direction."

German soldiers came out of the tree lines wearing white snowsuits, blending in with the snow. "It was tough to see them. Guys were firing in every direction!" Smuz exclaimed.

The 10th Armored had repulsed several infantry assaults by the time the sun was going down, but the enemy tanks kept coming. The Panzer tanks pounded the 101st's positions in Wardin and Marvie. The glow of burning buildings revealed Team O' Hara's foxholes, and they had to withdraw into the darkness to stay safe.

But the burning buildings also revealed the enemy positions. The Germans' snowsuits were of no use to them that night. When they tried to advance again, they were silhouetted by burning barns. The American soldiers picked them off until they fell back. Even with the attack repulsed, the men couldn't get any sleep. The sounds of screaming animals burning alive in the barns kept them awake.

The next morning, German half-tracks and tanks poured out of the woods. They attacked the paratroopers in Wardin so severely that the airborne troops had to retreat to the Tenth Armored perimeter. Team O'Hara did not have it any easier. The artillery was constant.

When the shelling ceased, a German Panzer tank began to make its way up the road. One of the roadblocks had been breached. "That road was our responsibility," Smuz said of the incursion. "Another soldier and I crawled toward a German tank to knock it out with a bazooka. It didn't do anything. We didn't want to be shot by its machine gun as we ran away, so we rolled right into another foxhole. The tank was so close it felt like it rolled right over us!" More bazooka shells bounced off the enemy tank until it reversed. "If it weren't for that frozen ground, we would have been crushed to death," Smuz reflected.

Without a break in the fighting, more white-camouflaged German infantry tried to push forward to take out the American bazooka teams. A long-lasting firefight broke out in the glow of burning buildings as the sun went down. "We called for more artillery, but it got denied because it was being used in Noville, another village north of us," Smuz said.

Smuz's platoon continued to engage the Germans where they could. "Germans were running at us, swearing in both English and German," Smuz told me, describing the fray. "They overran a couple of our forward machine guns."

The platoon continued to lob hand grenades and fire at anything that moved. The next morning, dead Germans littered the area. Men began to remove the snowsuits from the Germans and put them on. Lined with rabbit fur, they were much warmer than the American uniforms—in addition to being tactically useful. Other men took bedsheets from Belgian homes, creating their own white camouflage for their bodies and foxholes.

By this point, the Tenth Armored soldiers embedded at the Wiltz-Bastogne roadblock were running low on food and munitions. When they learned that the glider infantry holding the right side of the line had been wiped out, morale crashed. The situation was bleak: Germans were occupying a decent portion of the village of Marvie, and Smuz's company had to fall back to form a new line with what was left of the glider infantrymen.

"We fell back some several hundred yards, knowing our roadblocks were passable now. Our tanks were spread thin, supporting our ground units," Smuz said. "We were down to our last rounds of ammunition. At night we shivered in the foxholes." But come morning, the weather cleared, and the embattled American soldiers were given a ray of hope. It was clear enough for the Air Corps to take to the skies again. Smuz saw roughly ten men parachute into a nearby field. "They were pathfinders and informed us a whole lot of supplies were heading our way," Smuz told me. "We were so thrilled."

Sure enough, it was true. Later that morning, hundreds of planes dropped supplies to the besieged members of the 101st Airborne and 10th Armored Divisions, briefly lifting morale. Rearmed and no longer feeling isolated on the front lines, the American soldiers redoubled their efforts to hold the line. But the harsh combat quickly drained the men of their eager spirit again. The enemy onslaught continued, and casualties mounted.

But again, reinforcements came when the men on the line least expected them. Friendly tanks came out of nowhere. Smuz spotted the number four decaled on their turrets. The Fourth Armored Division had reached the men holding Bastogne.

On December 26, Smuz and the battle-weary men of the 101st Airborne and 10th Armored Divisions were reinforced by General Patton and the 4th Armored Division. The several-weeks-long defensive battle in Bastogne turned into an offensive push overnight. In the next days, Smuz walked past the foxholes he had once occupied, advancing into the woods the Germans had occupied. "We pushed forward with the 501st," Smuz said of the Allied advance. "Sure enough, the Krauts made their stand in those woods. I ran to jump into one of their foxholes when I saw a Panzer tank between the trees. It was disguised as a haystack and fired a round over my head, splintering the trees."

Smuz considered running back the other way but instead crouched in the German foxhole. "I tried to rise again, hoping our tanks were catching up to us," he remembered, "when a grenade went off to my left side. I fell back in the foxhole like a sack of potatoes." Dizzy and deaf, Smuz was useless. He couldn't even point his rifle in the correct direction. "Other soldiers saw me advancing the wrong way. I couldn't hear a thing."

Smuz was brought back to a field hospital in Bastogne. After over a month of holding the line, it was the first time he had ever been in the actual town of Bastogne. "It was bombed-out bad," Smuz said of the town. "They caught it as bad as we did on the outskirts. Men dug for survivors under destroyed churches and homes."

Smuz was relegated to the back lines for weeks, unable to recover his hearing from the grenade explosion. He was offered a return to England but refused to part from the action. Lying in a hospital cot, he received a letter from home. His brother John had been killed in action in the Pacific.

After several weeks in the Belgian hospital, Smuz finally started to get his hearing back. He vowed to return to his unit, which was now pushing into Germany. When he got back, Smuz was put in charge of a platoon. "There were a lot of replacements, young kids," he said of the soldiers under his command. "Again, I was thirty-two," he reminded me. "Those guys were all eighteen."

Smuz and his platoon attacked Trier, Germany, in March of 1945. As the platoon began to dig in outside the town, a Tiger tank and company-sized element of German SS attacked the Tenth Armored. The Tiger tank fired directly at the men, blowing soldiers out of their fox-holes. The fighting was gruesome. As Smuz fired his rifle at several Germans, he saw an American soldier to his right attempting to fire a bazooka with one of his arms dangling. "Someone move over there and help him out!" he shouted while shooting at the oncoming enemy. As Smuz turned to his left, he saw another soldier fighting with his jaw hanging off. The German tank continued to score direct hits on the American foxholes.

"I ducked down to reload, and I came back up to see the tank on fire," Smuz said of the action. "I still can't believe that that kid, missing an arm, took out that tank. I never did find out who he was or if he lived."

As the fighting subsided, the Americans succeeded in taking Trier. But there would be no break for the Tenth Armored Division. Almost as soon as they seized Trier, the men were loaded into the half-tracks and continued through Germany, liberating small concentration camps near Dachau. Men from the division spent all day on working parties, assisting the dying prisoners. They forced the local German civilians through what was essentially a guided tour of the camp. That night, the German mayor of Dachau and his wife hung themselves. "Talk about guilt!" Smuz exclaimed.

Physically exhausted, the men of the Fifty-Fourth Armored Infantry, Tenth Armored Division, were worn out. Their boots had holes, their uniforms were ripped, and their weapons were misfiring. They had been going nonstop since Bastogne all the way through Germany. When they found out that they had to capture one last hill before they would see a break from the action, depression set in.

"We knew it was close to the end," Smuz explained. "No one wanted to get killed this far into the war. Colonel O'Hara told us we had to take another hill, and none of the men wanted to. He said, 'Fine. I'll take the damn hill myself then!' He stormed out of the house. We followed him and mounted our half-tracks."

On the way to his last battle, Smuz's half-track hit an anti-tank mine. "I remember a flash and everyone getting thrown around. My rifle butt smashed me in the face, and my nose gushed blood. Of course, my hearing was gone again!" he said. The men went on to seize the hill with few casualties. It was late April of 1945, and the war would soon come to a close.

Smuz spent the rest of his life waking up with cold sweats and nightmares from his time in the Battle of the Bulge. He was my grandfather. Sadly, he died before he could sign the rifle, so I did it for him.

CHAPTER SEVENTEEN

Enemy Alien

Lawson Sakai
U.S. Army, 442nd Regimental Combat Team

Las Vegas, Nevada

Ninety-five-year-old Lawson Ichiro Sakai held his head high while reminiscing about the confusing time in our country when Japanese Americans were considered enemy aliens. Many were forced to leave their homes and the lives they knew and sent to one of the ten internment camps in the country. Others were similarly relocated, taking only what they could carry with them.

Lawson Ichiro Sakai wasn't angry. He didn't hold a grudge. Seventy-five years after the war, he was sitting next to me in his hotel room in Las Vegas, grinning. I guess you would be too if you had proved the whole world wrong by serving in one of the most highly decorated regiments of the U.S. Army during the war, a regiment made up exclusively of Japanese Americans.

Lawson Sakai. *Photo courtesy of Lawson Sakai*

I met Lawson at the California Hotel and Casino in Las Vegas, attending what could possibly be the last Japanese American World War II veteran gathering ever. As we talked in his room, I left the rifle lying across the table in case another World War II veteran happened to walk in. A banner hung over our heads. It read "442nd Regimental Combat Team Reunion."

Enemy Alien

The month of April was never hot in Los Angeles, but on this spring day the sun beat down on Southern California. Lawson Sakai watched as his father wiped beads of sweat off his forehead. The family had been working tirelessly all day moving furniture and packing up their belongings. They had known there would be consequences after the Japanese bombed Pearl Harbor, but they had never imagined it would come to this. The state of California was ordering an evacuation of all Japanese Americans from their homes. They would be relocated to internment camps.

As Lawson helped his father carry a trunk through the living room, the doorbell rang. On the porch were two men in suits. Lawson watched from the living room as his father answered the door. He couldn't hear the conversation, but the men handed his father a large envelope.

The men were from the FBI. The envelope held the proper documentation and permission for the Sakai family to relocate to Colorado. Relief poured over his father's face as he walked back into the room and opened the envelope. Being Christian had helped the Sakai family's case. A month earlier, Lawson's parents had discovered a church in Colorado willing to house Japanese Americans on their property. They applied and got approved just in the nick of time. It saved them from being placed in the camps.

Both the state and federal government were unsure of the allegiance of Japanese immigrants living in America now that the country was officially at war with Japan. Most of Lawson's friends and relatives were sent to the Manzanar internment camp, north of Los Angeles, even though they were born citizens. The Sakai family decided to stop at the camp before heading to Colorado to try to locate friends they knew.

The guards allowed Lawson and his family to enter. The camp was made up of wooden huts and barbed wire fences. Armed guards occupied towers that surrounded the facility. The Sakais' rendezvous with their friends didn't last long. Being at the camp only made the Sakai family worry that the guards would decide to keep them in there, too. Their friends suggested that they leave before it was too late. They took the good advice. The same guard that had allowed them in stood at the gate as they left. Luckily, he did not detain Lawson's family.

At the 442nd Regimental Combat Team reunion in Vegas in 2018, men and women of Japanese descent, too young to have served in World War II, walked around the room. It wasn't uncommon to hear them say, "I had five uncles with the 442nd," or "My father and his cousins were in the 442nd," or "Two of my dad's brothers were killed in the 442nd." The descendants in attendance were proud of their forebears' service and had come to pay their respects.

The fact that so many members of the same families had served in the same regiment was an anomaly by the time World War II began. The military did away with that practice after the Civil War, when entire families were wiped out serving together in the same outfits. Breaking up families across several regiments was a new policy designed to prevent that tragedy from happening again. But the Japanese Americans were an exception to the rule. They all had one thing in common: they and their relatives—because of their descent—were forced into a single regiment designed only for Japanese Americans: the 442nd Regimental Combat Team.

There hadn't always been a Japanese American segregated unit, but by the time Lawson went to enlist it was in full use. Lawson went down to the recruitment station with a group of his childhood friends. They were Caucasian, so they were welcomed right away. When the recruiter looked at Lawson's name on the paper, he realized he was Japanese and told him he couldn't join.

There was a pause as Lawson stood in front of the seated recruiter. He swallowed hard. "But I'm an American," he said.

"Doesn't matter. You're 4C!" the recruiter shot back, sliding him a piece of paper. As Lawson's friends celebrated being one step closer to being in the armed forces, they looked at Lawson. He wasn't smiling. "What's the matter?" they asked.

Lawson held up the piece of paper that the recruiters had handed him: Category 4C, "Enemy Alien," it read. The instant the Japanese attacked the United States, Lawson had lost the same rights other Americans had.

"They aren't going to let me join," Lawson said with difficulty.

"If they aren't going to let you join, we aren't joining either," his friends rejoined. Though happy to have his friends' support, Lawson knew that his friends wouldn't stay out of the military for long. Nobody was going to miss out on the war.

Before the attack on Pearl Harbor, thousands of Japanese Americans were serving in the American military. After the United States declared war on Japan, the men were stripped of their weapons and rank on a dime. These once honorable soldiers were forced to perform latrine duty, kitchen work, and other demoralizing jobs.

Upon hearing about the treatment of Japanese Americans in the military, the Japanese American Citizens League, a civil rights group established in 1929, demanded that Congress give these soldiers a chance. The group insisted that the young Japanese men would be loyal to the United States. The league succeeded in its appeal, and the military soon created the 100th Battalion, an element of 400 men initially designed to test whether the Japanese Americans were up for service. The success of the all–Japanese American unit led the Army to reconsider its decision. It upgraded the 400-man battalion to a regiment of 1,000 men. And so the 442nd Regiment was born.

The original members of the 100th Battalion were already fighting in Italy by the time Lawson started in basic training. General Mark Clark, who was in charge of the Italian campaign, reported back how impressed he was by the 100th Battalion to General Eisenhower. In fact, he demanded Eisenhower send him more Japanese soldiers.

So by 1943, Lawson was drafted and sent to Camp Shelby in Mississippi for basic training, where he met hundreds of other Japanese Americans from California and Hawaii. But things did not go smoothly for the newly formed regiment in Mississippi. The Japanese Americans from Hawaii clashed with California Japanese. "There were cultural differences," Lawson explained. "The Hawaiians were not put in internment camps. We were. The Hawaiian boys also loved to fight in packs. It was never a fair fight with them."

Things eventually calmed down when the Hawaiian Japanese got a tour of the internment camps their counterparts' families were in. This unified the men a little more before their deployment. With some tension still among the ranks, the regiment was soon attached to the Thirty-Fourth Infantry Division and deployed to Italy.

Lawson remembers the first action he saw on the Italian Peninsula like it was yesterday. He first saw fighting at "Hill 140," a position on the Italian coast north of Rome. By the time the 442nd joined up with the 34th Infantry, U.S. forces had already ousted the Germans from Rome and were now on the chase. "Those towns along the coast were all hills," Lawson told me. "Our first battle was in about July. We descended one hill cautiously, not taking fire at all. Then the Germans opened up on us. We got caught in interlocking fires."

Lawson's platoon in E Company, which hadn't heard shots fired in anger yet, began to panic. They did not know what was going on. They were being shot at from the slopes of two different hills. "I could see little puffs of dirt in front of me and didn't realize what it was," Lawson said of the chaos. Bullets suddenly snapped over Lawson's head. He was being shot at for the first time.

The 442nd Regiment immediately began to take casualties. Though Lawson's platoon crawled for cover, the men were still hit with bullets and shrapnel. Two men ran by, dragging another soldier. As Lawson peered over to see the helpless man, he realized it was his company commander. "Our captain was shot dead during the ambush," Lawson remarked. "He was killed right away."

As he told the story of that first day under fire, Lawson imitated the sound of the German burp gun. He remembered the sound of it as easily as if the gun had shot at him yesterday. "*Brrrrrp, Brrrrp*. I remember the rounds kept going over my head because the machine pistol was so powerful it would kick up in the shoulder of the German firing it," he said.

It was also the first time the soldiers of E Company experienced enemy artillery. As the men attempted to move out of the ambush zone and across the hillside, an artillery round exploded, sending shrapnel into Lawson's right leg. The enemy fire prevented Lawson from seeking out a medic. Luckily he was able to render aid to himself while pinned down.

As the green troops of the 442nd tried to orient themselves, the Japanese Americans who had already experienced combat as part of the 100th Battalion were able to outflank the enemy by taking the high ground. "They came out of nowhere and slaughtered the Germans," Lawson said, still in awe of his comrades' heroic actions.

When all was said and done, E Company emerged from their first engagement victorious. "We took a beating, but we didn't lose," Lawson said proudly. "We captured about fifty-six Germans and a lot of equipment." Lawson had met his enemy for the first time, been wounded, and lost friends in his first day in combat. But his involvement was still far from over. The 442nd had to push for Leghorn, the strategically important Italian port city of Livorno.

The men continued to clear the towns along the way. The Germans made their last stand before Leghorn in Luciano. Another officer, this time Lawson's platoon commander and lieutenant, was killed in the fighting.

As Lawson knelt with his squad in a covered position, a mortar round exploded next to them. The incoming shell was silent; the men didn't hear it coming in. When it detonated, five men were wounded. Lawson had shrapnel in his thigh and hip. "I looked over at my other buddy. He was wounded pretty bad," Lawson remembered. "Me and the other guys had minor wounds compared to him, so it made it easy for us to carry him to help."

By the end of July, the new Japanese American regiment had become battle-hardened. After crossing the Arno River and capturing the towns in and around Pisa, the regiment moved into Livorno, their division's objective. They still didn't get a break, just new orders. In August they found out that they would be attached to a new division and sent to France.

Attached to the 36th Infantry Division, the 442nd landed in Marseille, France, and continued to chase the Germans from there. Europeans from small villages saw Asian faces for the first time.

"We landed in France in August and got little to no opposition," Lawson said of the campaign in France. "The Air Corps was doing a great job. I saw whole German convoys destroyed. We made good progress until we reached a place called Bruyères in October."

Bruyères was a railway town. From Bruyères, the German Army used train tracks that spanned all the way to the Western Front to transport men and supplies. "I remember getting ready to enter the town. We were on each side of a flat highway, following it directly into the city, when we began to take heavy fire," Lawson recalled.

Enemy gunshots rang out. The only way for E Company to take cover was to run towards the hills, where there was some advantage of concealment. As they approached the wooded hills, E Company began to experience tree burst, something they hadn't witnessed in Italy. The German artillery, which usually exploded upon hitting the ground, was detonating in the trees above them, creating double the shrapnel due to the wooden shards from trees.

The Germans began to maneuver 88 mm anti-aircraft guns mounted on half-tracks toward the hills Lawson's company was hiding in. "I can still hear that high velocity 'boom' sound they made," Lawson bellowed, again describing the sounds of combat vividly. "It was hard to destroy them because they were on wheels. Once we called for artillery on them, they were already being moved into a different position."

With trees exploding all around, Lawson's company began to take casualties again. This area of France, known as the Vosges Forest, was a region known for its lumber and timber. The logging business was popular here because the trees in the area could be two feet in diameter. That made for tremendous tree burst.

Lawson's company hugged the ground during the bombardment. "If the shrapnel flying around everywhere wasn't bad enough," Lawson exclaimed, "the heavy tree branches were killing us." Lawson shook his head and swallowed hard as he described one of his own men being crushed by a falling chunk of wood. "I saw one man from my own company hugging the ground when a German shell exploded in the tree above him. A large piece of that tree fell and crushed his head. It must have been five hundred pounds or more."

The 442nd moved throughout the hills for another eight days, fighting the Germans at close quarters in the rain and mud. "In those eight days our casualties were high. It really was brutal," Lawson insisted, "but we finally took the city of Bruyères on October 23."

Lawson and the rest of his company expected to be taken off the line, but on October 24 they were given the depressing news that they would be sent back into the mountains again. "We were told there was a lost battalion. We looked around at each other wondering how that was even possible," Lawson said of the men's reaction to the new objective. "We had no idea another battalion was ahead of us, but that's because the generals were competing with one another to be the first to cross into Germany," he explained. "One of them pushed a whole battalion five miles too far ahead and got them surrounded in the mountains by the Germans."

The battalion in question was from the 141st Infantry of the 36th Division. They would go down in history as the "Lost Battalion." Their numbers had dwindled from 1,000 men to some 200. The fog over the French wilderness was so thick that no one could get their exact location. An observation plane crashed trying to spot them, killing one of the pilots. The other pilot survived. When I gave Lawson a puzzled look, he quickly explained, "I only mention the surviving pilot because his son is at this reunion right now."

The men of the Lost Battalion were surrounded, with little food or ammo. The Army thought it was a good idea to load supplies into howitzers and shell the vicinity with materials, but the men came over the radio and screamed that they were taking casualties from their own supplies hitting them at such a high velocity. Lawson thought on their situation with horror. In one attempt, fifty men of the Lost Battalion had tried to make a break for it. Their escape failed miserably. Just five men survived and fell back to the others. After a week of abortive sorties, the Army decided to send a rescue party.

The 442nd Regiment began their push into the Vosges Mountains in search of the Lost Battalion on Lawson's twenty-first birthday. "We were making this morning push, firing from the hip as we went," Lawson said of the action. "I was carrying a Browning automatic rifle when suddenly a German popped right out of a foxhole just feet in front of me."

The German, rifle in shoulder, fired a single shot at Lawson. "I closed my eyes and thought, 'Well, I'm dead,' but somehow the German missed," he told me. Lawson opened his eyes and squeezed the trigger to his BAR. Three rounds from his automatic rifle struck the German soldier in the chest. "The rounds drilled him. I ran right up on him as he fell back and his helmet rolled off."

Lawson squeezed his eyes shut while explaining how he had killed the enemy soldier. "I really hate talking about this," he confessed, "but when I saw his face, he was just a young boy. He was probably more scared than I was. How could he miss me from just ten feet away? But I survived my twenty-first birthday."

In the heat of battle, Lawson continued to push forward until a German hand grenade landed in front of him. He hit the ground, taking the blast from the front. "The potato masher explosion knocked me unconscious," he said. "When I woke up, I was covered in blood, with a massive headache."

A medic hovering over Lawson told him not to worry and that it looked worse than it actually was. He had cuts and scrapes but was able to recover quickly. It was the third time the battalion surgeon would see him in the field hospital.

Several days into the offensive, there was still no sign of the Lost Battalion. Lawson returned to E Company to assist, but the day he returned to the front would be his last day in the Vosges Mountains. "They got us zeroed in with artillery again," Lawson said of the fighting, "and a hunk of steel entered my back." The shrapnel lodged into the left side of his abdomen. He dropped to the ground in immense pain.

"I remember telling the medic just to let me die. I couldn't breathe and it was burning my insides," Lawson recalled. Using both hands, Lawson made out the shape of the shrapnel. "If it went through me and exited my chest, I would have died," he said with a shudder. "I was lucky it went out my side."

The medics hit Lawson with morphine, brought him to the rear, and placed him on a train to Dijon, France. He spent two months there in an Army hospital. "I was wounded on October 28, and on October 30, they finally rescued the Lost Battalion. They were down to 211 men, and we lost 200 just trying to reach them."

Two hundred men dead to save 200. On top of that, no one knew the men had been rescued by an all-Japanese segregated military outfit. It wouldn't be until after the war that this information would be revealed. This single mission helped to change the views of and discrimination against Japanese American soldiers forever. The bravery and sacrifice they displayed to rescue the same men who had judged them as traitors would go down in history.

The campaign in the Vosges Mountains, which lasted from October 15 to October 30, cost the 442nd 800 wounded and 200 KIA (killed in action). And their job still wasn't done. After Lawson healed up for two months, he rejoined the 442nd in January of 1945, just as they received orders to head back to Italy.

They moved through France under the cover of darkness and finally reached a staging area on the French–Italian border. "General Clark didn't want the Germans to know the 442nd was coming back into Italy," Lawson said with a smile on his face. This fact meant the Japanese Americans had made a name for themselves, so much so that they were now being called upon to do what other American regiments had failed to accomplish. "We had to push behind the Gothic Line to oust the remaining Germans on a mountain that had failed to be taken several times by other U.S. forces," Lawson told me, still beaming with pride.

Still only maneuvering at night, the 442nd infiltrated a tiny town called Azzano. There they received orders to strip down and take off packs and any extra gear. They were only allowed to carry their weapons and ammo, and had to cover their canteens and dog tags to prevent them from making noise.

The men began their stealthy hike up the impenetrable hill, Mount Folgorito. At eight o'clock that night, well after sunset, they began their advance, making as little noise as possible—they were barely allowed to breathe. "There was no moon that night," Lawson said of the stealth mission, "but we followed a couple of goat trails with the help of a fourteen-year-old Italian boy."

The men scaled the hill, pulling each other up in steep places one by one. When daybreak hit, they had already reached the top. With no time to sleep, E Company prepared to engage the enemy. "There was an outcropping where our 3rd Battalion could see the enemy guns," Lawson said. "As the sun came up, they caught the Germans still sleeping and opened fire, killing them."

The Germans frantically began to retreat down the hill, taking their equipment and vehicles with them. They made it all the way to the coast of Genoa and into the Po Valley before surrendering. "Three thousand of them surrendered to 300 of us!" Lawson belted out, laughing hysterically at the thought. "To me, that was one of the greatest accomplishments of our regiment. The war ended not too long after that."

I sat in the hotel room with Lawson, completely blown away. He was easily one of the greatest men I'd met. To have him sign the rifle filled me with pride. Today this man could laugh at the fact that he had received four Purple Hearts and turned down pursuing a fifth. He was cursed to be able to remember the exact day he had killed someone, because it fell on his birthday. Yet he was able to channel the negatives of war into a positive, a lesson that can be shown to every living veteran suffering any kind of regret.

Lawson Sakai with the rifle. *Photo courtesy of the author*

"It wasn't always easy for us. When we came home, we drank until we passed out at these reunions," Lawson said of civilian life. "One of my men died of alcoholism, homeless in the streets of Los Angeles."

We concluded our talk and re-entered the hospitality room for the 442nd Regimental Combat Team reunion. A younger Japanese man approached me with a book in his hand. It featured the history of the 442nd. "Would you mind signing this for me?" he asked.

I looked around, knowing that I was the last person in this room that should be asked about the story of the Japanese Americans in World War II.

"Whoa, man. I have no relation to these guys," I said. Nor was I even of the same generation.

"No, it's okay. I want all veterans to sign," the young man insisted.

Not feeling worthy, I flipped through the pages looking for somewhere to put my name. Instead of putting mine, I decided to offer homage to the man who had led me to this point: "In loving memory of PFC Andrew G. Biggio. KIA Sept. 17, 1944. Italy."

It was time to finish this rifle.

CHAPTER EIGHTEEN

Patton's Last Panther

Robert Andry
U.S. Army, 761st Tank Battalion

In November 1944, Robert Andry was the only black man lying in a field hospital in northern France. Both of his arms were splinted and bandaged. His face was covered in oil, and he had burns on his stomach and thighs. Pieces of shrapnel littered his body.

"Attention on deck!" someone screamed from farther down the tent. A colonel had made his way into the make-shift hospital.

"At ease. Relax, men; you all need to heal up," the colonel said as he entered. The Army leader began to make his way down the line of wounded white soldiers, commending all of them for their sacrifice.

As the colonel approached the soldier next to Robert, Robert could hear all the colonel's words to the soldier: "Your country is damn proud of you. We are all proud of you. You're a fine soldier. Great work out there, and get well."

Robert Andry. *Photo courtesy of Robert Andry*

Finally, the colonel reached Robert's cot. "What happened to you, boy, stumble over a bazooka?" The tent erupted in laughter. Somehow, the color of Robert's skin rendered his sacrifice and wounds a joke. The words stuck with Robert Andry forever, even after he was awarded the Purple Heart for wounds sustained in combat.

Seventy-five years later, I was sitting in Robert's living room. "I'm not a murderer. I never been a murderer," he repeated.

"What makes you think you're a murderer?" I replied.

Robert's eyes jolted to the corner of the room, where his wife, son, and daughter were sitting. I was never a fan of interviewing veterans with other people in the room, but I was so close to being done with the rifle project and I didn't want to push the envelope and upset a veteran's family. Plus, I didn't expect Robert's kids to trust some random guy in their house with a rifle.

Robert was holding back. He didn't want the image his family had had of him for over seven decades to be tarnished. He was a religious man; he attended church on both Saturday and Sunday. As he got older, he and his wife had begun to watch church services on television.

"You don't have tell me anything you don't want to," I assured him, "but I am here to share your story, and hopefully teach younger veterans how to live a successful life after combat."

Robert nodded his head up and down. When I began talking to veterans, I had vowed to myself that I would never prod veterans to speak of things they had worked hard to forget. I didn't travel all the way to Bucks, Alabama, to break that promise.

My mission with the rifle was rolling quickly to an end. In just a couple of years, I had gotten over 150 veterans to add their names to the weapon. As the popularity of my project grew, veterans began to reach out to me. A continuous stream of Facebook messages and emails from potential signatories of the rifle flooded my inbox. But while my hobby was gaining traction, my day job got increasingly tough.

In the summer of 2020, I was a white American police officer during the Black Lives Matter movement, in the middle of a controversial presidency, while a series of police brutality incidents occurred seemingly on a weekly basis. The environment of my job, along with the COVID-19 pandemic, was a mounting obstacle preventing me from meeting new veterans and capturing their stories.

My department demanded forced overtime, training, and remaining on constant standby for protests and riots. I had to choose wisely which veteran I would interview next. Although my wife was 100 percent supportive of my mission, we now had a one-year-old son. All these issues meant less time with my family. My next veteran I was going to see had to be a great story, because it could be one of my last interviews before calling a wrap on the project.

Race tensions were high in America, and as I gazed at my rifle with the television news streaming in the background, all I could hear was how relations between cops and black Americans were fragile. That was when I realized how many white men were on the rifle. Nearly all the signatures, with the exception of some of the Native American code talkers and some Japanese Americans, were those of white men.

This wasn't done intentionally. Black Americans were segregated in the 1940s military. They didn't make up a serious number of servicemen compared to white Americans, and many often served in non-combat, rear echelon duties as cooks, supply truck drivers, and stretcher bearers.

However, a handful of examples proved that there were exceptions. The Ninety-Second Infantry Division, also known as the "Buffalo Soldiers" for the buffalo patch they wore on their shoulder, was an entirely black infantry division that fought valiantly in Italy. Earlier in my travels, I had had the honor of meeting Rothacker Smith, who had been a medic with that division. Rothacker was wounded and captured by the Germans during the war. He signed my rifle, but he had already written his own book and had his own exhibit at the National WWII Museum. His story had already been told and preserved for the world to see.

There was also the Ninety-Third Division, another black segregated infantry unit that was sent to the Pacific. I had the honor of meeeting Asa Davison in his home in Morgantown, West Virginia. However, I was a few years too late. Mr. Davison was weak and on oxygen. We could not conduct a full interview. Still, having him sign the rifle to represent his division was fulfilling.

So here I was, close to being finished with my project, with limited divisions from which to find surviving black veterans to interview. To give a sense of scale, nearly 100 divisions were mobilized in World War II. It was already difficult to find living World War II veterans in general; narrowing the pool down to such a small window made finding these specific veterans who had served in segregated units almost impossible.

I was having a tough go at my research until I heard the phrase "Come Out Fighting," the motto of the 761st Tank Battalion, an African American tank unit that fought in Europe. As I did further research on this tank battalion, I became more intrigued. Their unit crest was, fittingly enough, a black panther baring its teeth.

During an overnight shift at work, I found an article written by a Gulf Power employee honoring his World War II veteran father. Lo and behold, his dad had served with the 761st Tank Battalion, and his name was Robert Curtis Andry, from Bucks, Alabama. I found a phone number for Mr. Andry but waited several days to call. I pondered whether he would be receptive to a random phone call from some kid way up north. As usual, I worried that he might write me off as another con artist looking to take advantage of his later years. I eventually gained the courage to call him. After explaining myself, Mr. Andry displayed typical southern hospitality and welcomed me to Alabama. Before I knew it, I was on a plane to the Deep South.

I flew into New Orleans and paid a visit to the National WWII Museum. I began to tear up, thinking that the rifle I had worked so hard on might be on display here one day as an exhibit.

The next morning came, and it was time to go meet Mr. Andry. When I pulled up to his home I was greeted by Robert himself, who looked like he was in his late seventies, not ninety-five. His Purple Heart was pinned to his polo. Robert was a handsome man and proud of his service. I met his daughter and son. Upon my arrival, his daughter immediately asked me the question all family members do: "How did you hear about my father?"

I explained that I had read an article by a man I presumed to be her brother. Her eyes lit up, and she walked over to her mother with a sense of urgency. "Mom, did you hear that?" she asked the frail old woman sitting in a recliner on the other side of the room. "He found dad because of Vincent!" Robert's daughter walked back over to me. "Vincent died of cancer three years ago."

It felt providential. Robert's son, although no longer with us, had something to do with my rendezvous with his dad. If not for him, I never would have found Robert Andry. I never would have had the chance to share his story with the world.

Robert and I got to talking right off the bat. He added a beautiful signature to the rifle and lifted the weapon in his arms. "We didn't carry this in a tank," he said, laughing.

"I know, too big," I shot back.

"But I did train with it at basic," he continued. Robert slapped the rifle with his palm. "761st Tank Battalion, Patton's Army!" he said to himself, his eyes glued to the weapon.

"Did you meet Patton personally?" I asked.

"Oh yes, he said some things to us," he replied. I did not want to get too far ahead of myself. I was keen to have Robert start at the beginning. I wanted to know about his early life, especially his experience of growing up black in the South. He told me that he had grown up in this very area with six siblings.

"The day I left for basic training was the same day my older sister left home, at 5:00 a.m.," Robert remembered. "We were both leaving home for the first time. She was going to become a nun, and I was going to Camp Shelby to be a soldier. We were both going to do God's mission for us," he said. "Quite frankly, I did not experience much racism growing up. It wasn't until I joined the military that I saw the brunt of it." While I was disappointed to hear this sad commentary on life in the armed forces, I understood that Robert's experience must have been very different from my own—and from that of many of the veterans I had interviewed. I often expect military service to be the best part of someone's life, but that is not the case for everyone. Robert was thrown into a government-run machine which segregated people of color. He was then sent to multiple states around the country and exposed for the first time to how black Americans were treated outside his little neighborhood in Alabama.

"I had to report to Camp Shelby, Mississippi. There I took a test with other black draftees. Those who scored high enough were transferred to Fort Knox, Kentucky, to Armor School. I happened to be one of those soldiers," Robert told me.

While at Fort Knox, southern black men and northern black men collided for the first time during basic training. "You don't sound like you're from the South," another black soldier said to Robert while standing in formation.

"I didn't know I was supposed to sound a certain way," he replied. The soldier questioning Robert was Roy King, a man from Michigan. Robert was educated and had attended Catholic school; he did not possess a deep southern drawl as seen in the movies, like the northern black soldiers had been expecting.

Over the course of training, Robert and Roy became friends as they transformed into soldiers. They spent several weeks learning the basics: marching, saluting, shooting, and map reading. Their role did not become evident until the day a 38-ton steel machine with tracks came roaring down the road and stopped in front of the men. It was an M4 Sherman tank. When the top hatch opened, the men, preparing to see a white officer, saw a black face instead. "This will be your new home. You will eat, sleep, and piss in this thing if you have to in combat," the battalion commander announced to the men.

The men were split up into different companies forming the 761st Tank Battalion. Robert and Roy were separated, as each of them was assigned to different platoons within Company B. Robert's platoon boasted a salty lieutenant named Jackie Robinson, the future MLB Hall of Famer.

"Wow," I exclaimed, interrupting Robert in the middle of his story. "But he didn't go to Europe with you guys, right?" I had read that Robinson was court-martialed for a racial incident in which he refused to go to the back of a bus while on liberty, and so he was transferred to a training unit, leaving the 761st Tank Battalion.

"We didn't know why he was transferred out of our unit at that time. We learned later when we came home from the war and he was running around a baseball field," Robert remarked.

As training continued, the men learned the ins and outs of being a true tanker. Robert was his tank's gunner: he would bear responsibility for the 76 mm cannon on the tank and operating the .50 caliber machine gun mounted on the turret if need be. The men were proud, and they impressed their white command staff as well. As their motivation grew, they pushed the envelope on Jim Crow laws when on liberty.

"Two men in our outfit were arrested for not obeying certain color laws when in town," Robert recollected. The men were prepared to fire up all the tanks and go down to the police station to get them out, but Army leaders were able to defuse the situation before it got out of hand.

As the 761st became a cohesive fighting unit, the entire tank battalion was transferred to Camp Hood, Texas, to perform war maneuvers. Racial tensions were no different there. Soldiers from the 761st were outraged to see German prisoners of war treated better than they were. Captured Germans served as warehouse clerks and could boss black Americans around when issuing gear.

While in Texas, Robert and the others learned about the D-Day invasion. It was no longer a matter of if the 761st would go to war, but when. After completing their training in late August of 1944, the tank battalion received orders to head to England. "We spent about a month in England. We let our tanks and gear catch up to us from the States," Robert said.

By early October, landing crafts loaded with tanks, half-tracks, and jeeps belonging to the first colored armored unit to fight in Europe crossed the English Channel and landed on Omaha Beach, Normandy.

The ship's ramp went down, and B Company's tanks made their way through low ocean water and up the sand, instantly making history.

Robert waited patiently for his Sherman tank's turn to exit the landing craft. The inside of the landing ship tank (LST) was filled with fumes as each tank fired up and made its way onto French soil. Robert's tank commander, Lieutenant John Long, stood proudly outside of the hatch as their turn to go ashore came. While the tank followed the others on a trail through the beachhead, Robert joined his commander on top of the tank, behind the mounted .50 caliber. "You could still see all the destruction from the battle months before," he said of the scene, "destroyed pill boxes, bomb craters, burnt vehicles."

The 761st had no time to waste. They drove four hundred miles in six days, trying to catch up to General Patton. French civilians crowded the men whenever they stopped. The French did not seem to care what color the soldiers were, just that they were liberators.

While the battalion staged in the town of Saint-Nicolas-de-Port, they were interrupted by a series of jeeps and half-tracks. The black tankers were ordered into formation, and suddenly a white officer with dual pistols stood up on the hood of a half-track. It was Patton himself.

"Men, you're the first Negro tankers to ever fight in the American Army. I would never have asked for you if you weren't good," Patton belted out from atop the tank. "I have nothing but the best in my Army. I don't care what color you are as long as you go up there and kill those Kraut sons of bitches. Everyone has their eyes on you and is expecting great things from you. Most of all, your race is looking forward to your success. Don't let them down, and damn you, don't let me down! They say it is patriotic to die for your country. Well, let's see how many patriots we can make out of those German sons of bitches!"

Patton descended from the tank and spoke to some of the men individually. "We were all proud to meet him," Robert remembered. "He told us were helping push towards Nancy, France, and were going to be attached to the 26th Infantry Division for their tank support." A few days later, the men of the 761st entered combat.

Starting the first week of November 1944, Robert's tank, commanded by Lieutenant John Long, buttoned up for combat in the vicinity of Nancy. Shells from the German heavy artillery landed in and around the columns of tanks, rocking the men inside. Robert held on to his rosary beads as the tanks formed a perimeter for A Company and C Company to complete their first attack on the towns. When they arrived at their rendezvous point, Robert and his men went out for fresh air. Robert took in the destruction around him. The first thing he noticed was a dead cow hanging from a tree. An artillery blast had tossed its carcass into the air like it was nothing. "If a shell could do that to a cow," Robert wondered, "what could it do to me?"

Robert hopped back into the tank and kept his eyes on his sights for fleeing Germans. Ambulances and jeeps rushed the wounded and dead in and out of the set perimeter as the 761st Tank Battalion lost its first tanks and, sadly, its first men. The tankers won their first battle later that day, taking a strategic hill, but it did not come without sacrifice.

The morning after their first triumph, Robert's tank was the first to roll into the village of Morville. His old buddy, Roy King, was in the tank behind them, followed by the rest of B Company. Once they arrived, it was time for Robert to let go of his rosary beads and look down the sights of his 76 mm cannon again. The weather was miserable from the start, with rain, wind, and sleet leaving little more for Robert to see than a silhouette around the tanks.

"Lieutenant Long had communication with infantry troops asking for tank support. We approached the town with them, destroying anything that was called out as a machine gun emplacement or troops in buildings. Aside from me and the lieutenant, there were three other men in the tank operating machine guns and helping me load my big gun," Robert recalled.

As Robert's column got closer to the town, the Twenty-Sixth Infantry Division soldiers darted from street to street. The infantrymen were continuously gunned down by Germans holding defensive positions in the town's buildings. Robert fired shell after shell into the structures, hoping to take out the hiding Germans. Other tanks from the company began to do the same. The wrath of several Sherman tanks wreaked havoc on a series of homes and dwellings. Smoke began to float in the air. When a single German soldier appeared through the cloud of smoke, fleeing from a smoldering building, Lieutenant Long called out "Fire!"

Robert hesitated, and Long called out again: "Fire!" Robert shot the German soldier with a single round from his 76 mm cannon. The enemy combatant, standing fifty meters away, turned into dust.

Robert sat back as friendly forces cleared out more buildings ahead of him. The tank gunners peppered .30 caliber machine gun fire into retreating Germans. There was a short break while the tanks waited for the infantry to catch up, but danger still lurked at every turn. Robert and his fellow soldiers dismounted to clear some roadblocks that the Germans had set up in their path. One of the men behind Robert got out of his tank to retrieve a Luger off a dead German. When he went down to pick it up, he found that it was booby-trapped with a makeshift bomb. The man tripped the detonator, and the explosion killed him instantly.

Once the infantrymen caught up, the American troops continued their push towards Morville. Constant artillery barrages forced the infantry to take cover. The artillery fire made the infantry less thorough in clearing the area of German soldiers. They were anxious to remain in cover from artillery fire and haphazardly kept track of which buildings they had already cleared of German foot soldiers and which they hadn't. Their carelessness would prove disastrous for Robert and his crew.

As Robert's tank approached a series of dwellings that should have been cleared by the infantry, a sudden attack came from an opening in a home. A group of rockets twirled their way towards Robert's tank. The enemy had fired German Panzerfaust guns, propelled explosives designed to take out armored vehicles.

By the time Robert saw the flaming rockets spinning towards the tank through his sights, it was too late. The warhead penetrated the front of the turret, and the accompanying explosion blew chunks of skin and flesh from Robert's arms and legs. His body was peppered with shrapnel and sprayed with hydraulic fluid from the tank's turret. The blast knocked him unconscious and blew the eye socket out of the gun loader sitting next to him. Robert's tank was out of the fight, and so was King's tank, which had been rolling behind him. Some fifteen American infantrymen lay dead or wounded on the street. German soldiers opened fire from roofs and cellar windows.

"I didn't come to until I was being pulled out of the turret," Robert said. "I was in pain all over." As Robert's limp, bleeding body was dragged out of his tank, the battle continued to rage. The only option for the medics was to stick him with morphine. They laid him down and temporarily buried him in the dirt, exposing only his face. "This protected me from the elements, and possibly any indirect fire landing around us," Robert explained. "My loader and I were buried around 10:00 a.m. and not recovered until 10:00 p.m. that night."

Robert's embarrassing encounter with the racist colonel in the American field hospital occurred soon after he was recovered from the battlefield. Within days, he was transferred to Paris, where he spent more time in a bigger hospital. In Paris, he came across another black tanker, a soldier from his buddy King's tank.

"That's when I found out King didn't make it," Robert grimaced. After being struck by a rocket, Sergeant Roy King exited his tank only to be shot by German machine gun fire while seeking cover. Although King's tank was unable to drive or fire its main gun, his crew reoccupied the vehicle multiple times in order to man the .30 caliber machine guns. Their brave fighting wasn't enough to save King, who had died on the spot.

Robert Andry was eventually evacuated to England with the other soldiers who had been wounded in the advance through France. His unit went on to fight in the Battle of the Bulge, the Rhineland, and Germany, liberating scores of concentration camp survivors. While his unit went on to make history as the first black tank outfit in the war, Robert faced a long road to recovery.

After his sojourn in England, Robert was transferred to a medical facility in Memphis, Tennessee. "While recuperating in the hospital, we

Robert Andry with the rifle. *Photo courtesy of the author*

were given passes to go home on convalescent leave," Robert recalled. "I had one arm in a sling, and the other bandaged up pretty good. I had to go to the bus terminal first in order to catch a train back to Alabama."

As Robert waited at the bus terminal, a tall white man approached him. "Hey nigger, you're supposed to wait for the bus over there! Get out back!" the man yelled. Robert could not believe it. After everything he had gone through, he was still being treated like a second-class citizen. Even with his wounds of war still visible, some racist civilian, not even a member of the armed forces, was harassing him.

It pained me deeply to hear this horrible memory still etched in Robert's brain after seventy-five years. My heart ached when I listened to white veterans' war experiences, but here in Alabama with Robert, my heart ached for what he had experienced on the home front.

It took over five years for Robert to be able to move his left wrist. Shrapnel remains in his body to this day. He had survived fighting the Eleventh and Thirteenth German Panzer Divisions. He stayed close to

God when he returned home. He has been married for seventy-two years and raised eight beautiful children.

Robert had never spoken about the war after he came back home. That is why his family gathered in the room for my interview—they were eager to learn of their father's heroic deeds for the first time. He lived his life the way his fallen comrades would have wanted him to. He was proud to be one of "Patton's Panthers."

CHAPTER NINETEEN

Finding Andy

Ed Hess and John Hymer
U.S. Army, Thirty-Fourth Infantry Division

Media, Pennsylvania

In December of 1946, Ed Hess was finally settling back in at home. Like many Americans who had served in the war, he hadn't seen his house since 1943. It was Christmastime in Media, Pennsylvania, and it was the first time in years that all the kids from the neighborhood were back together. Word spread that many of them would be gathering at the Veterans of Foreign Wars (VFW) post for a Christmas party.

Ed walked into the hall of the VFW and found it packed. Holiday decorations hung from the ceiling, and a Christmas tree stood lit up in the corner. The bar was full of men drinking, laughing, and conversing. Ed grabbed a beer and walked into a corner, where he saw a man he recognized from when he was in high school talking to a group.

"Cheers," Ed said as he approached, raising his glass to the man he remembered from his childhood.

"Yeah, cheers. Where were you in the war exactly?" the man asked.

"Italy," Ed replied.

The small group of men began to laugh. "Ha! How's the pope doing?" The men were all Marines and had served in the South Pacific.

"Man, I wish I could have hung out in Italy!" another Marine said. The men continued to make fun of the Italian campaign, downplaying it as if it had been some sort of vacation.

Ed, now ninety-nine years old, gazed down, reminiscing about the Marines who had embarrassed him seventy-five years before. It still bothered him that they had thought about his service as a joke. "I tried to laugh it off with them, but I couldn't," Ed said, still visibly upset by the interaction. "We all knew the Marines had it rough, no doubt, but Italy wasn't a picnic. I was pretty bitter after that and didn't get involved with veterans' activities for a long time."

Ed had a Rolling Rock beer in front of him. I had never had a drink with a man who was a few months away from turning one hundred years old. The rifle was on a table in front of us, almost entirely full of signatures at this point except for one or two spots. I knew that I had to make those spots count.

After hearing the stories of veterans who had served around the world, I knew I had to get serious about finding anyone who might have been on that hill in Italy on that fateful day when Andy Biggio, my great-uncle, was killed in action. After all, that was what had started this whole rifle project to begin with.

Ed had been there. I found Ed's name in an archived newspaper article from twenty years before, when he had served as the grand marshal in his local Memorial Day parade. He was quoted as being in the same division, same regiment, and same company as Andy. I called the phone number I found listed for him, and his son answered. Ed was still alive. I drove six hours to Pennsylvania to meet with them in the same VFW where Marines had laughed him off seven decades earlier.

When I got into town, I arrived at the VFW before Ed and his son. I ordered a beer, and the locals asked what had brought me there. Just as I finished explaining the purpose of my visit, the buzzer to the door went off. On the security camera behind the bar, I saw a man with a walker entering the bar. It was Ed.

I knew this could be the closest I would ever get to knowing what had happened on September 17, 1944, the day Andy lost his life. Ed would be one of the final pieces to this puzzle and one of the last men to sign the rifle.

As he walked into the bar with his son trailing him, I extended my hand. He shook it and proceeded into a separate room away from the bar, to avoid the noise and give us privacy. I went to pay for my drink. "Your money is no good here," the bartender insisted, sliding my twenty-dollar bill back to me.

Ed knew why I was there. He kept his head down and made himself comfortable in the room used for playing darts. Unlike the other veterans, who were prepared for a list of my questions, Ed leaned right in and started on his own.

Finding Andy

"I joined the 34th Division right before they attacked Monte Cassino," Ed Hess explained. "A shell blew up a house that I and four others were in. I was buried up to my armpits in debris before being pulled out. My other squad members were killed. I survived only to end up with a bad concussion." This event happened while he was serving with G Company of the 135th Regiment.

Shortly after this, Ed was transferred to Company B. "The same company as your uncle. They needed more bodies," he said. "The division was marching through liberated Rome."

It made perfect sense to me. According to Andy's letters, he had joined the 34th Division as a replacement just before taking Rome. Once they left the city, the 135th Regiment got into some intense fighting. While going up the west coast of Italy in June and July of 1944, they often caught up with the retreating German Army. I didn't need a history book to tell me that. It was in Andy's letters.

"In the outskirts of a town called Rosignano, if we knew where the Jerries were, we would sneak past their pillboxes on elevated terrain, lowering dynamite concealed in a suitcase down by rope," Ed told me. "The explosion would blow the face off the concrete pillboxes. We could see the Jerries trying to push the suitcase away, but it didn't do them any good."

His account of the fighting up the coast of Italy aligned with the stories from Carl DiCicco and Lawson Sakai, who were both also with the Thirty-Fourth Red Bull Division. "We had the month of August off to rest, then were ordered to a staging area outside the town of Barberino around September 12, 1944. We could see the hills in the distance that were our new objective. As we neared, it looked like someone had taken a chain saw to all the trees. The Germans had cut down everything so they would have a clear field of fire on us," Ed remembered.

The men were caked with mud because it was the rainy season. With all the incoming mortars, they were constantly diving onto their stomachs, but they had nowhere to seek cover, not even a tree to hide behind. The hill was littered with barbed wire entanglements and camouflaged pillboxes.

"Our company commander, Captain Drury, was the first one killed on September 14," Ed said. "He crept up with a few others to do some recon, and a sniper shot him." The sniper fire pinned the men down for several hours. The Germans were also lobbing grenades down at the men and calling in mortars.

"We were a decent way up the hill and began to dig in," Ed said of the fighting. "Company B had to disperse so much that they were now only communicating in platoon-size elements. We all felt it was a suicide mission. Some men considered mutiny."

As they lay dug in on the hillside, Ed reached his breaking point. "I just started saying to myself, 'Why should I have to die here? I have been carrying the BAR for nine months. I deserve a break. I shouldn't have to stay on the front line until I'm dead.'" He pleaded with his platoon commander to be sent back down the hill. "There are plenty of jobs I can do in the rear, sir, I have been carrying the BAR since Cassino," Ed said to him.

The lieutenant told Ed he would not be allowed off the front line. But for some reason, a few minutes later, another soldier came up to him and took his BAR away from him. The soldier informed Ed that the lieutenant wanted him to make his way back down the hill towards the company headquarters.

Ed walked a mile or so back down the hill. He was safe for now, and he worked in the company headquarters for several days. "After a few days, I began to hear how much of a hard time my company was having back up the hill," he remembered. Another officer in the command post approached Ed and aggressively asked why he was in the rear and not with the others up on the hill.

Ed explained what had happened and that his lieutenant had sent him down to the rear.

"Bullshit," the other lieutenant said. "Take the GRO men up to your company now!"

The GRO men were the grave registration officers. The men, along with some replacement troops, began to make their way up the slippery hill. It was Ed's first time back on the front line in a few days.

"As the hill flattened out a little, that's when I saw them. Thirty-seven of them," Ed said as he began to cry in front of me and his son. "Thirty-seven of them," he kept repeating, before explaining that he was speaking about the thirty-seven soldiers from his company he had found lying dead, lined up next to one another in dirty, blood-soaked uniforms, waiting to be collected.

One of them was Andy Biggio.

"The GRO men started picking them up. We carried them down the hill," Ed said through sobs. The men were forced to carry the bodies of their fellow comrades on stretchers down the slippery, muddy hill.

He hung his head. Did he feel guilt? Still, after all this time? After all, he never would have made it to ninety-nine years of age if he hadn't requested to come off the front line that day. "So many men got hurt or killed, and yet I never got a scratch," Ed said as he wiped tears from his eyes.

"Well, I'm sure you have been living your life the way they would have wanted you to," I said hesitantly. In the back of my mind, I knew

Ed Hess with the rifle. *Photo courtesy of the author*

some information was missing about exactly what had happened to Andy in those days Ed came off the line. I was proud and heartbroken that my nineteen-year-old uncle had stayed in his position on the hill until his death. Like Ed, he hadn't wanted to be up there either. In his last letter to my great-grandmother, Andy expressed not wanting to "go back up the hill," and begged for her to mail him a cross to wear around his neck.

Ed went on. "When I went up the hill, I passed John Hymer. He doesn't live too far from here."

"Wait? What?" I asked in disbelief.

"Yes, another man from our company lives an hour from here. He's still alive," he responded. Ed gave me the address in Bridgeton, New Jersey.

Ed continued talking, but I could no longer concentrate on what he was saying. I couldn't believe I had found two of these guys, an hour apart from one another, after I had spent months looking across the entire country for one. Would John have more answers about my great-uncle?

At the end of my interview with Ed, I was satisfied to see him sign the rifle. He had been living with survivor's guilt for an eternity. He had come home from the war, worked for forty years, gotten married, retired from two jobs, and had two kids. He had taken care of his disabled son until his death just two years before. Ed could have come home, drank at bars, and pounded his chest pretending to be someone he wasn't, but he remained quiet, humble, and honorable.

Bridgeton, New Jersey

The next morning, I drove straight to the Hymer residence in New Jersey. John and his wife knew I was coming and were delighted. "It's so great to have someone interested in all of this after all this time has passed," his wife said, letting me in the door. The two had been married for seventy-one years. John was now ninety-six years old. He shook my hand as I entered their small home.

"This rifle led me here," I explained, placing the plastic case on the living room floor. When I opened it, showing all the names, the couple was in awe. I pointed to the last available spot. "You, my friend, are going to sign right there," I told John.

"What did you say your uncle's name was?" John asked loudly. He was now hard of hearing,

I wrote down B-I-G-G-I-O on a piece of paper and showed him. He nodded, remembering the name but not the face of the boy who had been with the company for only a few months before being killed. John picked up where Ed had left off, telling me the story of the advance up that hill outside of Barberino in mid-September.

"I remember Barberino before we left the staging area," he began. "Some of the guys who were of Italian descent in the company were given civilian clothes. Our commander ordered them to walk into town and see what they could find out."

The soldiers who could speak Italian—mostly from New York, Philadelphia, and Boston—returned with some intelligence to report. "They were able to find out where the Jerries were," John said, "and the last time they were around."

In the second week of September, B Company patrolled through a village just before ascending its first hill. "One of the officers stepped on a mine, wounding him seriously," John told me. Aggravated that the locals hadn't warned the soldiers about the mines, one soldier released a farmer's sheep from their pen, herding them in the direction of the mine field.

"I remember the sheep stepping on the mines, exploding one after another," John told me. "It cleared most of the mines for us." As John walked through the rows of dead and dying sheep, some of them were still thrashing around violently with no legs. "It was a disturbing sight, but I continued to rush forward. There was scattered artillery enemy fire coming in."

Immersed in a macabre scene before they even reached their objective, Hill 650, the company advanced its way through the rest of the village. The Americans set up a command post at the base of the hill. There were already several goat paths leading up the terrain. "We began heading up," John said, "and as Ed told you, it really did seem like suicide."

The vegetation disappeared as they climbed the hillside. They were occasionally shot at but didn't know from where. "A few scouts would sneak up, then come back to inform us of pillboxes, trenches, and barbed wire ahead," John said of the climb. "We tried to stay off the paths, but we had no other option. You could see ropes hanging off the sides of the hill that the Germans had been using. Finally, we were pinned down by accurate sniper fire."

As the sun set, B Company began to advance under darkness before digging in. It was their first night on the hill. When the sun came up the next morning, it unveiled an intimidating sight. "Rows of barbed wire prevented access up the hill," John recalled. "Beyond the barbed wire were trenches and dugouts."

John was ordered to crawl up and start clipping the barbed wire with bolt cutters. He and another soldier crawled on their knees and elbows to the first strand of concertina wire. As they began to cut it, they looked up and saw two Germans standing over them, watching. John froze, but the Germans didn't shoot. They just walked away.

The other American soldiers who were watching began to whistle and waved them back. "They knew we were spotted," John explained. As soon as John got back to the foxhole, a mortar barrage began to rain down on B Company, continuing for several minutes. Most of the men were caught out of their foxholes. "We lay on our bellies and just prayed," John said of the shelling. "It was a barrage like no other!"

Several men were wounded. The Americans were in desperate need of counter-artillery fire, but they were not getting it. As the men backed their way down the hill, it became clear why they couldn't get friendly artillery fire returned. The radioman lay face down. Shrapnel had entered his lower body and penetrated the radio. When the medics rolled him over, they saw that it was Andy Biggio.

As John continued to paint the picture for me, I could only hope that Andy had died fast. The only people who might have heard his last words were the members of his platoon who surrounded him after the smoke cleared. But even they wouldn't survive the coming days.

In his last letter home, on September 12, 1944, Andy told his family that he had just volunteered to carry the radio. Andy had a bad feeling then, and he asked his mother to send him a gold cross to wear around his neck. He admitted to being scared and not wanting to go up those hills outside Barberino, but he did it anyway.

Andy was the only man killed in the barrage that day. While others hugged the ground or ran for their lives, he remained standing, attempting to keep his eyes on the enemy positions to relay messages over the radio. That's when a mortar shell landed behind him, killing him.

Andy died on September 17.

Company B made several more attempts to summit the hill and eventually penetrated the Gothic Line, but the victory came with a cost. "We took on so many casualties in the coming weeks up there, some guys just walked off—deserted!" John exclaimed. "Other men were refusing orders. It got ugly. The company had to send us replacements, but they weren't infantrymen; they were AA gunners and Gurkhas from India."

The AA gunners were men who often stayed in the rear and kept watch for enemy planes. They were not used to being on the front lines. "When the fighting became close quarters, I asked one of the AA gunner replacements in the foxhole behind me to keep watch while I cleaned the mud out of my rifle," John said, remembering the chaos on the front lines. "He didn't, and the Germans counterattacked. Suddenly someone was pulling me out of my foxhole. It was a German lifting me up by the back of my neck!"

A machine gunner in a foxhole fifty yards behind John fired a burst, killing the German. "I swear to God, if he hadn't shot that German, I wouldn't be here. They were either going to capture me or kill me," John remarked. "It was a lucky shot, too, for a machine gun." After the counterattack was repulsed, John cursed the replacement AA gunner.

The men were soon ordered to advance. B Company began to hook right around the hill again to avoid more barbed wire and mines. "The Germans had a U-shaped trench that wrapped around the hill. We tried to outflank it," John said.

While attempting to go around the enemy defensive position, John came across a series of foxholes. "I saw a man in a foxhole. I said, 'Hey buddy, are you with the Ninety-First Division?' I knew they were somewhere on the right side of us."

The man turned his head. He was wearing a German helmet.

"'Americana! Americana!' the Jerry started to yell," John told me, remembering his dangerous mistake. "I raised my rifle and shot him in the foxhole. My platoon sergeant, Sergeant Hart, jumped into the next foxhole and began stabbing the other German."

B Company had just infiltrated the German lines by accident, but it was a blessing in disguise. As soon as the Americans poured into the enemy trench, the soldiers began to hold their hands up and yell, "We Yugoslavs! We Yugoslavs!" Fifty-six Germans surrendered to John and his platoon. Although some of the enemy soldiers could have been Yugoslavian, the Americans had been fighting the German Fourth Paratrooper

Division. "They could have been Yugoslavian, but it didn't matter," John remarked. "None of us would know the difference anyway."

One of the Germans led John to a barn on the other side of the hill, where the men kept their blankets and food. The man reached under a blanket and handed John a heart-shaped watch. John refused to take the prisoner's souvenir. "I felt bad," he said of the experience. "He was a soldier just like me, and probably didn't want to be there either. I let him keep his personal belongings."

John and the German, who had been trying to kill each other just minutes before, shared a moment at the top of the hill. "Next thing you know, another American came into the barn and ripped the watch out of his hands and kept it for himself," John told me. The German kept his head down and was forced out of the barn at gunpoint. "I felt bad for him, but there was nothing I could say."

The prisoners were marched down the hill to battalion headquarters. Americans collected the enemy machine guns that were strewn about. The Americans had suffered serious casualties, but they had accomplished their objective. "We went up that hill with 180 men," John said, shaking his head, fighting back emotions. "We had 25 men left by October."

The Gothic Line was finally penetrated. Hitler's stronghold in Italy collapsed, but it took as many Americans down with it as it could.

Private First Class Andy Biggio was one of them.

These were the last pieces of the puzzle I needed. I buckled the rifle in its case for the last time. John was the last interview on my journey. My mission was complete. I thanked him and his wife. They were sad to see me go.

"I hope I helped you understand a little more about how it was," John said.

Trying to hold it together, all I could say was, "You did, John. You did."

CHAPTER TWENTY

Saying Goodbye

Boston, Massachusetts

On the long drive back to Boston, I thought about Andy's last days. He was only one of the hundreds of thousands of other eighteen- and nineteen-year-old Americans whose names we will never know. They were just starting to live. They were young men with a sense of patriotic duty and courage they didn't know they had. To this day, some of them still lie where they fell seventy-five years ago. They remain in Italy, France, Belgium, Luxembourg, and the Pacific Islands, countries that host our cemeteries that hardly anyone visits anymore.

On my mission to hear these soldiers' stories, I was able to say good-bye to some of America's last veterans of World War II. They passed on some of life's most important lessons to me.

They taught me that there is life after war. They showed me how to be a survivor, not a victim. They encouraged me to find something after the military to keep myself occupied. They told me not to dwell on things that can't be changed. And they drilled it in me that veterans owe it to the men who didn't come home to carry on with integrity, even when times get tough—and to live a good life, have a family, another career, and a purpose.

I met these veterans in the final stages of their lives. I met them when they were hardly able to walk, eat, answer the door, or care for themselves. They weren't always as vulnerable as they were when I met them. They wore the uniform honorably. Without question, every one of them lived out lives that exhibit how military service creates strong character.

One day I'll tell my kids how I was able to meet these men who helped save the world. They became my brothers. Now when I see the street sign dedicated to Private First Class Andy Biggio, I don't just see his name. I see all the men on the rifle.

Of the nearly two hundred veterans featured on the rifle, twenty passed away before this book was finished. As I write this passage, only 300,000 of the 16 million World War II veterans remain. They will only be able to tell their own stories for another few years. Then it will be up to us to tell those stories for them so that they are not forgotten.

The World War II veterans will join the rank of Frank Buckles, America's last World War I veteran. And though I regrettably dismissed that particular World War I veteran as boring on that fifth grade field trip so long ago, I now understand the importance of paying respect to people who sacrificed life and limb for their fellow citizens. We can all honor our veterans by showing them the time and attention they deserve, thinking about their stories and what they have to offer us. Their heroism, duty, courage, and sacrifice still have a lot to teach us about our own lives—both those of us who have worn our country's uniform and those who haven't.

The last stop for the rifle is a museum—which one, I have yet to decide. The once-clean M1 Garand is completely covered in names, places, and battles written on the gun by a generation of warriors. Those names, places, and battles come with stories of spirit, grit, and courage. I spent several years on a journey to get the rifle filled with names; my journey now is to carry on their legacy even when the rifle is not by my side.

The World War II veterans may have signed it as old men, but they were once the strongest warriors of all time. That is how they will always be remembered. As generations fade, history constantly shifts. It's important to keep the facts, stories, and truth alive, because no matter your age, war never leaves you.

ACKNOWLEDGMENTS

The Rifle Signatures, the Warriors

To the men and women who taught me so much, trusted me, and allowed me to bring up the worst of memories in the last stages of their life:

1. **CWO2 HERSHEL "WOODY" WILLIAMS–U.S. MARINES**
   Unit: C Company, 1st Battalion, 3rd Marine Division
   Battles: Gaum, Iwo Jima
   Medals: Medal of Honor, Purple Heart

2. **ROBERT MAXWELL–U.S. ARMY**
   Unit: HQ Company, 7th Infantry Regiment, 3rd Infantry Division
   Battles: North Africa, Casablanca, Salerno, Anzio, Monte Cassino, southern France
   Medals: Medal of Honor, Silver Star (2x), Bronze Star, Purple Heart (2x), Combat Infantryman Badge

3. **SANTO DISALVO–U.S. ARMY**
   Unit: G Company, 143rd Infantry Regiment, 36th Infantry Division
   Battles: Salerno, San Pietro, southern France
   Medals: Distinguished Service Cross, Purple Heart, Bronze Star, Combat Infantryman Badge

4. **LEVI OAKES–U.S. ARMY**
    Unit: Mohawk Code Talker of the 442nd Signal Battalion
    Battles: Leyte, Luzon, Philippines
    Medals: Silver Star, Bronze Star, Combat Infantryman Badge, Congressional Gold Medal

5. **CARL DICICCO–U.S. ARMY**
    Unit: G Company, 135th Infantry Regiment, 34th Infantry Division
    Battles: Anzio, North Apennines, Po Valley
    Medals: Silver Star, Bronze Star, Purple Heart (4x), Combat Infantryman Badge

6. **JOHN PRIMERANO–U.S. ARMY**
    Unit: HQ Company, 501st Parachute Infantry Regiment, 101st Airborne
    Battles: Holland, Belgium, Germany
    Medals: Bronze Star, Combat Infantryman Badge, Combat Parachutist Badge

7. **FRANK MINISCALCO–U.S. ARMY**
    Unit: D Company, 506th Parachute Infantry Regiment, 101st Airborne
    Battles: Normandy, Holland
    Medals: Bronze Star, Purple Heart (2x), Combat Infantryman Badge, Combat Parachutist Badge (2 Stars)

8. **FREEMAN JOHNSON–U.S. NAVY**
    Unit: USS *St. Louis*, USS *Iowa*
    Battles: Pearl Harbor, Okinawa
    Medals: Combat Action Ribbon

9. **GEORGE HURSEY–U.S. ARMY**
    Unit: Battery G, 64th Coast Artillery
    Battles: Pearl Harbor, Guadalcanal
    Medals: Bronze Star, Purple Heart, Combat Infantryman Badge

10. **BOB NOBLE–U.S. ARMY**
    Unit: 347th Infantry Regiment, 87th Division
    Battles: northern France, Stalag XIB
    Medals: Prisoner of War Medal, Bronze Star, Combat Infantryman Badge

11. **ROBERT NODGREN–U.S. ARMY**
    Unit: K Company, 329th Regiment, 83rd Infantry Division
    Battles: Ardennes, Rhineland, Central Europe
    Medals: Bronze Star, Combat Infantryman Badge

12. **ROY ROUSH–U.S. MARINES**
    Unit: 2nd Battalion, 6th Marines, 2nd Marine Divison
    Battles: Guadalcanal, Tarawa, Saipan, Tinian
    Medals: Purple Heart, Combat Action Ribbon

13. **WILLIAM GRIFFITHS–U.S. MARINES**
Unit: 1st Tank Battalion
Battles: Cape Gloucester, Peleliu, Okinawa
Medals: Purple Heart, Combat Action Ribbon

14. **EDWARD E. PARSONS–U.S. ARMY**
Unit: 4th Engineer Battalion, 4th Infantry Division
Battles: Ardennes, Rhineland
Medals: Bronze Star, Combat Infantryman Badge

15. **JIM BAKER–U.S. ARMY**
Unit: 15th Infantry Regiment, 3rd Infantry Division
Battles: Anzio, Southern France
Medals: Purple Heart, Bronze Star, Combat Infantryman Badge

16. **MIKE MAGLIO–U.S. ARMY**
Unit: HQ Company, 28th Infantry Regiment, 8th Infantry Division
Battles: Normandy, northern France, Rhineland
Medals: Bronze Star, Combat Infantryman Badge

17. **WALTER LIPINSKI–U.S. ARMY**
Unit: HQ Company, 20th Armored Infantry, 10th Armored Division
Battles: Ardennes, Rhineland, Central Europe
Medals: Bronze Star, Combat Infantryman Badge

18. **QUINTIN BUSSOLARI–U.S. ARMY**
Unit: F Troop, 90th Cavalry, 10th Armored Division
Battles: northern France, Rhineland
Medals: Purple Heart, Bronze Star, Combat Infantryman Badge

19. **EDWIN SWIRTEK–U.S. NAVY**
Unit: USS *Wasp* CV18
Battles: Saipan, Philippine Sea, Iwo Jima, Chichi Jima, Guam, Rota, Leyte, Luzon

20. **FRANK DELESPRO–U.S. NAVY**
Unit: USS *Cabot*–3 kamikaze strikes
Battles: Marianas Island, Philippine Sea, Iwo Jima, Guam, Wake Island

21. **LEO BRUNO–U.S. NAVY**
Unit: ADP 102, USS *Rednaud* –2 kamikaze strikes
Battles: Okinawa

22. **VINNY TAGLIAMONTE–U.S. ARMY**
Unit: HQ Company, 80th Infantry Division
Battles: Rhineland, Central Europe
Medals: Bronze Star, Purple Heart, Combat Action Badge

23.   **LOU SAN MIGUEL–U.S. ARMY**
Unit: 103rd Cavalry Reconnaissance, 103rd Infantry Division
Battles: Ardennes, Rhineland, Central Europe
Medals: Purple Heart, Combat Infantryman Badge

24.   **ANTHONY DABROSCA–U.S. ARMY**
Unit: 38th Infantry Division
Battles: Luzon, Philippines
Medals: Combat Infantryman Badge

25.   **ENOCH WOODY WOODHOUSE–U.S. ARMY**
Unit: Tuskegee Airman
Medals: WWII Victory Medal

26.   **DELBROOK BINS–U.S. ARMY**
Unit: Tuskegee Airman
Medals: WWII Victory Medal, Korean Service Medal

27.   **MANUEL ALMEIDA–U.S. ARMY**
Unit: 81st Armored Reconnaissance, 1st Armored Division
Battles: Tunisia, North Africa, Sicily, Monte Cassino
Medals: Purple Heart, Bronze Star, Combat Infantryman Badge

28.   **ROD HANLON–U.S. MARINES**
Unit: 2nd Marine Amphibious Corps
Battles: Guam
Medals: Purple Heart, Combat Action Ribbon

29.   **FRANCES XIE MURPHY–U.S. ARMY**
Unit: HQ Company, 83rd Airdrome Squad
Battles: Normandy, northern France, Rhineland

30.   **BUDDY MARINO CUOZZO–U.S. MARINES**
Unit: AA Gunner, 6th Marine Division
Battles: Okinawa
Medals: Combat Action Ribbon

31.   **BERNARD POTHIER–U.S. ARMY AIR CORPS**
Unit: Headquarters Squadron, 24th Pursuit Group
Battles: Bataan Death March, Camp Fukuoka, Prison Camp #17 Honshu, Japan
Medals: Silver Star, Bronze Star, Prisoner of War Medal

32.   **VINCENT "BILL" PURPLE–U.S. ARMY AIR CORPS**
Unit: B-17, 379th Bomber Group, 8th Air Force
Battles: England
Medals: Distinguished Flying Cross, Air Medal (four Oak Leaf Clusters)

33.   **RAY MALLEY–U.S. ARMY AIR CORPS**
Unit: B-24, 450th Bomber Group, 15th Air Force
Battles: Italy
Medals: Distinguished Flying Cross, Purple Heart, Air Medal

34.   **STEVEN VACILIOU–U.S. NAVY**
Unit: USS *Chapultepec*–torpedoed
Battles: South America
Medals: Combat Action Ribbon

35.   **ROCCO TELESE–U.S. ARMY**
Unit: K Company, 339th Regiment, 85th Infantry Division
Battles: Rome-Arno, North Apennines, Po Valley
Medals: Purple Heart, Bronze Star, Combat Infantryman Badge

36.   **JOSIAH BENATOR–U.S. ARMY**
Unit: 20th Armored Infantry, 10th Armored Division
Battles: Ardennes
Medals: Bronze Star, Purple Heart, Combat Infantryman Badge

37.   **CLARENCE CORMIER–U.S. ARMY**
Unit: HQ Company, 422nd Regiment, 106th Infantry Division
Battles: Ardennes
Medals: Bronze Star, Prisoner of War Medal, Purple Heart, Combat
Infantryman Badge

38.   **FRANK POLEWARCZYK–U.S. ARMY**
Unit: A Company, 315th Regiment, 79th Infantry Division
Battles: Normandy, northern France, Rhineland, Central Europe
Medals: Bronze Star, Purple Heart, Combat Infantryman Badge

39.   **FRANCIS GAUDERE–U.S. ARMY**
Unit: HQ Company, 119th Infntry Regiment, 30th Infantry Division
Battles: Normandy, Holland, Ardennes, Rhineland, Central Europe
Medals: Bronze Star, Combat Infantryman Badge

40.   **STANLEY SASINE–U.S. ARMY**
Unit: 5307th Composite Unit, "Merrill's Marauders"
Battles: India, Burma
Medals: Bronze Star, Purple Heart, Combat Infantryman Badge

41.   **HAROLD SHEFFIELD–U.S. MARINES**
Unit: 1st Raider Battalion
Battles: Solomon Islands, Guadalcanal, Tulagi, Bougainville
Medals: Combat Action Ribbon

42.   **JACK FOY–U.S. ARMY**
Unit: A Company, 347th Regiment, 87th Infantry Division
Battles: northern France, Ardennes, Rhineland, Central Europe
Medals: Bronze Star, Purple Heart (3x), Combat Infantryman Badge

43.   **CHUCK SOZIO–U.S. MARINES**
Unit: VMF 525
Battles: Ulithi

44.   **PAUL PERRY–U.S. ARMY**
Unit: 351st Infantry Regiment, 88th Infantry Division
Battles: Sicily, Naples-Foggia, Rome-Arno
Medals: Bronze Star, Combat Infantryman Badge

45.   **LARRY KIRBY–U.S. MARINES**
Unit: 2nd Battalion, 9th Marines, 2nd Marine Division
Battles: Guam, Iwo Jima
Medals: Silver Star, Combat Action Ribbon

46.   **ALFRED WILLETT–U.S. ARMY**
Unit: 227th Field Artillery, 29th Infantry Division
Battles: Omaha Beach, Normandy, northern France, Rhineland
Medals: Bronze Star, Combat Infantryman Badge

47.   **JOHN MCAULIFFE–U.S. ARMY**
Unit: M Company, 347th Infantry Regiment, 87th Infantry Division
Battles: Ardennes, Rhineland, Central Europe
Medals: Bronze Star, Combat Infantryman Badge

48.   **ERNEST ROBERTS–U.S. ARMY**
Unit: M Company, 347th Infantry Regiment, 87th Infantry Division
Battles: northern France, Ardennes, Rhineland, Central Europe
Medals: Silver Star, Bronze Star, Purple Heart, Combat Infantryman
Badge.

49.   **BERNARD RUCHIN–U.S. MARINES**
Unit: 2nd Battalion, 2nd Marine Division
Battles: Saipan, Tinian
Medals: Purple Heart (2x), Combat Action Ribbon, Korean War Campaign Medal

50.   **KENNETH GAY–U.S. ARMY**
Unit: 65th Armored Infantry Battalion, 20th Armored Division
Battles: Central Europe
Medals: Bronze Star, Combat Infantryman Badge

51. **ROBERT OLIVER–U.S. NAVY**
Unit: LST 309
Battles: North Africa, Salerno, Normandy, Japan
Medals: Combat Action Ribbon

52. **JOE MILONE–U.S. ARMY**
Unit: 701st Tank Destroyer Battalion, 10th Mountain Division
Battles: Po Valley
Medals: Bronze Star, Combat Infantryman Badge

53. **NICK FRANCULLO–U.S. ARMY**
Unit: HQ Company, 330th Infantry Regiment, 83rd Infantry Division
Battles: Normandy, northern France, Ardennes, Rhineland, Central
Europe
Medals: Bronze Star, Purple Heart (2x), Combat Infantryman Badge

54. **JOHN KATSAROS–U.S. ARMY AIR CORPS**
Unit: B-17, 401st Bomber Group, 8th Air Force
Medals: Purple Heart, Distinguished Flying Cross, Air Medal with Cluster, French Resistance and WWII Victory Medals, Prisoner of War Medal, Bronze Star, British Flying Boot

55. **NELSON BRYANT–U.S. ARMY**
Unit: D Company, 508th Parachute Infantry Regiment, 82nd Airborne
Division
Battles: Normandy, Holland, Ardennes
Medals: Bronze Star, Purple Heart, Combat Infantryman Badge, Combat
Parachutist Badge (2x)

56. **FRED MORGAN–U.S. ARMY**
Unit: A Company, 505th Parachute Infantry Regiment, 82nd Airborne
Battles: Sicily, Normandy, Holland, Ardennes, Rhineland, Central Europe
Medals: Bronze Star, Purple Heart (2x), Combat Medical Badge, Combat
Parachutist Badge (4x)

57. **EDWARD HESS–U.S. ARMY**
Unit: B Company, 135th Infantry Regiment, 34th Infantry Division
Battles: Anzio, Monte Cassino, Rome-Arno, North Apennines, Po
Valley
Medals: Bronze Star, Combat Infantryman Badge

58. **CURTISS BURWELL–U.S. ARMY**
Unit: HQ Company, 11th Infantry Regiment, 5th Infantry Division
Battles: northern France, Ardennes, Rhineland, Central Europe
Medals: Bronze Star, Purple Heart, Combat Infantryman Badge

59.   **SHARLAND LEAVITT–U.S. ARMY AIR CORPS**
       Unit: B-17, 95th Bomber Group, 8th Air Force
       Medals: Distinguished Flying Cross, Bronze Star, Air Medal

60.   **JOHN HYMER–U.S. ARMY**
       Unit: B Company, 135th Infantry Regiment, 34th Infantry Division
       Battles: Anzio, Rome-Arno, North Apennines, Po Valley
       Medals: Bronze Star, Combat Infantryman Badge

61.   **MARSHALL HEYMAN–U.S. ARMY**
       Unit: 3rd Tank Battalion, 10th Armored Division
       Battles: Alsace-Lorraine, Ardennes, Rhineland, Central Europe
       Medals: Bronze Star, Purple Heart, Combat Infantryman Badge

62.   **PETER MACDONALD–U.S. MARINES**
       Unit: Navajo Code Talker, 6th Marines
       Battles: China Occupation

63.   **YOSHIO NAKAMURA–U.S. ARMY**
       Unit: 442nd Regimental Combat Team, Heavy Weapons Platoon
       Battles: southern France, Italy
       Medals: Bronze Star, Combat Infantryman Badge

64.   **LAWSON SAKAI–U.S. ARMY**
       Unit: 442nd Regimental Combat Team, 100th Battalion
       Battles: Rome-Arno, North Apennines, Southern France
       Medals: Bronze Star (2), Purple Heart (3x), Combat Infantryman Badge

65.   **EVA WAGNER–U.S. ARMY**
       Unit: Nurse Corps, England
       Medals: WWII Victory Medal

66.   **MASMENO DELROSSI–U.S. ARMY**
       Unit: B Company, 54th Armored Infantry Battalion, 10th Armored
       Division
       Battles: Alsace-Lorraine, Ardennes, Rhineland, Central Europe
       Medals: Bronze Star, Purple Heart (2x), Combat Infantryman Badge

67.   **JERRY GUSTAFSON–U.S. ARMY**
       Unit: Cannon Company, 442nd Regimental Combat Team
       Battles: Italy, southern France
       Medals: Bronze Star (2x), Purple Heart, Korean War Medal, Vietnam
       Campaign Medal, Combat Infantryman Badge (2x)

68.   **THOMAS H. BEGAY–U.S. MARINES**
Unit: Navajo Code Talker, 5th Marine Division
Battles: Iwo Jima, Chosin Reservoir
Medals: Combat Action Ribbon, Korean War Medal

69.   **DONALD STRATTON–U.S. NAVY**
Unit: USS *Arizona*, USS *Stack*
Battles: Pearl Harbor, Leyte Gulf, Lingayen Gulf, Okinawa
Medals: Purple Heart, Combat Action Ribbon

70.   **STEVEN DOMITROVICH–U.S. ARMY**
Unit: 575th Ambulance Company
Battles: Ardennes, Rhineland (Malmedy massacre survivor)

71.   **ROCCO DIGLORIA–U.S. ARMY**
Unit: 9th Infantry Division
Battles: Northern France, Ardennes, Rhineland, Central Europe
Medals: Bronze Star, Purple Heart (2x), Combat Infantryman Badge

72.   **CHARLES SANDERSON–U.S. ARMY**
Unit: 552nd Heavy Field Artillery Battalion, Red Ball Express
Battles: Normandy, Ardennes, Rhineland, Central Europe
Medals: Bronze Star, Combat Infantryman Badge

73.   **MARVIN GILMORE–U.S. ARMY**
Unit: A Company, 458th Anti-Aircraft Battalion
Battles: Normandy, Ardennes, Rhineland
Medals: Bronze Star, Combat Infantryman Badge

74.   **ROD STROHL–U.S. ARMY**
Unit: Easy Company, 501st Parachute Infantry Regiment, 101st
Airborne
Battles: Normandy, Holland, Ardennes, Rhineland, Central Europe
Medals: Bronze Star, Purple Heart, Combat Infantryman Badge, Combat
Parachutist Badge (2x)

75.   **LAWRENCE HUNEWILL–U.S. NAVY**
Unit: Bomber Patrol Squadron, VPB 19
Battles: Iwo Jima, Pacific Islands

76.   **ALLAN ATWELL–U.S. ARMY**
Unit: 28th Infantry Division, 28th Military Police Company
Battles: Hurtgen Forrest, Ardennes, Rhineland
Medals: Bronze Star, Purple Heart, Combat Infantryman Badge

77.   **AL BUCHARELLI–U.S. ARMY**
Unit: HQ Company, 15th Regiment, 3rd Infantry Division
Battles: Salerno, Arme-Arno
Medals: Bronze Star, Purple Heart, Combat Infantryman Badge

78.   **TOM BRISTOL–U.S. ARMY AIR CORPS**
Unit: 12th Bomber Group; 490th Bomber Squad, 10th Air Force
Battles: China, Burma, India
Medals: Distinguished Flying Cross, Purple Heart, Air Medal

79.   **JAMES HACKENBERG–U.S. ARMY**
Unit: 20th Field Artillery, 5th Infantry Division
Battles: northern France, Ardennes, Rhineland, Central Europe

80.   **HANK BAGGS–U.S. ARMY**
Unit: 359th Regiment, 90th Infantry Division
Battles: Ardennes, Rhineland, Central Europe
Medals: Bronze Star, Combat Infantryman Badge

81.   **AL HULSTRUNK–U.S. ARMY AIR CORPS**
Unit: Glider Pilot, 5th U.S. Army, Special Operations Group 12
Battles: Operation Varsity, Rhineland
Medals: Air Medal, Bronze Star, Combat Glider Badge

82.   **PETER PAICOS–U.S. ARMY AIR CORPS**
Unit: Glider Pilot, 305th Troop Transport
Battles: Operation Varsity, Rhineland
Medals: Air Medal, Bronze Star, Combat Glider Badge

83.   **ALFRED SIDAL–U.S. NAVY**
Unit: USS *Bunker Hill* (severely damaged by two kamikazes)
Battles: Okinawa, Philippine Sea, Solomon Islands, Marshal Islands

84.   **JAMES HANLEY–U.S. MARINES**
Unit: I Company, 22nd Marines, 6th Marine Division
Battles: Okinawa
Medals: Purple Heart, Combat Action Ribbon

85.   **RUSS LANG–U.S. ARMY**
Unit: I Company, 423rd Infantry Regiment, 106th Infantry Division
Battles: Ardennes, Stalag XIIA
Medals: Bronze Star, Prisoner of War Medal, Combat Infantryman Badge

86.   **LOUISE MCROBERTS** (present when Patton died)

87.   **JOE TERENZIO–U.S. ARMY**
Unit: 169th Infantry Regiment, 43rd Infantry Division
Battles: New Guinea, Philippines
Medals: Silver Star, Bronze Star, Purple Heart (3x)

88.   **JOE DRAGO–U.S. MARINES**
Unit: I Company, 3rd Battalion, 22nd Marines, 6th Marine Division
Battles: Okinawa
Medals: Purple Heart, Combat Action Ribbon

89.   **SAM YANKU–U.S. ARMY**
Unit: D Company, 229th Infantry Regiment, 75th Infantry Division
Battles: Ardennes, Rhineland, Central Europe
Medals: Bronze Star, Combat Infantryman Badge

90.   **ERNIE DEEB–U.S. ARMY**
Unit: 150th Engineer Battalion
Battles: Normandy, northern France, Ardennes, Rhineland
Medals: Bronze Star

91.   **ANTHONY DEFUSCO–U.S. MARINES**
Unit: I Company, 3rd Battalion, 25th Marines, 4th Marine Division
Battles: Saipan, Tinian, Iwo Jima
Medals: Combat Action Ribbon

92.   **ALLISON BLANEY–U.S. ARMY**
Unit: Medical Aid Man, 1st Army
Battles: Normandy, Holland, Ardennes, Rhineland, Central Europe
Medals: Bronze Star, Combat Medical Badge

93.   **HERMAN STREITBURGER–U.S. ARMY AIR CORPS**
Unit: 343rd Bomb Squad, 98th Bomb Group, 15th Air Force (prisoner in
Stalag Luft IV)
Medals: Distinguished Flying Cross, Air Medal, Bronze Star, Purple
Heart, Prisoner of War Medal

94.   **ALFRED CONSIGLI–U.S. ARMY**
Unit: 774th Tank Battalion
Battles: Normandy, northern France, Ardennes, Rhineland, Central
Europe
Medals: Bronze Star

95.   **DAN DONOVAN–U.S. MARINES**
Unit: 17th Anti-Aircraft Battalion, 2nd Marine Divison
Battles: Tinian
Medals: Combat Action Ribbon

96. **GERALD GLOOKASIAN–U.S. ARMY**
Unit: 3rd Tank Battalion, 10th Armored Division
Battles: Alsace-Lorraine, Ardennes, Rhineland, Central Europe
Medals: Bronze Star, Purple Heart

97. **DOMINIC DAVOLIO–U.S. ARMY**
Unit: 86th Infantry Division
Battles: Central Europe
Medals: Bronze Star, Combat Infantryman Badge

98. **TED ACKROYD–U.S. ARMY**
Unit: 18th Regiment, 1st Infantry Division
Battles: Ardennes, Rhineland
Medals: Bronze Star, Combat Infantryman Badge

99. **MIKE LINQUATA–U.S. ARMY**
Unit: D Company, 134th Regiment, 35th Division
Battles: northern France, Ardennes, Stalag 12A
Medals: Bronze Star, Prisoner of War Medal, Combat Medical Badge

100. **WALTER GILBERT–U.S. ARMY**
Unit: 101st Infantry Regiment, 26th Infantry Division
Battles: northern France, Ardennes, Rhineland, Central Europe
Medals: Silver Star, Bronze Star, Purple Heart (2x), Combat Infantryman
Badge

101. **WALTER "MIZ" O'MALLEY–U.S. MARINES**
Unit: 2nd Battalion, 27th Marines, 5th Marine Division
Battles: Iwo Jima
Medals: Purple Heart, Combat Action Ribbon

102. **LOUIS ZOGHBY–U.S. ARMY**
Unit: F Company, 194th Regiment, 17th Airborne Division
Battles: Ardennes, Operation Varsity, Rhineland, Central Europe
Medals: Bronze Star, Combat Infantryman Badge, Combat Glider Badge

103. **WAYNE FIELD–U.S. ARMY**
Unit: 86th Cavalry Reconnaissance, 6th Armored Division
Battles: Ardennes, Rhineland, Central Europe
Medals: Bronze Star, Purple Heart, Combat Infantryman Badge

104. **ARMAND SEDGELEY–U.S. ARMY AIR CORPS**
Unit: 97th Bomber Group, 15th Air Force
Battles: Italy, North Africa
Medals: Distinguished Flying Cross, Silver Star, Bronze Star Purple Heart,
Air Medal

105. **BOB WEBER–U.S. ARMY**
Unit: A Company, 54th Armored Infantry, 10th Armored Division
Medals: Bronze Star, Combat Infantryman Badge

106. **BOB WHITE–U.S. ARMY**
Unit: HQ Company, 507th Parachute Infantry Regiment, 17th Airborne
Division
Battles: Ardennes, Operation Varsity, Rhineland, Central Europe
Medals: Bronze Star, Purple Heart, Combat Infantryman Badge, Combat
Parachutist Badge

107. **RODNEY PERKINS–U.S. ARMY**
Unit: B Company, 345th Regiment, 87th Infantry Division
Battles: Ardennes, Rhineland, Central Europe
Medals: Bronze Star, Purple Heart, Combat Infantryman Badge

108. **LEN KIELEY–U.S. ARMY**
Unit: 8th Tank Battalion, 4th Armored Division
Battles: Normandy, northern France, Rhineland, Ardennes, Central
Europe
Medals: Silver Stars (2x), Bronze Star, Purple Heart

109. **DOUG BRYANT–U.S. NAVY**
Unit: USS *Dogfish* SS-350 (submarine)
Battles: Pacific war patrols (sinking twelve enemy vessels)
Medals: Combat Submarine Patrol Badge

110. **WINSTON PATRICK FLYNN–U.S. ARMY**
Unit: F Company, 157th Regiment, 45th Infantry Division
Battles: Anzio, Italy, southern France
Medals: Bronze Star (2x), Purple Heart (3x), Korean War Medal, Vietnam
Campaign Medal, Combat Infantryman Badge (3x)

111. **MILDRED COX–U.S. MARINES**
Unit: 1st Marine Division stenographer (one of the first woman Marines)

112. **RUSSELL ERICKSON–U.S. ARMY AIR CORPS**
Unit: B-24, 44th Bomb Group, 8th Air Force
Battles: Ardennes, Rhineland, Central Europe
Medals: Distinguished Flying Cross (2x), Air Medal (4x)

113. **DON HALVERSON–U.S. ARMY**
Unit: Weapons Company, 168th Regiment, 34th Infantry Division
Battles: Monte Cassino, Anzio, Rome-Arno, North Apennines, Po
Valley
Medals: Bronze Star, Combat Infantryman Badge

114.   **VINCENT SPERANZA–U.S. ARMY**
Unit: H Company, 501st Parachute Infantry Regiment, 101st Airborne
Battles: Ardennes, Rhineland, Central Europe
Medals: Bronze Star, Purple Heart, Combat Infantryman Badge

115.   **CLAYTON CHRISTIANSEN–U.S. ARMY**
Unit: A Company, 324th Combat Engineer Battalion, 99th Infantry
Division
Battles: Ardennes, Rhineland, Central Europe

116.   **ROBERT THOMPSON–U.S. ARMY**
Unit: A Company, 23rd Infantry Regiment, 2nd Infantry Division
Battles: Normandy, northern France, Ardennes, Rhineland, Central
Europe
Medals: Bronze Star, Combat Infantryman Badge

117.   **RAYMOND WALLACE–U.S. ARMY**
Unit: B Company, 507 Parachute Infantry Regiment, 82nd Airborne
Battles: Normandy, Stalag 12A
Medals: Bronze Star, Combat Infantryman Badge

118.   **CHET ROHN–U.S. ARMY**
Unit: C Company, 56th Engineers, 11th Armored Division
Battles: Ardennes, Rhineland, Central Europe

119.   **FRED WHITAKER–U.S. ARMY**
Unit: B Company, 347th Regiment, 87th Infantry Division
Battles: Ardennes, Rhineland, Central Europe
Medals: Bronze Star, Purple Heart, Combat Infantryman Badge

120.   **KENNETH GILLPATRICK–U.S. ARMY**
Unit: HQ Company, Glider Signal Corps, 82nd Airborne
Battles: Sicily, Normandy, Holland, Ardennes, Rhineland, Central Europe
Medals: Bronze Star, Combat Infantryman Badge, Combat Glider Badge
(2x)

121.   **GEORGE ARNSTEIN–U.S. ARMY**
Unit: 76th Cavalry Troop, 76th Infantry Division
Battles: Rhineland, Ardennes, Central Europe
Medals: Bronze Star, Combat Infantryman Badge

122.   **RICK SPOONER–U.S. MARINES**
Unit: F Company, 2nd Battalion, 8th Marines, 2nd Marine Division
Battles: Saipan, Tinian, Okinawa
Medals: Bronze Star, Purple Heart (3x), Combat Action Ribbon (3x),
Korean War Medal, Vietnam Campaign Medal

123. **ROBERT SMITH–U.S. ARMY**
Unit: A Company, 746th Tank Battalion
Battles: Normandy, northern France, Rhineland, Ardennes, Central
Europe
Medals: Bronze Star

124. **VINCE TERRILL–U.S. ARMY**
Unit: C Company, 381st Infantry Regiment, 96th Infantry Division
Battles: Okinawa
Medals: Bronze Star, Purple Heart, Combat Infantryman Badge

125. **HARVEY SEGAL–U.S. ARMY**
Unit: 37th Field Artillery, 2nd Infantry Division
Battles: Normandy, northern France, Ardennes, Rhineland, Central
Europe

126. **EDWIN WAITE–U.S. ARMY**
Unit: 259 Infantry Regiment, 65th Infantry Division
Battles: Rhineland, Central Europe
Medals: Bronze Star, Combat Infantryman Badge

127. **LUIGI PASQUALE–U.S. ARMY**
Unit: 184th Regiment, 7th Infantry Division
Battles: Okinawa
Medals: Bronze Star, Combat Infantryman Badge, Purple Heart

128. **CHARLES SAHAGIAN–U.S. ARMY**
Unit: 347th Regiment, 87th Infantry Division
Battles: Ardennes, Rhineland, Central Europe
Medals: Bronze Star, Purple Heart, Combat Infantryman Badge

129. **RAYMOND GOULET–U.S. ARMY**
Unit: 259th Field Artillery, Red Ball Express
Battles: Normandy, northern France, Ardennes, Rhineland

130. **RICHARD MINICHIELLO–U.S. ARMY AIR CORPS**
Unit: 1333rd Army Air Force Base Unit
Battles: India, China, Burma
Medals: Air Medal with Oak Leaf Cluster

131. **JOHN LEONCELLO–U.S. ARMY**
Unit: E Company, 345th Regiment, 87th Infantry Division
Battles: Ardennes, Rhineland, Central Europe
Medals: Bronze Star, Purple Heart, Combat Infantryman Badge

132. **BENNET BARD–U.S. MARINES**
Unit: 29th Marine Regiment, 6th Marine Division
Battles: Okinawa
Medals: Purple Heart, Combat Action Ribbon

133. **CHARLES SWAIN–U.S. ARMY**
Unit: I Company, 345th Regiment, 87th Infantry Division
Battles: Ardennes, Rhineland, Central Europe
Medals: Bronze Star, Combat Infantryman Badge

134. **HAROLD ANGLE–U.S. ARMY**
Unit: 112th Regiment, 29th Infantry Division
Battles: northern France, Ardennes, Rhineland
Medals: Bronze Star, Combat Infantryman Badge

135. **JACK MYERS–U.S. ARMY**
Unit: 692nd Tank Battalion
Battles: Holland, Rhineland, Ardennes, Central Europe
Medals: Bronze Star

136. **THOMAS HOKE–U.S. ARMY**
Unit: 312th Medical Company, 347th Regiment, 87th Division
Battles: northern France, Ardennes, Rhineland, Central Europe
Medals: Bronze, Star Combat Medical Badge

137. **JOHN DICLIMENTE–U.S. ARMY**
Unit: 413th Anti-Aircraft Battalion, 1st Infantry Division

138. **CHARLES COGGIO–U.S. ARMY**
Unit: 88th Infantry Division
Medals: WWII Victory Medal, Occupation Medal

139. **PHILLIP SCHWARTZ–U.S. ARMY**
Unit: 125th Field Artillery, 34th Infantry Division
Battles: Salerno, Monte Cassino, Anzio, North Apennines, Po Valley

140. **CLIFFORD TENNEY–U.S. ARMY**
Unit: A Company, 54th Armored Infantry, 10th Armored Division
Battles: Rhineland, Central Europe
Medals: Bronze Star, Combat Infantry Badge

141. **DAVID STEVENS–U.S. ARMY**
Unit: 350th Infantry Regiment, 88th Division
Battles: Salerno, Rome-Arno, North Apennines, Po Valley
Medals: Purple Heart, Bronze Star, Combat Infantryman Badge

142.   **SAM HANNA–U.S. NAVY**
Unit: LST 308
Battles: North Africa, Salerno, Normandy, Japan
Medals: Combat Action Ribbon

143.   **SAM BOIKE–U.S. ARMY**
Unit: 740th Field Artillery Battalion
Battles: Normandy, northern France, Ardennes, Rhineland, Central
Europe
Medals: Purple Heart, Bronze Star

144.   **JACK LANGTON–U.S. NAVY**
Unit: LCI(R) 643
Battles: Okinawa
Medals: Combat Action Ribbon

145.   **BILL ALLEN–U.S. NAVY**
Unit: LST 523 (sunk)
Battles: Normandy
Medals: Purple Heart, Combat Action Ribbon

146.   **ROTHACKER SMITH–U.S. ARMY**
Unit: 366th Infantry Regiment, 92nd Infantry Division
Battles: Rome, North Apennines
Medals: Purple Heart, Bronze Star, Prisoner of War Medal, Combat
Medical Badge

147.   **RALPH PAINTER–U.S. ARMY**
Unit: 83rd Armored Field Artillery Battalion
Battles: Normandy, northern France, Rhineland, Ardennes, Central
Europe
Medals: WWII Victory Medal

148.   **TONY VACCARO–U.S. ARMY**
Unit: 83rd Infantry Division
Battles: Normandy, northern France, Rhineland, Ardennes, Central
Europe
Medals: Purple Heart, Bronze Star, Combat Infantryman Badge

149.   **EDWARD HANSBERRY–U.S. MARINES**
Unit: 1st Marine Division
Battles: Cape Gloucester, Peleliu, Okinawa
Medals: Navy Cross, Purple Heart, Combat Action Ribbon

150.   **BOB CHASE–U.S. ARMY**
Unit: 102nd Infantry Division
Battles: Holland, Rhineland, Central Europe
Medals: Bronze Star, Combat Infantryman Badge

151. **LAWRENCE BATLEY–U.S. ARMY**
      Unit: 95th Infantry Division
      Battles: Normandy, northern France
      Medals: Purple Heart, Bronze Star, Combat Infantryman Badge

152. **RAY CARDINALE–U.S. ARMY**
      Unit: C Company, 330th Regiment, 83rd Infantry Division
      Battles: Ardennes, Rhineland
      Medals: Bronze Star, Purple Heart, Combat Infantryman Badge

153. **CHARLES KETCHAM–U.S. ARMY**
      Unit: A Company, 54th Armored Infantry Battalion, 10th Armored
      Division
      Battles: Rhineland, Central Europe
      Medals: Bronze Star, Combat Infantryman Badge

154. **PETER MANNA–U.S. ARMY**
      Unit: L Company, 163rd Regiment, 41st Division
      Battles: New Guinea, Philippines
      Medals: Combat Infantryman Badge, Philippine Liberation

155. **ANTHONY BARRASSO–U.S. ARMY**
      Unit: HQ Company, 101st Regiment, 26th Division
      Battles: northern France, Ardennes, Rhineland, Central Europe
      Medals: Bronze Star, Combat Infantryman Badge

156. **ROBERT ANDRY–U.S. ARMY**
      Unit: B Company, 761st Tank Battalion
      Battles: northern France
      Medals: Bronze Star, Purple Heart

157. **MAURICE DIAMOND–U.S. ARMY**
      Unit: F Company, 347th Regiment, 87th Division
      Battles: northern France, Ardennes, Rhineland, Central Europe
      Medals: Bronze Star, Purple Heart, Combat Infantryman Badge

158. **NORMAN MENARD–U.S. ARMY AIR CORPS**
      Unit: 8th Air Force, 457th Bomb Group
      Medals: Air Medal, WWII Victory Medal

159. **PETER CARDINALE–U.S. NAVY**
      Unit: SS *John Bell*, Armed Guard (torpedoed)
      Battles: North Africa
      Medals: Combat Action Ribbon

160. **MEDERICK ZAHER–U.S. MARINES**
      Unit: 1st Marines, Field Artillery
      Medals: Combat Action Ribbon

161. **STANLEY FRIDAY–U.S. ARMY**
Unit: HQ Company, 80th Division, 317th Regiment
Battles: northern France, Rhineland, Ardennes, Central Europe
Medals: Bronze Star, Purple Heart, Combat Infantryman Badge

162. **JOHN TREZZA–U.S. MARINES**
Unit: 5th Marine Division, 13th Artillery
Battles: Iwo Jima
Medals: Purple Heart, Combat Action Ribbon

163. **LAWRENCE GROVE–U.S. ARMY AIR CORPS**
Unit: 15th Air Force, 7th Bomb Group
Battles: China, Burma, India, bridge over the River Kwai
Medals: Air Medal (2x)

164. **ASA DAVISON–U.S. ARMY**
Unit: 93rd Infantry Division
Battles: Guadalcanal, New Guinea, Philippines
Medals: Bronze Star, Combat Infantryman Badge

165. **EDDIE GUARALDI–U.S. ARMY**
Unit: 296th Engineer Battalion
Battles: Normandy, northern France, Ardennes, Rhineland, Central
Europe
Medals: European Campaign Medal

166. **CURT SHAW–U.S. ARMY**
Unit: 150th Combat Engineer Medics
Battles: Normandy, northern France, Ardennes, Rhineland, Central
Europe
Medals: Bronze Star, Combat Medical Badge

167. **JAMES STERNER–U.S. ARMY**
Unit: K Company, 84th Infantry Division, 333rd Regiment Battles:
Ardennes, Rhineland
Medals: Purple Heart, Bronze Star, Combat Infantryman Badge

168. **BILL HALLEY–U.S. NAVY**
Unit: USS *Hoggatt Bay*, Avenger Arial Gunner, Torpedo 14
Medals: Combat Action Ribbon, Air Medal

169. **HENRY NARUSZEWICZ- U.S. ARMY**
Unit: 276th Armored Field Artillery
Battles: northern France, Ardennes, Rhineland, Central Europe
Medals: WWII Victory Medal

170. **HENRY BENGIS–U.S. ARMY AIR CORPS**
Unit: 379th Bomb Group, 8th Air Force
Medals: Air Medal, Prisoner of War Medal

171. **PHILLIP WALSH–U.S. ARMY**
Unit: I Company, 2nd Armored Division, 66th Armored Regiment
Battles: Normandy, northern France, Ardennes, Rhineland
Medals: Bronze Star, Combat Infantryman Badge

172. **ARTHUR COLACHICO–U.S. ARMY**
Unit: 156th Infantry Regiment, Medical Detachment
Battles: northern France
Medals: Combat Medical Badge

173. **EMILIO MAGLIACANE–U.S. MARINES**
Unit: 1st Battalion, 5th Marines, 1st Marine Division
Battles: Peleliu, Okinawa
Medals: Combat Action Ribbon

174. **DOMINIC FRENI–U.S. ARMY**
Unit: 82nd Airborne, 80th Airborne Anti-Aircraft Battalion, B Battery
Battles: Normandy, Holland, Ardennes, Central Europe
Medals: Purple Heart, Bronze Star, Combat Infantryman Badge

175. **ALBERT ST. GEORGE–U.S. ARMY**
Unit: 2nd Armored Division, 82nd Armored Reconnaissance Battalion
Battles: Sicily, Rome, southern France, Rhineland
Medals: WWII Victory Medal

176. **PETER BUCCI–U.S. ARMY**
Unit: 257th Combat Engineer Battalion
Medals: WWII Victory Medal

177. **JIM MARTIN–U.S. ARMY**
Unit: 506th Parachute Infantry Regiment, G Company, 101st Airborne
Medals: Purple Heart, Bronze Star, Combat Infantryman Badge

178. **DAN MCBRIDE–U.S. ARMY**
Unit: 502nd Parachute Infantry Regiment, F Company, 101st Airborne
Medals: Purple Heart (3x), Bronze Star, Combat Infantryman Badge

179. **TOM RICE–U.S. ARMY**
Unit: 501st Parachute Infantry Regiment, C Company, 101st Airborne
Medals: Purple Heart (2x), Bronze Star, Combat Infantryman Badge

180. **LAWRENCE MCCAULEY–U.S. ARMY**
Unit: 63rd Armored Field Artillery
Medals: WWII Victory Medal

181. **CHARLES DAVIS–U.S. ARMY**
Unit: 17th Airborne Division, 517th Parachute Infantry Regiment, Signal Company
Medals: Glider Badge, WWII Victory Medal

182. **PAUL SHEAFFER–U.S. ARMY**
Unit: 1182nd Combat Engineer Battalion
Medals: WWII Victory Medal

183. **CLAIR GUEY–U.S. ARMY**
Unit: 260th Combat Engineer Battalion
Medals: WWII Victory Medal

184. **CARL TRINGALI–U.S. NAVY**
Unit: USS *Barber* USN DE-161

185. **RICHARD HEINL–U.S. ARMY**
Unit: 94th Infantry Division, 376th Regiment
Medals: Bronze Star, Combat Infantryman Badge

186. **ANGELO OLIVARI–U.S. MARINES**
Unit: 29th Regiment, 6th Marine Division
Medals: Combat Action Ribbon, Purple Heart

187. **RUSSEL MOULASION–U.S. NAVY**
Unit: 6th Naval Beach Battalion
Medals: Combat Action Ribbon

188. **EVERETT ALLEN–U.S. ARMY AIR CORPS.**
Unit: 458th Bomb Group, 8th Air Force
Medals: Prisoner of War Medal, Air Medal (2x)

189. **DAVID FISHER–U.S. ARMY AIR CORPS**
Unit: 20th Air Force, 39th Bomb Group
Medals: Air Medal

190. **VERNON LOPEZ–U.S. ARMY**
Unit: 214th Military Police
Medals: WWII Victory Medal

191. **JERRY DUNHAM–U.S. ARMY**
Unit: 91st Infantry Division
Medals: Silver Star, Bronze Star

192. **HARRY N. WHISLER–U.S. ARMY**
Unit: 10th Armored Division
Medals: Combat Medical Badge

193. **PAUL FLYNN–U.S. NAVY**
Medals: WWII Victory Medal

194. **UBERT TERREL–U.S. ARMY AIR CORPS**
Unit: 100th Troop Carrier Squadron, 441st Troop Carrier Group
Medals: Air Medal

195. **ANTHONY GRASSO–U.S. ARMY**
Unit: 112th Regiment, 28th Infantry Division
Medals: Purple Heart (2x), Bronze Star, Combat Infantryman Badge

196. **ARTHUR MINICHIELLO–U.S. NAVY**
Unit: USS *New Jersey*
Medals: Combat Action Ribbon, WWII Victory Medal

197. **ARNALD GABRIEL–U.S. ARMY**
Unit: 175th Regiment, 29th Infantry Division
Medals: Bronze Star, Combat Infantryman Badge

198. **LAMPTON TERREL–U.S. ARMY**
Unit: 1st Engineer Special Brigade
Medals: WWII Victory Medal

199. **JOE CROTTY–U.S. NAVY**
Unit: USS *Helena*
Medals: WWII Victory Medal

200. **WALLACE MATTISON–U.S. ARMY**
Unit: 29th Infantry Division, 115th Regiment
Medals: Purple Heart, Combat Infantryman Badge

201. **ED COTTRELL–U.S. ARMY**
Unit: 48th Fighter Group, 493rd Squadron
Battles: Ardennes, Rhineland, Central Europe

Commendations

Chapter One
James L. Day, Corporal, U.S. Marine Corps Reserve
Purple Heart

For conspicuous gallantry and intrepidity at the risk of his life above and beyond the call of duty as a squad leader serving with the Second Battalion, Twenty-Second Marines, Sixth Marine Division, in sustained combat operations against Japanese forces on Okinawa, Ryukyu Islands from 14 to 17 May 1945. On the first day, Corporal Day rallied his squad and the remnants of another unit and led them to a critical position forward of the front lines of Sugar Loaf Hill. Soon thereafter, they came under an intense mortar and artillery barrage that was quickly followed by a fanatical ground attack of about forty Japanese soldiers. Despite the loss of one-half of his men, Corporal Day remained at the forefront, shouting encouragement, hurling hand grenades, and directing deadly fire thereby repelling the determined enemy.

Reinforced by six men, he led his squad in repelling three fierce night attacks but suffered five additional Marines killed and one wounded whom he assisted to safety. Upon hearing nearby calls for corpsman assistance, Corporal Day braved heavy enemy fire to escort four seriously wounded Marines, one at a time, to safety. Corporal Day then manned a light machine gun assisted by a wounded Marine, and halted another frenzied night attack. In this ferocious action, his machine gun was destroyed, and he suffered multiple white phosphorus and fragmentation wounds.

Assisted by only one partially effective man, he reorganized his defensive position in time to halt a fifth enemy attack with devastating small arms fire. On three separate occasions, Japanese soldiers closed to within a few feet of his foxhole, but were killed by Corporal Day.

During the second day, the enemy conducted numerous unsuccessful swarming attacks against his exposed position. When the attacks momentarily subsided, over 70 enemy dead were counted around his position. On the third day, a wounded and exhausted Corporal Day repulsed the enemy's final attack and dispatched around 12 of the enemy at close range. Having yielded no ground and with more than 100 enemy dead around his position, Corporal Day preserved the lives of his fellow Marines and made a primal contribution to the success of the Okinawa campaign.

By his extraordinary heroism, repeated acts of valor, and quintessential battlefield leadership, Corporal Day inspired the efforts of his outnumbered Marines to defeat a much larger enemy force, reflecting great credit upon him and upholding the highest traditions of the Marine Corps and the United States Navy.

Chapter Two
Ernest E. Roberts, Staff Sergeant, U.S. Army
Silver Star

Company M, 147th Infantry Regiment, for gallantry in action against an armed enemy of the United States near Germany, on 1 March 1945. In order to cover the advance of his company, Staff Sergeant Roberts led his squad under mortar barrage to an open position on a knoll. They were immediately fired upon by an enemy machine gun located in a pillbox. Staff Sergeant Roberts set up his machine gun and gave effective counter-fire, forcing the enemy to close his embrasures. His heroic actions enabled his company to successfully assault the pillbox and continue its mission. Entered military service from Rhode Island.

Chapter Six
Hershel Williams, Corporal, U.S. Marine Corps
Medal of Honor

For conspicuous gallantry and intrepidity at the risk of his life above and beyond the call of duty as Demolition Sergeant serving with the First Battalion, Twenty-First Marines, Third Marine Division, in action against enemy Japanese forces on Iwo Jima, Volcano Island, 23 February 1945. Quick to volunteer his services when our tanks were maneuvering vainly to open a lane for the infantry through the network of reinforced concrete pillboxes, buried mines and black, volcanic sands, Corporal Williams daringly went forward alone to attempt the reduction of devastating machine-gun fire from the unyielding positions. Covered only by four riflemen, he fought desperately for four hours under terrific enemy small-arms fire and repeatedly returned to his own lines to prepare demolition charges and obtain serviced flame throwers, struggling back, frequently to the rear of hostile emplacements, to wipe out one position after another. On one occasion he daringly mounted a pillbox to insert the nozzle of his flame thrower through the air vent, kill the occupants and silence the gun; on another he grimly charged enemy riflemen who attempted to stop him with bayonets and destroyed them with a burst of flame from his weapon. His unyielding determination and extraordinary heroism in the face of ruthless enemy resistance were directly instrumental in neutralizing one of the most fanatically defended Japanese strong points encountered by his regiment and aided in enabling his company to reach its' [sic] objective. Corporal Williams' aggressive fighting spirit and valiant devotion to duty throughout this fiercely contested action sustain and enhance the highest traditions of the United States Naval Service.

Chapter Seven
Carl D. DiCicco, Sergeant, U.S. Army
Silver Star

Carl D. DiCicco, Sergeant, Infantry United States Army. For gallantry in action, on 17 September 1944, in the vicinity of Barberino, Italy. While a platoon was crawling through barbed wire entanglement, a murderous volume of machinegun, rifle and grenade fire wounded Sgt. DiCicco and ten comrades. As the platoon attempted to withdraw, the enemy fire intensified while Germans began shooting red flares, apparently calling for mortar support. The men of Sgt. DiCicco's squad hugged the ground, unable to move. Realizing the necessity of decisive action, Sgt. DiCicco crawled through the barbed wire [and] poured an intense volume of automatic rifle fire in the opening of a German pillbox, to wound five of the enemy and force the surrender of nineteen others. Although severely wounded, Sgt DiCicco had saved his platoon and had eliminated a difficult obstacle in the path of his company's advance. His indomitable fighting spirit is a tribute to the gallantry of the American Infantryman. (GO 4, Hq FIFTH Army, dtd 6 Jan '45).

Chapter Eleven
Santo DiSalvo, Private First Class, U.S. Army
Distinguished Service Cross

The President of the United States takes pleasure in presenting the Distinguished Service Cross to Santo J. DiSalvo, Private First Class, U.S. Army, for extraordinary heroism in connection with military operations against an armed enemy while serving with Company G, 143rd Infantry Regiment, 36th Infantry Division, in action against enemy forces on 18 December 1944. When his squad was pinned down by heavy enemy fire, Private First Class DiSalvo, by rising drew all enemy fire upon himself, enabling his men to withdraw to cover. Then, although a target for enemy machine gun fire, he single-handedly captured the enemy emplacement. HQ Seventh Army.

References

8th Air Force Historical Society.

34th Infantry Division Association.

106th Infantry Division Association.

American Ex–Prisoners of War Organization.

Bryant, Nelson. *Mill Pond Joe: Naturalist, Writer, Journalist, and NY Times Columnist*. New York: YBK Publishers Inc., 2014.

Chapman, Dean M. *Growl of the Tiger: 10th Armored Tiger Division*. Nashville, Tennessee: Turner Publishing Company, 1994.

Charlton, Craig. President of the 10th Armored Division Veterans.

Collins, Michael and Martin King. *The Tigers of Bastogne: Voices of the 10th Armored Division in the Battle of the Bulge*. Philadelphia, Pennsylvania: Casemate Publishers, 2017. Reprint Edition.

Katsaros, John. *Code Burgundy: The Long Escape*. Perth, Scotland: Oakford Media, 2012. 2nd Edition.

Lamberty, Joel. "Ardennes 44: The Battle of the Bulge Guide." Bastogne and Bulge Battlefields Guided Tours.

Marshall, S. L. A. *Bastogne: The First Eight Days*. CreateSpace, 2014.

McAuliffe, John. President of the Battle of the Bulge Veterans Association.

Mohawk Nation American Tribe Council.

Patterson, Eugene. *Patton's Unsung Armor of the Ardennes: The Tenth Armored Division's Secret Dash to Bastogne*. Bloomington, Indiana: Xlibris, 2008.

Roush, Roy William. *Open Fire!* Front Line Press, 2003.

Second Marine Division Association.

Sixth Marine Division Association.

Valera, Charley. *My Father's War: Memories from Our Honored WWII Soldiers*. Bloomington, Indiana: iUniverse, 2017.

Veterans History Project.

Veterans Affairs.

Witness to War.

**Most importantly, all the family members of the veterans featured on the rifle.

Index

About the Author

Andrew Biggio is a U.S. Marine, historian, writer, biker, and Massachusetts police officer. He is a veteran of Iraq and Afghanistan and currently serves as president of the nonprofit New England's Wounded Veterans, Inc. His efforts in assisting injured war veterans have gained national attention, including acknowledgements from two U.S. presidents.

Andrew graduated from Suffolk University. He earned a master's in homeland security at Northeastern University in Boston, Massachusetts.

From 2017 to 2018, Andrew interviewed roughly 200 of America's last World War II veterans in order to compile a series of stories to motivate young veterans to live successful lives after combat. A portion of each book sold supports severely wounded veterans and their families.